Contents

Section 1
Menu Cost Control   5

Section 2
Purchasing Cost Control   59

Second Edition
Food, Labor, and Beverage Cost Control

A Concise Guide

Edward E. Sanders

New York City College of Technology, CUNY

Contributing Authors

Jean F. Claude
Karen Goodlad
Robert Walljasper

New York City College of Technology, CUNY

WAVELAND

PRESS, INC.

Long Grove, Illinois

For information about this book, contact:

Waveland Press, Inc.
4180 IL Route 83, Suite 101
Long Grove, IL 60047-9580
(847) 634-0081
info@waveland.com
www.waveland.com

10-digit ISBN 1-4786-3976-8
13-digit ISBN 978-1-4786-3976-3

Printed in the United States of America

7   6   5   4   3   2   1

Section 3
Food Production Cost Control   115

6   Controlling Food Production 117

Section 4
Labor Cost Control   145

Section 5
Beverage Cost Control   185

Website Resources............................321

Foreword

Food, Labor, and Beverage Cost Control: A Concise Guide, 2nd Edition, focuses on maintaining budget goals and operational profitability. The material is presented in a concise format that is easy to understand. It allows readers to quickly grasp cost-control methods and procedures applicable to all types of foodservice operations. The examples, forms, and charts are among the most commonly used in the industry. Analyzing, costing, and tracking of food, labor, beverage, and sales are vital to having a restaurant be profitable. Understanding these basic control procedures creates a smooth transition to many of the advanced POS and software applications used today.

In order to make informed management decisions one is required to have all the facts. Costing and management formulas like the ones presented here allow managers and team players to optimize financial objectives. This combined text and hands-on workbook is the foundation for novice culinary and hospitality management students as well as a refresher for those working in the industry. Included in the appendix are helpful case studies for a full-service Tuscan-style restaurant, catering business, brick-oven pizza restaurant, and an operational and marketing plan for a food truck.

Experienced restaurateurs know how to effectively manage costs and meet financial goals in a competitive foodservice environment and *Food, Labor, and Beverage Cost Control*, 2nd Edition is the guide on how to accomplish those objectives.

John Avella, Ed.D.
Executive Director
Sustainable Hospitality Management Program
California State University, Monterey Bay

Former vice president of human resources for
Marriott Corporation, The Rainbow Room, and Windows on the World,
and consultant to many major hospitality organizations.

Preface

While various POS (point of sale) and tablet applications process cost control and accounting information, to be able to comprehend that information begins with understanding the purpose and use of the information and how it is derived.

The material presented in this book represents a thorough coverage of the most essential cost-control categories. There are 14 chapters within the six cost-analysis sections of the Operating Cycle of Control. The sections flow in a logical sequence that presents a path for understanding cost control from menu concept to financial reporting. The six cost-analysis sections are self-contained, so that the reader (student) can go to any section for specific cost-control procedures. Therefore, the book can be taken from the classroom to the workplace.

The textbook also functions as a hands-on learning workbook with 21 assignments within the 14 chapters that can be completed on cost-analysis forms provided in the book. There are key terms and definitions at the beginning of each chapter that accelerate the understanding of chapter content and become the foundation for comprehending commonly used terms within the foodservice industry as applied to managing costs.

New to This Edition

The second edition updates include the following:

- Clearly defined chapter learning objectives with end-of-chapter discussion questions that can assess readers (students) level of comprehension.

- Project exercises following each chapter that are designed to test applied knowledge.

- Restaurant Reality Stories that reflect upon what often occurs in restaurant businesses are appropriately placed within each of the 6 sections of the Operating Cycle of Control.

- Mobile foodservice (food trucks and trailers) is presented in the Appendix—Restaurant Case and concludes with a project exercise to create a food-truck menu, as well as operational and marketing plans for a mobile foodservice as an additional business revenue source for the existing three-tiered restaurant operation case.

- Key Cost and Analysis Formulas (Quick Reference)

- Website Resources

The Operating Cycle of Control is clearly explained in the following order:

Section 1: Menu Cost Control

Chapter 1 Standardized Recipes begins with a quick math review followed by a brief introduction to identifying food styles and themes along with the selection of recipes. The purpose of standardizing recipes includes a detailed explanation with an assignment to complete a Standardized HACCP (Hazard Analysis Critical Control Point) Recipe. Weight and volume measures used in recipes are explained and how to determine the portion size when a recipe only lists the number of servings, plus converting (sizing) recipes is explained. Includes assignments to determine portion size and recipe conversion.

Chapter 2 Portion Control introduces portion costing options that include the Recipe Cost Card, Plate Cost Card, Butcher Test, and Cooking Loss Test. The Spice Factor is explained along with the application of Recipe Cost Cards and calculating product yield amounts followed by a step by step assignment. The application and use of Plate Cost Cards for determining menu pricing includes an application assignment. NEW—Common Product Yields.

Section 2: Purchasing Cost Control

Chapter 3 Purchasing Functions explains the process of identifying and determining what items to buy, then outlines the procedure for writing product specifications in the major categories of meats, poultry, seafood, dairy, bakery, grocery, and produce with detailed examples. The option of convenience products is presented, along with a make or buy (convenience product) decision assignment. Services offered by foodservice distributors and wholesale foodservice suppliers are reviewed along with the role of foodservice brokers. Inventory management procedures, determining par stock amounts, order sheets, standing orders, bid sheets, and contract services are explained with examples.

Chapter 4 Receiving, Storing, and Issuing Products and Processing Invoices reviews the basic requirements to properly receive products and in dealing with potential problems in receiving those products. Purchases that are "directs" and "stores" are defined. Safe and proper storage procedures are reviewed. The use of requisitions for issuing products, the purpose and function of transfers, and processing and paying invoices are explained.

Chapter 5 Food Cost clearly explains how the actual purchase cost of food products and ingredients that generate sales is measured and expressed in terms of a percentage—the food cost percentage. Typical food cost percent averages are presented for the major foodservice categories; also, the circumstances attributed to increasing or fluctuating food costs are defined and discussed. The procedure to prepare a food cost report is shown in a step-by-step example. A physical inventory is an important component to accurate food cost percentage reporting and is discussed in detail along with calculating inventory turnover rates—includes assignments and project exercises.

Section 3: Food Production Cost Control

Chapter 6 Controlling Food Production begins by discussing the importance of a complete sales history that tracks the number of customers served—customer counts, and the menu items they selected—menu items sales report with popularity percentages, during a specific period of time (month, week, days). Then the process of preparing a menu item sales forecast to determine the daily food production schedule (quantities to prepare) is explained, followed by a portion control report that tracks food portions available, sold, void orders, and remaining quantities. Includes assignments and project exercises.

Chapter 7 Menu Analysis and Seat Turnover focuses on menu profitability and how to use the seat turnover rate to determine the number of customers served during the course of a meal period. The menu sales mix is discussed along with providing an understanding of menu engineering as shown in the menu sales mix report example. Daily and weekly seat turnover rate assignment and project exercises included.
NEW—Menu Sales Mix Report (a version of menu engineering).

Section 4: Labor Cost Control

Chapter 8 Controlling Payroll Costs discusses the primary factors that affect payroll costs, and with examples provided, analyzes work schedules for kitchen, dining room staff and management. The payroll budget estimate is explained in a step-by-step manner with an emphasis toward achieving a designated payroll cost percentage goal established by management. A review of the direct and indirect costs associated with employee turnover along with an example of how to calculate the employee turnover rate is provided—includes assignment and project exercises.

Chapter 9 Measuring Performance and Productivity presents the key factors in creating and maintaining high productivity in any type of foodservice operation. A kitchen productivity report and server productivity report that track performance and productivity are both explained with examples. The procedure for reporting server tips, minimum wage laws, and the formulas for applying tip credit are discussed. Briefly reviews the speed, accuracy, and efficiency of tabletop tablets and apps and the effect on customer guest check averages.

Section 5: Beverage Cost Control

Chapter 10 Alcohol Beverage Service provides a brief overview of how and where alcohol beverages are served. Alcohol beverage portion control is presented, beginning with an example of a standardized drink recipe followed by an explanation of the various pour and service methods. The procedure for determining liquor portion cost is explained along with the function of the drink cost card which includes a completion assignment. A review of liquor sales and liability as well as responsible beverage service is covered in detail.

Chapter 11 Purchasing and Selling Alcohol Beverages reviews purchasing procedures applied to alcohol beverages and the function of alcohol beverage distributors within a "license state" or a "control state" system. The function of alcohol beverage and supply requisitions along with transfers in tracking beverage costs is explained with examples. Alcohol beverage sales and cost analysis is reviewed with an explanation of the alcohol beverage sales report and category sales and cost report with a focus on cost percentages for liquor, beer, and wine. Includes assignment and project exercises.

Chapter 12 Alcohol Beverage Inventory and Control discusses the factors that identify the alcohol beverage products to stock with adequate quantities. Inventory turnover rate calculations are explained and identified by liquor, wine, and beer, with assignment and project exercises. Alcohol beverage inventory and sales control determines if the inventory has been properly used and calculates the value of the alcohol beverage storeroom inventory. Also includes a review of potential areas of theft by managers, bookkeepers, bartenders, servers and customers as well as the control procedures that can discourage and prevent theft.

Chapter 13 Espresso Drink Control begins with a basic explanation of how espresso drinks are prepared and served. An espresso drink cost analysis chart reflects the average cost and drink cost percentage for a latte, cappuccino, and mocha served in the typical drink serving sizes, and includes assignment and project exercises. Popular spirited espresso and coffee drinks that are often served in fine dining are discussed.

Section 6: Financial and Operating Reporting

Chapter 14 Income Statements and Budgets—Cash and Card Reporting clearly explains the functions and components of the income statement and how it is used in foodservice operations. Assessing the performance of income statement categories—sales, cost of goods sold, controllable expenses, occupation costs, and profit or loss. Calculations are explained for expense detail line items in food cost and beverage cost. Comparing favorable and unfavorable variances from forecasted amounts and budgeted goals and identifying possible reasons for the unacceptable variances—includes assignments and project exercises. Tight controls and documentation are explained for cash and card transactions with the use of a cash turn-in report and a cash and card sales report as shown by examples. NEW—Cash and Card Reporting.

Appendix: A Restaurant Case with Applied Exercises

The restaurant case provides students with the opportunity to step into the management role of a three-tiered restaurant operation. The ten exercises are designed to stimulate critical thinking, require practical applications, and help to determine the student's level of understanding. The operation consists of an Italian (Tuscan-style menu) casual-dining table service restaurant, full-service catering business, and its "about to be opened" brick-oven pizza place. NEW—A current review of mobile foodservice (food trucks and trailers) that concludes with a project exercise to create a food truck menu and operational and marketing plans.

NOTE: This book is designed to provide accurate and authoritative information with regard to the subject matter covered. It is provided with the understanding that the author is not engaged in rendering legal, accounting, or other professional services. If legal advice or other expert assistance is required the services of a competent professional should be sought. The author has made every effort to provide accurate Internet addresses and other contact information at the time of publication—neither the author nor the publisher assumes any responsibility for errors, or changes that occur after publication.

Instructor's Resources

Instructor's resource materials can be found on the book's webpage at waveland.com. New materials are available to aid online class instruction that include end-of-chapter quizzes, completion assignments, and comprehensive exams—sample syllabus included.

Acknowledgments

The contributing authors to the second edition have added new insight and refinement in their respective areas of expertise. I would like to acknowledge and thank the following dedicated professional educators from the Hospitality Management Program at New York City College of Technology, CUNY: Jean F. Claude, MA, CHE, CCE to the Online Content, Robert Walljasper, MSET, CEC, CCE, CHE, AAC to the Menu Cost Control chapters, and Karen Goodlad, MA, CSW to the Beverage Cost Control chapters.

A special thanks to Gerald Van Loon, MBA, PhD, CHIA, CHE for reviewing the Financial and Operating Reporting section, John V. Muzio, Jr., MBA, CHE, CHA, adjunct professor, for continually providing suggestions, and Rosa Abreu, MA for bringing the important topic of Food Trucks to my attention.

To my son, Mark, for his financial expertise that brought forth and improved many of the control and reporting forms, and to my wife, Linda, for her methodical proofreading and thoughtful suggestions —son, Jay, and daughter Katherine for quickly responding to calls for tech support. Love always.

A sincere thank you to Waveland Press—Neil Rowe, publisher, for the guidance and direction provided during the publication process, and Deborah Underwood, graphics and composition, for editing and clearly presenting the topics, formulas, and examples in a concise format throughout the book.

From the Author

In memory of chef and restaurateur, Nick Drossos, for having shared his decades of management experience in food, labor, and beverage cost control, often conveyed as "restaurant reality stories" with various outcomes. All valuable lessons by someone taking the time to be a mentor to a young manager.

I am now celebrating 50 years (1971–2021) in various positions within the hospitality industry, and have shared some of my own "restaurant reality stories" in each section of the book. There is no greater honor to have been mentored well and then to become a mentor to others.

About the Author

EDWARD E. SANDERS is an adjunct professor of Hospitality Management at New York City College of Technology, CUNY. He is a Certified Food Executive and Certified Purchasing Manager and has a Master of Science in International Management from Thunderbird School of Global Management and a Doctor of Business Administration degree in Management and Organization. Through his career in business and education he has been associated with Xerox, Sky Chefs–American Airlines, Marriott, Delaware North, Brigham Young University, Oregon State University, and Southern Oregon University. Ed owned a restaurant, operated a chain of restaurants, founded and operated *Hospitality News* (1988–2006), has been an associate professor of business, and cofounded and directed a hospitality and tourism management university program. He is also the lead coauthor of *The Professional Server: A Training Manual*, 3rd Edition, 2018 (Pearson), and *Catering Solutions for the Culinary Student, Foodservice Operator, and Caterer*, 2000 (Prentice Hall / Pearson).

Contributing Authors

JEAN F. CLAUDE is a professor of Hospitality Management at New York City College of Technology, CUNY, and has been part of the education team since 2001. He is a Certified Hospitality Educator and a Certified Culinary Educator and has a Master of Arts degree in International Business Management from Webster University. Jean is an accomplished hospitality and tourism professional, having held responsible positions with Ogden Aviation Services, Russian Tea Room, Marriott International, and Walt Disney World. He is vice president of the Société Culinaire Philanthropique and an active member of the American Culinary Federation. Professor Claude is dedicated to advancing student learning at every level and has adopted the content for online class instruction.

KAREN GOODLAD is an Associate Professor at New York City College of Technology, CUNY and is a Certified Specialist of Wine with the Society of Wine Educators and is an active member of Les Dames d'Escoffier International, New York Chapter. She was among hospitality educators recognized by *Total Food Service* and named in the Top Woman in Metro New York Foodservice & Hospitality 2019 and 2020. Professor Goodlad is the lead coauthor of "Place-Based Learning across Disciplines: A Living Laboratory Approach to Pedagogy," *InSight: A Journal of Scholarly Teaching*, vol. 66 no. 3 (2018), and "Comparing Faculty and Student Perception of Academic Performance, Classroom Behavior, and Social Interactions in Learning Communities," *College Teaching*, vol. 13 (2018). Her professional experience in food and beverage management is leveraged in the classroom, where she teaches beverage management courses and is the faculty advisor to students participating in the Walt Disney World College Program.

ROBERT WALLJASPER is an Assistant Professor at New York City College of Technology, CUNY and is a hospitality educator with over 10 years of teaching experience and 20-plus years of leadership roles in professional culinary establishments. He is a Certified Executive Chef and Certified Culinary Educator through the American Culinary Federation (ACF), and in 2019 was inducted into the honor society of the American Academy of Chefs. He was awarded Chef Educator of the Year by Chef de Cuisine in 2016 and by the International Chefs Association–ACF Big Apple Chapter in 2019. Robert is also a Certified Hospitality Educator through the American Hotel and Lodging Educational Institute. He is an active member of the American Culinary Federation (serving as president of the New York City "Big Apple" chapter), World Chefs, and Chef de Cuisine. Professor Walljasper has presented his research at various conferences including the annual conference of the Association for the Study of Food & Society. He continues to work with students and partner with industry leaders on cost control issues that focus on profitability, controlling food waste, and sustainability.

Introduction

Successful foodservice operators understand the value of an integrated information system, the **Operating Cycle of Control** that supports the operation and management of the business, commonly known as—**Internal Functions**. The information may be communicated verbally, in writing, electronically, or with a combination of methods. The quality of the system will vary, depending on the skill of its designer and the resources available to implement it. Ideally, the information system will support the business operation with timely and accurate data to help it operate efficiently. Much of the necessary information will be generated as transactions occur during the normal course of business operations. Additional information, such as *local market conditions, supplier pricing, weather conditions, government regulations, labor market conditions, economic conditions, new technology, and social media* will originate outside the confines of the business, often referred to as—**External Factors**.

Operating Cycle of Control

Internal Functions

The Operating Cycle of Control is defined as a control cycle that divides a food and beverage operation into a series of coordinated functions. Those functions are the basic activities, procedures, and data reporting necessary to efficiently and profitably provide food and beverage products and services to customers.

Additional Information—External Factors

Foodservice operators are affected by ongoing external factors. Therefore, being aware of and monitoring those factors is critical, given the potential impact or changes that can interrupt or advance the normal flow of business activities and sales revenue. The following are the main external factors that can affect foodservice operations:

> ▶ **Local Market Conditions.** Business is affected when demographic changes occur, tourism increases, road and street improvements are made, traffic patterns change, and new competitors open or existing competitors close.

> ▶ **Supplier Pricing.** Product and supply availability is often affected by seasonal patterns and by economic and weather conditions, resulting in price increases or decreases.

▶ **Weather Conditions.** Supplier-scheduled delivery times can be delayed, and projected sales revenues and the forecasted number of customers can be reduced as a result of extreme weather conditions.

▶ **Government Regulations.** Federal, state, and local governments require timely compliance with a variety of licensing, inspection, current and new regulatory, and reporting requirements. A delay or violation in compliance may result in a fine or interruption of business.

▶ **Labor Market Conditions.** Recruiting and hiring practices along with wage and salary rates are influenced by the availability of qualified job applicants.

OPERATING CYCLE
OF CONTROL

Menu Cost Control

1 Standardized Recipes
2 Portion Cost

Financial and Operational Reporting

14 Income Statements and Budgets— Cash and Card Reporting

Purchasing Cost Control

3 Purchasing Functions
4 Receiving, Storing, and Issuing Products and Processing Invoices
5 Food Cost

Beverage Cost Control

10 Alcohol Beverage Service
11 Purchasing and Selling Alcohol Beverages
12 Alcohol Beverage Inventory and Control
13 Espresso Drink Control

Food Production Cost Control

6 Controlling Food Production
7 Menu Sales Analysis and Seat Turnover

Labor Cost Control

8 Controlling Payroll Costs
9 Measuring Performance and Productivity

► **Economic Conditions.** Local, regional, and national economic conditions can affect the flow of business in both positive and negative ways. A strong economy can produce increased sales revenue, contrasted with a weak economy and declining sales revenue.

► **New Technology.** Advancements in POS (point of sale) systems software, tablet applications, and new developments in kitchen equipment continue to support operational efficiencies that can further add to profitability.

► **Social Media.** An effective website, frequently updated Facebook page, especially with positive customer reviews, can support a good reputation that promotes increased sales revenue.

The additional information available to foodservice operators can be helpful in setting goals, planning strategies, implementing procedures, and evaluating results.

The diagram on the following page represents the relationship of internal functions and external factors.

Management Control Procedures

The responsibility of a foodservice manager is to observe, monitor, and control the various aspects of the foodservice operation. The manager knows when something should be done in a specific way (the standard); observes and monitors whether that is actually occurring (measures performance); and if it is not, makes the necessary adjustment or correction and then continues to monitor and evaluate the process. Therefore, the steps are as follows:

1. Set standards.

2. Measure performance.

3. Determine whether standards have been met.

4. Take corrective action, as needed.

5. Continue to monitor and evaluate.

The standards are to be maintained. Everything from the workplace to the employees to the financial objectives must be based on sound operating practices and industry norms.

The operating system (system software) collects timely information about what has actually occurred. Prepared data reports allow the manager to compare actual results to established standards. Generally, this is easiest to understand when evaluating financial results. However, the same activity transpires when evaluating the daily work of employees. The manager knows the standard and evaluates what is actually occurring.

Managers understand the standards and criteria to be met. Simply stated, it means looking at what happened, looking at what was supposed to happen, identifying those things that need attention, and determining what to do about it.

If data reports indicate that a standard is repeatedly not being met or is exceeded, an inquiry as to "why" should reveal that either the standard is too difficult or too easy to achieve; therefore the standard is not an acceptable measure. In either situation, the standard needs to be reevaluated and possibly reestablished.

Management sets standards based on specific criteria for all aspects of the foodservice operation.

An ongoing or periodic measure of performance occurs for each of the set standards, using the same measure that defined the standard.

Managers determine whether things are on track or if corrective action is needed.

A manager finds solutions to problems revealed through the evaluation process.

Monitoring and evaluating is an ongoing process.

Foodservice operators must decide what information they need to operate their establishment and the format in which they wish to receive it. The following sections (chapters) suggest the procedures and forms needed to support specific management controls, following the functions in the Operating Cycle of Control. These procedures and forms accomplish the immediate objective of demonstrating efficient food, labor, and beverage cost-control techniques.

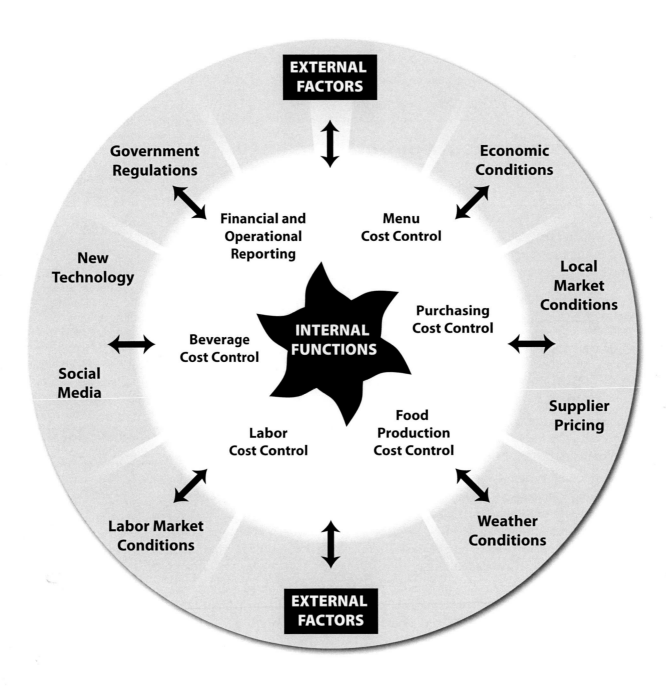

Menu Cost Control

1 Standardized Recipes

2 Portion Cost

Management's decisions regarding menu content are the most important decisions made in a foodservice operation. The menu drives the business in terms of what is to be purchased, prepared, cooked, and served.

A well-crafted menu targets customers that the restaurant wants to attract with appropriate food and beverage selections. The menu reflects the restaurant concept: fine dining, casual-dining table service, fast casual, quick service (fast food), catering full service, cafeteria, or buffet.

The menu must consider the capacity of the foodservice facility and kitchen equipment along with the skills and abilities of the staff. A POS (point of sale) system with a recipe file bank that updates the cost of recipes with current pricing as products are purchased is a fast and convenient way to maintain food cost percentages.

Serving consistent quality menu items and identifying and controlling recipe costs and menu item costs require standardized recipes.

Contributing Author

Robert Walljasper
CEC, CCE, CHE

ROBERT WALLJASPER Assistant Professor, New York City College of Technology, CUNY is a hospitality educator with over 10 years of teaching experience and 20-plus years of leadership roles in professional culinary establishments. He is a Certified Executive Chef and Certified Culinary Educator through the American Culinary Federation (ACF), and in 2019 was inducted into the honor society of the American Academy of Chefs. He was awarded Chef Educator of the Year by Chef de Cuisine in 2016 and by the International Chefs Association–ACF Big Apple Chapter in 2019. Robert is also a Certified Hospitality Educator through the American Hotel and Lodging Educational Institute. He is an active member of the American Culinary Federation (serving as president of the New York City "Big Apple" chapter), World Chefs, and Chef de Cuisine. Professor Walljasper has presented his research at various conferences including the annual conference of the Association for the Study of Food & Society. He continues to work with students and partner with industry leaders on cost control issues that focus on profitability, controlling food waste, and sustainability.

Quick Math Review

Rounding a decimal number

The process of rounding begins with determining the number of digits that will follow after the decimal point—typically, one, two, or three digits as illustrated by the following examples:

28.7	one digit	tenths
28.76	two digits	hundredths
28.764	three digits	thousandths

When rounding up or down, the rule to remember is as follows:

- If the number is 5 or more, round up
- If the number is less than 5, round down

Therefore:

28.76 would be rounded to 28.8 if rounding to the tenth's place (one digit right of decimal)

28.764 would be rounded to 28.76 if rounding to the hundredth's place (two digits right of decimal)

28.7649 would be rounded to 28.765 if rounding to the thousandth's place (three digits right of decimal)

NOTE: POS costing programs may often follow the decimal with 3 digits.

Converting a decimal number to a percentage:

A decimal number is converted to a percentage if multiplied by 100. The decimal point is moved two places to the right followed by a percentage sign.

Example: $0.318 \times 100 = 31.8\%$

Converting a fraction to a decimal:

Example: 2/3 cup to decimal ounces $(2 \div 3 = 0.666$ ounces$)$

Example: 1/8 teaspoon to decimal ounces $(1 \div 8 = 0.125$ ounces$)$

NOTE: A "pinch" of a certain ingredient can also be expressed as 1/8 tsp (0.125 ounces).

Determining the total amount when a percentage is added:

When a number is multiplied by 1 plus the added percentage it will quickly determine a total amount. Example: 10 % (expressed as 0.10) is added to 1 resulting in 1.10 as the multiplier.

$$42.39 \times 1.10 = 46.629$$

This method saves a step in the normal two-step process of multiplying and then having to add that 10% number to the original number as follows: $42.39 \times 0.10 = 4.239$

$$42.39 + 4.239 = 46.629$$

NOTE: The answer is the same but the method is quicker.

1

Standardized Recipes

Introduction

Once the menu is determined, recipes need to be developed for each menu item. Developing standardized recipes is the first step to controlling product quality and cost. From the standardized recipe comes all the food costing and control activity crucial to the financial success of a foodservice operation.

Learning Objectives

1. Know the questions to ask when identifying a restaurant's primary customers.
2. Identify a food style or theme for a restaurant.
3. Define the criteria for the selection of a recipe.
4. Explain the purpose of standardized recipes in a foodservice operation.
5. Identify the elements of a Standardized HACCP (Hazard Analysis Critical Control Point) Recipe.
6. Explain the difference between weight and volume measures used in recipes.
7. Determine the portion size when a recipe only lists the number of servings.
8. Understand how to convert recipe sizes (sizing recipes).

Chapter Outline

Determining the Menu
Standardized Recipes
Standardized HACCP Recipes
Weight and Volume Measures
Determining Recipe Serving Portion Sizes

Recipe Conversion (Sizing)
Summary
Discussion Questions
Project Exercises

Key Terms and Definitions

Begin by first reading the key terms and their definitions. An advanced understanding of the terms will be helpful prior to reading the chapter.

Cooking Temperature and Time	The temperature and amount of time required to finish cooking an item.
Cooling and Storing	The amount of time and at temperature food can be safely stored. (Includes attaching an item label with the date for all food items that are cooled and stored.)
Food Holding Temperatures and Times	Hot food is held at 135°F or higher, cold food at 41°F or lower; the length of time an item can be held before quality is compromised.
Food Safety Statement	A statement used to outline the sanitation procedures employees must carry out before beginning production.
Method of Preparation	The procedural steps to produce a recipe item according to HACCP safe food principles.
Nutritional Analysis	Commonly includes the number of calories, and the amount of protein, fat, cholesterol, carbohydrates, fiber, and sodium content in one serving.
Portion Size	Determined by methods that leave little or no room for error, such as exact weight, exact measure, exact count, and even division or pan cuts.
Preparation Time	The time needed to prepare an item.
Recipe Conversion	Sizing a recipe written for a certain number of servings to accommodate a different number of servings.
(Recipe) Conversion Multiplier	New Yield (number of portions) divided by Original Yield (number of portions).
Recipe Source	Recipes may be created and developed in-house (within the foodservice operation); may be family recipes; or may be taken from cookbooks, newspapers, magazines, or the Internet.
Recipe Sub-Recipes	Recipes for products used within a number of other recipes, such as sauces or fresh pastas.
Recipe Yield	Expressed with three separate descriptions: number of servings, serving portion size, and the total quantity a recipe produces.
Standardized HACCP Recipe	Principles of time, temperature, and procedures integrated into a recipe to ensure the safety of the food being produced throughout preparation and serving.
Standardized Recipe	Recipe tested, adjusted, and retested until it produces a menu item as management wants the item produced; tested three consecutive times with the same result.
Volume	Measures space—measured by teaspoons, tablespoons, pints, quarts, and gallons.
Weight	Measures density or heaviness—measured by a scale.

Determining the Menu

Foodservice establishments typically appeal to certain types of customers—their primary customers.

Who are the primary customers? By answering the following questions, foodservice operators can develop a business instinct for recognizing menu items that are most desired by their customers:

1. What are customers doing prior to coming to the restaurant?
2. How much time do customers have to eat?
3. How price sensitive are customers?—Every restaurant has a price threshold, a range of acceptable prices for menu items.
4. What is the reason for the customer's presence—special occasion, a matter of convenience, or to experience the menu?
5. What is the customer's food expertise and expectation?

LEARNING OBJECTIVE 1
Know the questions to ask when identifying a restaurant's primary customers.

What is the primary food style or theme? Generally, food style or theme indicates foods that are based on the following:

▶ Style or flavor—bistro, barbecue, Cajun, Tuscan

▶ Theme or ethnic—Italian, Mexican, Asian, Indian

▶ Food trend—vegetarian, gluten-free, organic

▶ Specific food item—beef, seafood, pastas, bakery

▶ Cooking method or technique—fusion, grilled, broiled, steamed

LEARNING OBJECTIVE 2
Be able to identify a food style or theme for a restaurant.

What is the facility and equipment capacity? Knowing the capacity of the kitchen and equipment is a key factor when deciding the menu selection. Also, new menu (recipe) items may require the operation to purchase additional food products that may affect storage space and inventory costs.

Recipes

Recipes may be created and developed in-house (within the foodservice operation) or may be family recipes or taken from cookbooks, newspapers, magazines, or the Internet.

Recipe sites:
www.allrecipes.com
www.foodnetwork.com
www.cooking.nytimes.com

A recipe, when selected, should be based on the following criteria:

1. The preferences and tastes of the customers to be served with the recipe
2. The existing kitchen capacity and equipment to produce the recipe
3. The skill level of the kitchen staff to prepare the recipe

The practice of using standardized recipes allows the foodservice operation to deliver a consistent product to customers, regardless of who is preparing the items.

LEARNING OBJECTIVE 3
Define the criteria for the selection of a recipe.

All recipes must be standardized.

Non-standardized recipes often:

1. Cause confusion because they leave out essential information
2. Awkwardly mention time and temperature settings, and preparation method details
3. Neglect to specify accurate measurements or clearly state ingredients
4. Neglect to specify serving sizes, leaving employees to guess how much to serve on a plate
5. Use unfamiliar terminology
6. Have a poorly written method of preparation that could lead to an inconsistent product
7. Waste employees' and management's time

The consequences of not using standardized recipes can result in:

Increased labor cost	Inaccurate recipe yield	Customer dissatisfaction
Increased food cost	Inaccurate portion cost	Potential health code violations
Inconsistent product	Server confusion	Lost revenue

Standardized Recipes

LEARNING OBJECTIVE 4
Explain the purpose of standardized recipes in a foodservice operation.

A standardized recipe is one that has been tested, adjusted, and retested again and again until it produces a menu item as management wants the item produced.

A standardized recipe has to fit management's plan for quality, taste, portion size, cost, selling price, purchasing, production, profitability, and appearance on the plate—all with the objective of pleasing the customers.

Procedure to standardize a recipe:

1. Produce the recipe exactly as it is written, without changing or adjusting anything.
2. Analyze the outcome for the following:
   - Appearance—balance of color, texture, and flavor
   - Method of preparation—clarity of steps, accuracy of cooking times, and proportions of ingredients
   - Serving size—cost per serving for the item as prepared—menu fit

A recipe is standardized when it is produced three consecutive times with the same result.

3. If needed, adjust the recipe to reflect the customers' preferences and record the changes.
4. Produce the recipe a second time—analyze according to the same criteria listed in Step 2.
5. If necessary, further adjust the recipe to reach the desired results and record the changes.
6. Produce the recipe a third time and analyze according to the same criteria listed in Step 2.
7. Repeat this process until satisfied with the results.

NOTE: A recipe has to be retested any time the ingredients or equipment change.

Standardized HACCP Recipe

HACCP—Hazard Analysis Critical Control Point is a familiar term for those who have been certified through the National Restaurant Association's ServSafe program. HACCP principles of time, temperature, and procedures when integrated into a recipe are what determine a Standardized HACCP Recipe.

Developing a recipe into a Standardized HACCP Recipe is an investment of time and effort to produce a recipe that is:

▶ Consistent

▶ Easy-to-follow—has clearly written instructions

▶ Comprehensive—includes all necessary information

▶ Safe in cooking and handling procedures

▶ Readily available at all times—is easily accessed from the kitchen computer screen

The following explanations refer to a Standardized HACCP Recipe like the one in Figure 1.1 on pp. 14–15:

> **LEARNING OBJECTIVE 5**
> Identify the elements of a Standardized HACCP Recipe.

▶ **Recipe Name:** Farfalle Arrabbiata

▶ **Recipe Source:** Recipes may be created and developed in-house (within the foodservice operation); may be a family recipe; or may be taken from cookbooks, newspapers, magazines, or the Internet. The source of the recipe should be listed.

▶ **Recipe File Code:** Typically, recipe file systems are organized by menu category (appetizers, soups, salads, pastas, entrées, desserts), and recipes are filed alphabetically or numerically within the category.

   ▷ **Sub-Categories:** Menu categories can be expanded to include sub-categories, such as entrées—beef, veal, seafood, poultry, and vegetarian selections; soups—clear soups, cream soups, thickened soups, or seasonal soups.

   ▷ **Sub-Recipes:** Recipes for products used within a number of other recipes, such as stock, sauces, or fresh pastas (example: chicken stock, pomodoro sauce, and pasta dough).

▶ **Recipe Yield:** The recipe yield is the amount available after all in-house processing has been completed, and may be expressed as:

   ▷ **A quantity produced**—example: 1.5 gallons of soup or sauce—sub-recipes are often in quantities.

   ▷ **A number of servings**—example: 20 servings of pasta—recipes are often in number of servings. A serving portion size by:

      Exact Weight—example: one 6-ounce portion of salmon

      Exact Measure—example: 8-ounce portion of soup or 3-ounce portion of peas

      Exact Count—example: five grilled shrimp per portion. The exact number of pieces for the portion size serving.

The use of accurate portion scales assures a consistent portion weight.

The use of sized ladles, spoodles, and scoops assures consistent portion measure.

The use of scored (marked) sheet pans and pie or cake scorers assures consistent cuts.

The recipe preparation time is necessary in order to prepare food production schedules.

The length of time an item can be held before quality is compromised should also be included on the recipe.

Improper holding times and temperatures can result in food-borne illness. For resources for preventing food-borne illness, see www.servsafe.com.

Kitchen equipment sites:
www.vollrath.com
www.hobartcorp.com

Each ingredient amount is recorded in both WEIGHT (density or heaviness) and MEASURE (volume).

Even Division or Pan Cuts—example: 18-inch by 26-inch sheet pan of brownies, cut 6 by 8 for 48 brownies (3-inch by 3¼-inch each piece); 10-inch pie or cake, cut 8 slices.

▶ **Preparation Time:** The amount of time that is normally needed to prepare the recipe item is easily determined during the recipe-testing phase.

▶ **Cooking Time:** The cooking time is the amount of time required to finish cooking the item. This information is especially important for items requiring roasting, simmering, or reducing. Temperature stated in degrees (example: 350°F) may also be listed.

▶ **Holding Temperature and Time** (Safe Food Temperatures):

▷ Hot holding equipment must hold food at 135°F or higher.

▷ Cold holding equipment must hold food at 41°F or lower.

▷ Monitoring and tracking the time and temperature of products must be a standard operating procedure.

▷ Temperature logs are often used to record holding temperature on a scheduled basis, such as every hour or specified number of hours (example: every 4 hours). Temperature logs are kept on file for 3 to 6 months or longer as determined by management.

▶ **Equipment to Be Used:** The necessary preparation and cooking equipment to produce the recipe item—such as cutting boards, knives, graters, pots, pans, and serving utensils—are listed.

▷ This allows employees to prepare their work station (*mise en place*) prior to beginning the preparation process and be ready to promptly serve the item after cooking or when ordered.

▷ It further eliminates wasted time and energy due to multiple trips to retrieve pots, pans, knives, etc., which contribute to frustration and increase labor costs.

▶ **Ingredients and Quantities:** Ingredients and quantities may be listed by:

▷ **The largest quantities first** and the method of preparation described below.

▷ **The order of use** during the preparation procedure.

▷ **The ingredients that are combined or worked on together** with the method of preparation listed below or to the right side of the ingredients.

▷ **Recording each ingredient amount in weight and measure** enables staff to correctly measure everything.

▷ **All recipe quantities must be recorded in the same unit (pound, ounce, etc.) the item is purchased in.** This is essential to be able to accurately determine the cost of the recipe.

▶ **Food Safety Statement:** This is a statement used to outline the basic sanitation procedures employees must carry out before beginning production.

▶ **Method of Preparation:** The method of preparation records the procedural steps to produce the recipe item and should include *Critical Control Points (CCP)* where applicable—noting required temperatures and the use of plastic gloves or tongs.

▸ **Plating and Garnish Instructions:** The plating and garnish instructions are a description of the actual placement of the food item and garnish onto the plate.

▹ The garnish must be part of the ingredient list so it can be included with the items to be purchased for the recipe, and must be eatable—adding to the plate appearance.

▸ **Proper Cooling and Storing:** Detailed instructions for cooling and storing of leftover items must include time, temperature, and procedural standards, along with attaching an item label with the date and time the item was placed in storage.

▸ **Nutritional Analysis:** The nutritional analysis information commonly includes the number of calories (1 g. protein = 4 calories, 1 g. fat = 9 calories, 1 g. carbohydrates = 4 calories) and the amount of protein, fat, cholesterol, carbohydrates, fiber, and sodium content in one serving.

▹ Some foodservice operators are including nutritional analysis information with menu item descriptions.

> Association of Nutrition & Foodservice Professionals
>
> www.ANFPonline.org

▸ **Photos:** Many foodservice operations are using digital cameras for sequential photos to detail preparation procedures and for final plate presentation; computer screens are often conveniently placed in kitchens for quick access to recipes and plate presentations.

▹ A growing number of restaurants utilize digital photography to show menu plate presentations on the restaurant's website, for lighted menu boards, and for menus presented on tablets.

> Unclear wording for procedural steps can lead to misinterpretation.

▸ **The use of clear and definitive wording** when writing or rephrasing procedural steps in a recipe is absolutely necessary in order to remove any confusion or misinterpretation in the preparation and plating of a recipe item. See the box below for an example.

Writing Procedural Steps in a Recipe

Confusing wording	Rephrased wording
Stir until well blended	Stir until uniform consistency, with no streaks.
Lightly brown	Cook until light brown in color, 3 to 5 minutes.
Steam, bake, boil until done	Steam, bake, boil for___ (a specific length of time).
Slightly undercook	Cook for a maximum of ___ minutes. Product should remain firm to the bite.
Adjust seasonings	(Phrasing is fine if a minimum quantity for each seasoning)
Hold in a warm spot	Place food in a warming oven or steam table set at 140°F.
Pierce the skin	Using a paring knife, make 1/4 inch cuts in the surface of the product.
Toss lightly	Toss ingredients together until the product is well coated with dressing or sauce mixture.

Standardized HACCP Recipe

Recipe Name: Farfalle Arrabbiata   **Source:** In-house recipe   **File Code:** Entrée - 8

Yield: 20 Servings   **Portion:** 14-ounce   **Prep. Time:** 20 minutes   **Cooking Time:** To order at the cooking line

Holding Temperature and Time: 135°F or higher and 41°F or lower at the cooking line during serving hours

Equipment:	vegetable cutting board	(2) sauté pans	cheese grater	½ hotel pan
	chef's knife	(2) 6-qt stock pots	tongs	⅛ hotel pan
	small strainer	6-oz. ladle		

Ingredients	Measure
Mixed vegetables:	
Peppers, red, sliced ¼"	8.5 cup
Peppers, green, sliced ¼"	8.5 cup
Calamata olives (pitted)	1.5 cup
Button mushrooms, whole	12 cup
Shrimp, 16/20 count, deveined tail on	100 each
Bow-tie Pasta, fresh (sub-recipe: Pasta)	5.5 lb
Olive oil	2.5 cup
Pomodoro Sauce (sub-recipe: Sauce)	1.5 gal
Parsley, chopped	1.25 cup
Parmesan cheese	1.5 cup
Bread sticks, thin, 7.5"	40 each

Food Safety Statement

• Before beginning this recipe, clean and sanitize work station—wash hands, paying attention to fingers and nails.
• Gather all equipment and utensils needed to complete the recipe. All must be clean and sanitized before proceeding.
• To avoid the possibility of spoilage, only work on as much food product as you can process in 20 minutes or less.

Method of Preparation:

1. Add 5.5 quarts of water to a 6-quart stock pot and bring to a boil; hold at the serving line until ready to cook pasta.

2. Add 1 gallon of the pomodoro sauce to another 6-quart stock pot; reheat to 165° F and hold at 135°F.

3. Wash the red and green peppers and mushrooms in the vegetable sink using cold running water. With gloved hands, slice the peppers into ¼-inch strips on the vegetable cutting board; place the peppers and mushrooms in a covered ½ hotel pan and refrigerate at 41°F or lower until needed.

4. With gloved hands, wash the parsley in the vegetable sink; place on paper towels. With gloved hands, finely chop the parsley on the vegetable cutting board; place the chopped parsley in a covered ⅛ hotel pan and refrigerate at 41°F or lower until ready to serve.

Figure 1.1   Standardized HACCP Recipe

Standardized HACCP Recipe
(continued)

To prepare one order of Farfalle Arrabbiata:

1. Sauté 1.5 ounces each of red and green peppers, 2 ounces of mushrooms, and 6 olives in 0.5 ounce of olive oil for 2 minutes or until vegetables are softened; using a 6-ounce ladle, add 6 ounces of pomodoro sauce to the vegetable mix and simmer over low heat for 5 minutes.

2. Using tongs, place 5 shrimp in a broiler and broil for 2 minutes or until lightly browned. Shrimp must be cooked to 145°F or higher for 15 seconds.

3. In the 6-quart stock pot of boiling water at the serving line, place 4 ounces of pasta into a small strainer and immerse in the boiling water for 30 seconds. Drain pasta and transfer to a sauté pan.

4. Sauté pasta in 0.5 ounce of olive oil over medium heat for 30 seconds. Transfer pasta to a 10-inch rimmed pasta bowl that has been warmed to 90°F in a plate warmer.

Plating and Garnish:

   Serviceware: 10-inch rimmed pasta bowl, warmed to 90°F in a plate warmer

Plate Presentation	Quantity
Freshly chopped parsley	0.125 ounce (a pinch = 1/8 tsp)
Parmesan cheese, grated	0.5 ounce (1 tbsp)
Breadsticks, thin, 7.5"	2

1. Pour the Pomodoro and vegetable sauce mixture over the center of the pasta.

2. Place the cooked shrimp in an evenly spaced pinwheel arrangement, backs up, tails down, into the pasta, sauce, and vegetables.

3. With gloved hands, sprinkle 0.125 ounce (a pinch) of parsley around the rim of the bowl and lightly over the pasta.

4. Grate 0.5 ounce of Parmesan cheese over the pasta.

5. **Just before server pickup,** with gloved hands, insert 2 breadsticks 2 inches into the pasta; one at 2 o'clock and the other at the 10 o'clock position; breadsticks will cross at the top of the bowl (12 o'clock position).

Proper Cooling and Storing of Leftovers	Nutritional Analysis	Photo
Note: Follow HACCP safe food-handling procedures for all recipes and sub-recipes	Optional	Optional

Figure 1.1   Standardized HACCP Recipe (continued)

Convenience Food Products

Convenience food products require a Standardized HACCP Recipe procedure for handling. Convenience food products, such as prepared bakery items—cheesecakes, pies, cakes, tortes, and so on—may need little or no preparation but need to be handled and served safely and according to the standards established by management for plate presentation.

LEARNING OBJECTIVE 6
Explain the difference between weight and volume measures used in recipes.

Weight and Volume Measures

The foodservice industry in the United States uses two units of measure—weight and volume. Every country uses the metric system except the United States, where English units are commonly used. When weight and volume measures are committed to memory it saves time to accurately calculate and convert recipe ingredient amounts.

The term "ounce" is a unit that measures smaller amounts of both weight and volume measurements. *Fluid ounce* measures volume; *ounce* measures weight..

▶ **Weight** measures density or heaviness, measured on a scale. The standard *English* unit of measure for weight is a **pound (lb),** with smaller quantities weighed by the **ounce (oz).** There are 16 ounces in a pound.
The standard *metric* unit of measure for weight is a **gram.** Large quantities are measured in **kilograms (kg),** or "kilos," which is 1000 grams.

▶ **Volume** measures space and can be wet and dry. Standard *English* units of measure are **teaspoons, tablespoons, fluid ounces, pints, quarts,** and **gallons.**
The standard *metric* unit of measure is a **liter (L).** Small quantities are measured in **milliliters (mL), or "mils"** equivalent to 1/1000 of a liter. One mil equals one **cubic centimeter (cc).**

▶ Temperature is measured in **degrees Fahrenheit (°F)** or **degrees Celsius (°C).** The freezing point of water is 32°F = 0°C. The boiling point of water registers 212°F = 100°C.

Determining the Portion Size When a Recipe Only Lists the Number of Servings

LEARNING OBJECTIVE 7
Determine the portion size when a recipe only lists the number of servings.

Recipes provided in the food section of newspapers, magazines, cookbooks, and on the Internet often just list the number of servings that a recipe will produce, such as servings for 4 to 6, 8, 12, or 25. This becomes difficult to use when needing to prepare for a larger or smaller number and to accurately identify costs. The following procedure determines the portion size and can be applied to any recipe to quickly find the portion size when it is not given.

To determine the portion size do the following:

STEP 1 **Convert the quantity for each main ingredient into ounces and then add them all up to determine *total ounces.***

▶ Use the main ingredients only—not the spices, herbs, or garnishes.

Soups and liquids would be converted into liquid ounces.

Meats and similar solid products would be converted into scaled ounces.

English Volume Measure Equivalents

1 tablespoon	1/8 cup	1/4 cup	1/2 cup	1 cup	1 pint	1 quart	1 gallon
3 teaspoons	2 tablespoons	4 tablespoons	8 tablespoons	16 tablespoons	2 cups	2 pints	4 quarts
	6 teaspoons	12 teaspoons					8 pints
						4 cups	16 cups
1/2 fluid ounce	1 fluid ounce	2 fluid ounces	4 fluid ounces	8 fluid ounces	16 fluid ounces	32 fluid ounces	128 fluid ounces

English to Metric Conversion

WEIGHT CONVERSION		VOLUME CONVERSION		TEMPERATURE CONVERSION	
ENGLISH	METRIC	ENGLISH	METRIC	ENGLISH	METRIC
ounce (oz)	gram (g)	liquid / dry	milliliters (mL) / liters (L)	Fahrenheit (°F)	Celsius (°C)
½ oz	14	1 teaspoon	5 mL	225°	105°
¾	21	1 teaspoons	10 mL	250°	120°
1	28	1 tablespoon	15 mL	275°	135°
1½	43	2 tablespoons	30 mL	300°	150°
2	57	¼ cup	59 mL	325°	165°
2½	71	⅓ cup	79 mL	350°	180°
3	85	½ cup	118 mL	375°	190°
3½	99	¾ cup	177 mL	400°	200°
4	113	1 cup	237 mL	425°	220°
4½	128	1¼ cup	296 mL	450°	230°
5	142	1½ cup	355 mL	475°	245°
6	170	2 cups (1 pint)	473 mL		
7	196	2½ cups	591 mL		
8	227	3 cups	710 mL		
9	255	25.4 fl oz	750 mL		
10	283	4 cups (1 qt)	0.95 L		
12	340	33.8 fl oz	1 L		
16 (= 1 lb)	454	59.2 fl oz	1.75 L		
2.2 lb	1000 g (= 1 kg)	1 gal (4 qt)	3.8 L		

Quick Formula for Converting Temperatures:
°F to °C   subtract 32, then multiply by .55
°C to °F   multiply by 1.8, then subtract 32

Liquid Volume Measure Equivalents

Dividing in Half	Doubling Up
1 gallon = 128 ounces ÷ 2 = 64 oz. (½ gal)	**1 cup** = 8 ounces × 2 = 16 oz. (1 pt)
1/2 gallon = 64 ounces ÷ 2 = 32 oz. (1 qt)	**1 pint** = 16 ounces × 2 = 32 oz. (1 qt)
1 quart = 32 ounces ÷ 2 = 16 oz. (1 pt)	**1 quart** = 32 ounces × 2 = 64 oz. (½ gal)
1 pint = 16 ounces ÷ 2 = 8 oz. (1 cup)	**1/2 gallon** = 64 ounces × 2 = 128 oz. (1 gal)
1 cup = 8 ounces	**1 gallon** = 128 ounces

STEP 2 Divide the *total ounces* the recipe produces by the *number of servings* to determine the *portion size.*

$$\frac{\text{Total Number of Ounces the Recipe Produces}}{\text{Number of Servings}} = \textbf{Portion Size}$$

NOTE: This method determines *an initial approximation of the portion size* that can be refined once the recipe is actually produced. The portion size can then be evaluated for conformity with other similar menu items.

The Chicken Noodle Soup recipe example (see Step 1 in the box below) shows the quantities of all ingredients converted into measure equivalencies, regardless of the normal purchasing or serving unit (except for garnishes, spices, and seasonings). The following steps show how to determine the serving portion size for 25 servings.

STEP 1 Determine the total ounces.

Example: Chicken Noodle Soup Recipe
Yield: 25 Servings

Ingredients	Amount Measure		Ounces per Unit		Total Ounces
Chicken Stock	1.5 gal	×	128 (oz per gal)	=	192 ounces
Chicken breast, shredded	5 cup	×	8 (oz per cup)	=	40 ounces
Bow-tie egg noodles	5 cup	×	8	=	40 ounces
Onion, Spanish, ¼″ dice	1.5 cup	×	8	=	12 ounces
Carrots, thin slice	1.75 cup	×	8	=	14 ounces
Bay Leaf	3 each				
Parsley, chopped	3 tbsp				
Celery Salt	1.5 tsp				
Pepper	1.5 tsp				
				+	
				TOTAL:	**298 ounces**

This recipe yields a total of **approximately 298 ounces** of uncooked Chicken Noodle Soup. Given the soup will simmer out and reduce—and the onions, carrots, noodles, and all ingredients will cook down on average 10 to 15 percent—it is fair to say that the recipe will probably **yield about 253 servable ounces** after the cooking loss (298 × .85 = 253.3; round to 253). The exact yield would be determined when the recipe is actually cooked and tested.

STEP 2 Determine the *serving portion size:*

Total Number of Ounces the Recipe Produces	÷	Number of Servings	=	**Portion Size**
253	÷	25	=	10.12 rounded to **10 oz**

NOTE: A 10-ounce portion (large bowl) would typically be served as a soup entrée.

> When calculating portion size, always round down.

Complete Assignment 1 beginning on p. 21.

Recipe Conversion

Recipes often have to be converted (sized) to yield a different number of servings. Recipe software programs can quickly adjust the quantities of ingredients needed to yield a greater or lesser number of servings. When converting recipe yield *without* the use of a computer, use the conversion procedure as shown in the following example. (Refer also to Figure 1.2 on the following page.)

NOTE: This is also commonly known as *scaling a recipe.*

Example: Recipe Conversion for Chicken Noodle Soup

The Chicken Noodle Soup recipe on page 18 yields 25 servings. The yield needs to be reduced to 15 servings (with the same serving portion size) in order to accommodate a catered lunch group. The following steps need to occur to size the recipe down to 15:

STEP 1 Determine the conversion multiplier:

New Yield (number of servings)	÷	Original Yield (number of servings)	=	Conversion Multiplier
15	÷	25	=	0.6

STEP 2 Convert each ingredient's original recipe quantity into ounces:

Ingredient's Original Measure	×	Number of Ounces per Unit of Measure	=	Number of Ounces of Ingredient
1.5 Gallons Chicken Stock	×	128 Ounces per Gallon	=	192 Ounces Chicken Stock

STEP 3 Multiply the ingredient quantity in ounces by the conversion multiplier to determine the amount needed for the new yield:

Ingredient Quantity (ounces)	×	Conversion Multiplier	=	Sized Amount (in ounces)
192	×	0.6	=	115.2 ounces Chicken Stock

STEP 4 Convert each ingredient quantity back to standard units of measure:

115.2 ounces ÷ 32 ounces per quart = 3.6 quarts

0.6 quart × 32 ounces per quart = 19.2 ounces

19.2 ounces ÷ 8 ounces per cup = 2.4 rounded to 2.5 cups

115.2 ounces converts to 3 quarts + about 2.5 cups Chicken Stock

3 quarts (32 oz per quart)	=	96 ounces
2.5 cups (8 oz per cup)	=	+ 20 ounces
Total:		**116 ounces**

Rounding of numbers to make the measured amounts easier to work with will not significantly affect the product or cost.

Follow the same procedure in Steps 2, 3, and 4 for the remainder of ingredients.

▸ **When the serving portion size changes**—for example, if the original 25-serving portion size for the Chicken Noodle Soup was 10 ounces (bowl), and the new 15-serving portion size is 6 ounces (cup), the conversion multiplier would be calculated as follows:

Original Yield: 25 servings × 10 ounces each = 250 ounces

New Yield: 15 servings × 6 ounces each = 90 ounces

$$\textbf{Conversion Multiplier} = \frac{\text{New Yield}}{\text{Original Yield}} = \frac{90 \text{ ounces}}{250 \text{ ounces}} = \textbf{0.36}$$

▸ When increasing the size of a standardized recipe to many times the original quantity (example: 25 servings to 200 servings), care must be taken to **select the correct size cooking equipment** in order to accommodate the increased food quantity; **preparation and cooking times** may need to be increased and care must be taken to **adjust the amount of spices and herbs needed.** If a recipe is significantly reduced in size, then **the cooking temperature** may need to be adjusted in order to keep the food from drying out. The end goal is to assure that the new recipe amount produces the same quality as the original recipe.

▸ **Baked items that use a leavening agent** must also be carefully adjusted because they rely on precise interactions with other ingredients to achieve the proper chemical reaction.

Complete Assignment 2 on p. 25

Recipe Conversion

Recipe: Chicken Noodle Soup   **Portion Size:** 10 ounces

New Yield	÷	Original Yield	=	Conversion Multiplier
15	÷	25	=	0.6

A	B	×	C	=	D	E
Ingredients	**Total Ounces**		**Conversion Multiplier**		**Sized Amounts**	**Standard Unit of Measure**
Chicken stock	1.5 gal × 128 = 192 oz		0.6		115.2 oz	3 qt + 2.5 cup
Chicken breast, shredded	5 cup × 8 = 40 oz		0.6		24.0 oz	3 cup
Bow-tie egg noodles	5 cup × 8 = 40 oz		0.6		24.0 oz	3 cup
Onions, ¼" dice	1.50 cup = 12 oz		0.6		7.2 oz	1 cup
Carrots, thin slice	1.75 cup = 14 oz		0.6		8.4 oz	1 cup
Bay leaf	3 each		0.6		2 bay leaf	2 bay leaf
Parsley, chopped	3 tbsp		0.6		1.75 tbsp	1.75 tbsp
Celery salt	1.5 tsp		0.6		0.9 tsp	1 tsp
Pepper	1.5 tsp		0.6		0.9 tsp	1 tsp

Figure 1.2 Recipe Conversion

Assignment 1

The purpose of Assignment 1 is to actively demonstrate how to write a Standardized HACCP Recipe, adjust it for specific serving portions, and write clear instructions. The assignment is divided into 4 steps. The recipe below is your starting point.

This is an example of a recipe that is typically obtained from the Internet.

Recipe Name: Golden Potato Soup   **Source:** Internet

Yield: 8 to 10 servings   **Prep. Time:** 25 minutes   **Cooking Time:** 50 minutes

Ingredients:

3 cups peeled and cubed potatoes
½ cup chopped celery
½ cup chopped onion
1 cup chicken stock
1½ teaspoon chopped parsley
½ teaspoon salt
1 pinch ground black pepper
2 teaspoons flour
1½ cups milk
1½ cups shredded cheddar cheese
1 cup chopped ham

Method of Preparation:

1. In a large stock pot, add potatoes, celery, onion, chicken stock and parsley. Season with salt and pepper and simmer until vegetables become tender.

2. In a separate bowl mix flour and milk. Once it is well blended, add to soup mixture and cook until soup becomes thick.

3. Stir in cheese and ham; simmer until cheese is melted.

STEP 1. **Determine the total ounces for the Standardized HACCP Recipe for Golden Potato Soup below.**

NOTE: The ingredients for a thickened soup will cook down, on average 5 to 10%.

Recipe: Golden Potato Soup
Yield: 8–10 servings   **Portion Size:**

Ingredients	Amount Measure		Ounces per Unit		Total Ounces
3 cups peeled and cubed potatoes	3.00 cup	×	8 (oz. per cup)	=	24 oz
½ cup chopped celery	0.50 cup	×	8	=	4 oz
½ cup chopped onion	0.50 cup	×	8	=	4 oz
1 cup chicken stock	1.00 cup	×	8	=	8 oz
1½ teaspoon chopped parsley	1.50 tsp				
½ teaspoon salt	0.50 tsp				
1 pinch ground pepper	0.125 tsp				
2 teaspoons flour	2.00 tsp				
1½ cups milk	1.50 cup	×	8	=	12 oz
1½ cups shredded Cheddar cheese	1.50 cup	×	8	=	12 oz
1 cup chopped ham	1.00 cup	×	8	+ =	8 oz
				TOTAL:	72 oz*

* The recipe yields a total of approximately 72 uncooked ounces. Given the ingredients will cook down—on average 5–10 percent, to about 90 percent of its original quantity—the recipe will probably yield about **65 servable ounces.** [72 × .90 = 64.8 rounded to 65 ounces]

STEP 2. **Review the "Standardized HACCP Recipe" section beginning on p. 11 as a guide. Also, review the section entitled "Determining the Portion Size When a Recipe Only Lists the Number of Servings" that begins on p. 16 to determine an initial approximation of the recipe portion size.**

To determine the serving portion sizes, divide the recipe yield by the desired number of servings.

_____ ÷   8   servings   =   _____ ounce portion
_____ ÷   9   servings   =   _____ ounce portion
_____ ÷ 10 servings   =   _____ ounce portion

STEP 3. **Method of Preparation: This would need to be rewritten with clear and defined wording after preparing and cooking the recipe—documenting cooking times, temperatures, and rephrasing the procedural wording. (Use the space provided on the following page to practice writing the Method of Preparation based on just the information provided in the recipe instructions.) Refer to Writing Procedural Steps in a Recipe on p. 13.**

The example that follows is from the recipe at this point—all that remains is to identify the needed kitchen equipment. Cooking times will not be known until the cooking begins and the actual times are recorded.

Example:

1. In a large stock pot (what size?) add potatoes, celery, onion, chicken stock, and parsley; (then what?) stir and season with salt and pepper, and (simmer for how long?) cook over medium heat for (how many?) minutes or until vegetables become tender.

2. In a separate bowl (what size?), using a whisk, blend flour and milk to a uniform consistency, then add to vegetable mixture frequently stirring for (how many minutes?) or until the soup becomes thick.

3. Stir in shredded cheese and chopped ham, and cook for (how many minutes?) or until cheese is melted.

NOTE: To standardize a recipe, the recipe is tested, adjusted, and retested until it produces a menu item as management wants the item produced; tested three consecutive times with the same result.

Method of Preparation:

_____

_____

_____

_____

_____

_____

_____

_____

_____

_____

_____

_____

_____

_____

_____

_____

STEP 4. Complete the Standardized HACCP Recipe form on the following page by using 8 servings with the serving portion size that you determined. So the yield should read: 8 servings, _____ ounce portion. Also complete the following:

Holding Temperature and Time: The HACCP temperature for holding hot foods

Equipment: The equipment needed based upon the recipe

Method of Preparation: The specific method, based on the recipe information (not having prepared or cooked the recipe at this point), used for 8 servings of the portion size determined. Fill in the blank spaces with as much information that is known at this point

Serviceware: The size of the soup bowl based upon the serving portion size

Standardized HACCP Recipe

Recipe Name: Golden Potato Soup   Source: Internet   File Code: Soup - Thickened

Yield: _____   Portion: _____   Prep. Time: 25 min.   Cooking Time: 50 min.

Holding Temperature and Time: _____

Equipment: _____

_____

_____

_____

Ingredients	Amount Measure
Potatoes, Yukon Gold, chop, ½-inch cube	3 cup
Celery, dice, ¼ inch	0.5 cup
Onion, Spanish, dice, ¼ inch	0.5 cup
Chicken stock	1 cup
Parsley, chopped	1.5 tsp
Salt	0.5 tsp
Pepper, ground	0.125 tsp
Flour, all-purpose	2 tsp
Milk, whole	1.5 cup
Cheddar cheese, shredded	1.5 cup
Ham, baked, chop, ½ inch cube	1 cup

Food Safety Statement
• Before beginning this recipe, clean and sanitize work station— wash hands, paying attention to fingers and nails.
• Gather all equipment and utensils needed to complete the recipe. All must be clean and sanitized before proceeding.
• To avoid the possibility of spoilage, only work on as much food product as you can process in 20 minutes or less.

Method of Preparation:

1. In a _____ stock pot, add potatoes, celery, onion, chicken stock, and parsley. Using a _____ stir and season with salt and pepper, and _____ for _____ minutes or until vegetables become tender.

2. In a _____ mixing bowl, using a whisk, blend flour and milk to a uniform consistency then add to vegetable mixture, frequently stirring for _____ minutes or until the soup becomes thick.

3. Stir in shredded cheese and chopped ham and cook for _____ minutes or until the cheese is melted.

Serviceware:

NOTE: The ingredients are further defined, such as Potatoes, Yukon Gold, chop, ½-inch cube. Section 2, Chapter 3, "Purchasing Functions" will explain product specifications.

Assignment 2

Convert the recipe from Assignment 1 to increase the yield to 24 servings with the same serving portion size determined in Assignment 1, Step 4, p. 23.

Recipe Conversion

Recipe: Golden Potato Soup   Portion Size:

New Yield: _____   ÷   Original Yield: _____   =   _____ (Conversion Multiplier)

A Ingredients	B Total Ounces	× 	C Conversion Multiplier	= 	D Sized Amounts	E Standard Unit of Measure

---

Summary

A restaurant's menu should always be in sync with its primary customers, and represent a certain food style or theme. The menu item recipes should be based on the preferences and tastes of the customers, fit with the kitchen capacity and equipment, and meet the skill level of the staff preparing the recipes.

The time and effort invested to develop and produce Standardized HACCP Recipes is returned with the following benefits: Recipes that are consistent, easy-to-follow, comprehensive by including all of the necessary information, safe in cooking and handling procedures, and readily available at all times when accessed from a kitchen computer screen.

When weight and volume measures are committed to memory it becomes a time saver in accurately calculating and converting recipe ingredient amounts. Weight measures density or heaviness, and is measured on a scale. Volume measures space and can be wet or dry.

The recipe cookbooks that are developed for commercial kitchens typically list the number of servings and serving "portion size" that a recipe produces. Apart from those cookbooks, the portion size for most recipes has to be determined by a specific procedure. That procedure begins with an approximate estimate based upon the recipe ingredient amounts, and is then further checked for accuracy when the recipe is actually produced.

Recipes sizes quite often need to be converted to produce more or less of the original recipe, or to produce a different serving "portion size." When this occurs, a specific procedure needs to be followed, initially by determining the recipe conversion multiplier. Also, additional cooking factors must be considered, such as the amount of time needed to prepare the new amount and any changes to the size of the cooking equipment.

It all begins with determining the best menu items to serve to the customers, which is then supported by Standardized HACCP Recipes that will assure consistency and safe food handling and procedures.

Discussion Questions

1. What is the essential information that must be determined when identifying the primary customers for a restaurant?
2. Discuss the factors that define a particular food style of theme.
3. When selecting a recipe what should be considered?
4. List the function and purpose of standardized recipes.
5. Describe some of the consequences that may occur when not using standardized recipes.
6. A recipe is standardized when it is produced how may consecutive times with the same result?
7. What is the result when a recipe is developed into a Standardized HACCP Recipe?
8. Contrast the difference between weight and volume measures in recipes.
9. What is an easy way to remember liquid volume measure equivalents?
10. Explain the two-step procedure to determine the portion size when a recipe only lists the number of servings.
11. When converting a recipe to yield a different number of servings, how is the conversion multiplier determined?
12. Explain the four-steps to simply convert any recipe. Also, what happens if the new serving portion size changes — for example, from a 10-ounce bowl to a 6-ounce cup.

Project Exercises

These exercises are further added upon in Chapter 2 Portion Cost.

1. Create a semi á la carte menu that reflects a primary food style or theme. The menu must include one item from each of the following categories: Soup, Salad, Entrée (with sides), and Dessert. The menu should be typed (Times New Roman or Courier typeface) on a single-page of white bond paper. A brief ingredient description should follow each menu item.

   NOTE: An example of an (Italian) Tuscan semi á la carte menu, with menu item ingredient descriptions, begins on page 278, "The Menu" in the Appendix.

2. Prepare a Standardized HACCP Recipe for each of the semi á la carte menu items. Some menu items may require a sub-recipe, such as fresh pasta or sauce, which should be a separate Standardized HACCP Recipe. Each recipe and sub-recipe must be typed and submitted on the Standardized HACCP Recipe form that is available in Excel format for this text / work book.

Kitchen Essentials

The Vollrath Company, LLC

SEE MORE AT vollrathuniversity.com

Portion Control Menu Planner

Delivering proper nutrition and controlling your food costs demands accurate, repeatable portion sizing. The trouble is, how do you ensure that your kitchen staff and servers are using the proper size utensil? Vollrath simplifies portion control with a complete system of serving utensils, color-coded for quick and easy size selection. Your menu calls for 2 ounces of vegetables, tell your staff to use the blue Spoodle˚. Serving 4 ounces of stuffing? Use a gray disher. It's that simple. No more searching through a drawer of look-alike utensils trying to read the capacity stamps.

Color	CAPACITY (ounces)	CAPACITY (cups)	APPROX. SERVINGS PER QUART	DISHER②③ VOLLRATH ITEM NUMBER	ROUND SPOODLE② VOLLRATH ITEM NUMBER ONE-PIECE SOLID/PERF. TWO-PIECE SOLID/PERF.	OVAL SPOODLE② VOLLRATH ITEM NUMBER ONE-PIECE SOLID/PERF	LADLE② VOLLRATH ITEM NUMBER ONE-PIECE TWO-PIECE
	3/4	3/32	40	47147			
	1	1/8	30	47146	6433120/6432120 61147/61145	6412120/6422120	4980120 58011
	1 1/3	1/6	24	47145			
	1 5/8	7/32	20	47144			
	2	1/4	16	47143	6433230/6432230 62157/62155	6412230/6422230	4980230 58322
	2 2/3	1/3	12	47142			
	3①	3/8①	10	47141	6433335/6432335 62167/62165	6412335/6422335	4980335 58333
	4	1/2	8	47140	6433445/6432445 62172/62170	6412445/6422445	4980445 58344
	5 1/3	2/3	6	47139			
	6	3/4	5		6433655/6432655 62177/62175	6412655/6422655	4980655 58355
	8	1	4		6433865/6432865 62182/62180	6412865/6422865	4980865 58366

①Disher Capacity: 3 1/4 oz. (2/5 cup)   Additional disher capacities available

STEAM TABLE PAN	SERVING SIZE (OZ)	FULL SIZE 20¾" X 12¾" DEPTH (INCHES)			TWO THIRDS SIZE 13⅞" X 12¾" DEPTH (INCHES)			HALF SIZE 10⅜" X 12¾" DEPTH (INCHES)			HALF SIZE LONG 20¾" X 6⅜" DEPTH (INCHES)			ONE THIRD SIZE 6⅞" X 12¾" DEPTH (INCHES)			ONE FOURTH SIZE 6½" X 10⅜" DEPTH (INCHES)			ONE SIXTH SIZE 6⅞" X 6¼" DEPTH (INCHES)		
		2½	4	6	2½	4	6	2½	4	6	2½	4	6	2½	4	6	2½	4	6	2½	4	6
Super Pan V	1	268	452	684	176	296	452	136	214	322	120	184	264	85	134	197	60	96	146	40	60	87
Super Pan 3	1	294	448	672	182	270	402	128	202	301	125	192	277	81	125	185	57	84	128	37	55	78
Super Pan V	2	134	226	342	88	148	226	68	107	161	60	92	132	42	67	98	30	48	73	20	30	43
Super Pan 3	2	147	228	338	91	135	201	64	101	151	62	96	138	40	62	92	28	42	64	18	28	39
Super Pan V	3	89	150	228	58	98	150	45	71	107	40	61	88	28	44	66	20	32	48	13	20	29
Super Pan 3	3	98	149	224	60	90	134	42	67	100	41	64	92	27	41	61	19	28	42	12	18	26
Super Pan V	4	67	113	171	44	74	113	34	53	80	30	46	66	21	33	49	15	24	36	10	15	21
Super Pan 3	4	74	112	168	45	67	100	32	51	75	31	48	69	20	31	46	14	21	32	9	14	20
Super Pan V	6	44	75	114	29	49	75	22	35	53	20	30	44	14	22	32	10	16	24	6	10	14
Super Pan 3	6	49	75	112	30	45	67	21	34	50	20	32	46	13	20	30	9	14	21	6	9	13
Super Pan V	8	33	56	85	22	37	56	17	26	40	15	23	33	10	16	24	7	12	18	5	7	10
Super Pan 3	8	37	56	84	22	33	50	16	25	38	15	24	34	10	15	23	7	10	16	4	7	10

Light Blue = Super Pan V
Dark Blue = Super Pan 3

8-5

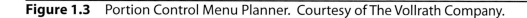

Figure 1.3   Portion Control Menu Planner. Courtesy of The Vollrath Company.

2

Portion Cost

Introduction

The portion cost for each menu item is the basis for determining the menu selling price for those items. A POS system with a menu management software program integrates purchasing functions with Recipe and Plate Cost Cards in a way that keeps Recipe Cost Cards and Plate Cost Cards current. Although experienced foodservice managers understand how to manually maintain effective portion costing through the use of procedural controls, the portion cost for each menu item should be identified and kept current in order to effectively control menu costs. This chapter presents procedures that identify portion costs, and butcher and cooking loss yields, as well as for determining minimum menu selling prices.

Learning Objectives

Upon successfully completing this chapter, readers will be able to:

1. Know the portion costing options that can be used by foodservice operators.
2. Discuss the application and use of Recipe Cost Cards.
3. Explain how the Spice Factor is determined and calculated.
4. Understand how to calculate product yield amounts when determining ingredient quantities to purchase for menu items.
5. Demonstrate the application and use of Plate Cost Cards for determining menu pricing.
6. Prepare a Plate Cost Card for a salad bar or buffet menu.
7. Understand the purpose of a Butcher Test and know what it identifies.
8. Explain the importance of the Cooking Loss Test and how it functions.

Chapter Outline

Portion Costing Options	Menu Pricing
Recipe Cost Card	Butcher Test
Spice Factor	Cooking Loss Test
Product Yield Amounts	Summary
Purchasing Quantities	Discussion Questions
Plate Cost Card	Project Exercises

Key Terms and Definitions

Begin by first reading the key terms and their definitions. An advanced understanding of the terms will be helpful prior to reading the chapter.

À la Carte Pricing	All menu items priced individually.
AP (As Purchased)	Acronym for raw food products received from suppliers.
AS (As Served)	Acronym for food that has been processed, prepared, cooked, and ready to serve to customers.
Buffet	Menu selections that may include a variety of soups, salads, entrées, pastas, potatoes, rice, vegetables, desserts, and beverages for a set price.
Butcher Test	Used for food products that can be measured for a set quality standard and quantity yield, such as beef, pork, lamb, veal, and fish.
Cooking Loss Test	Used for menu items that will experience shrinkage during the cooking process.
Minimum Menu Price	The lowest menu price or *minimum selling price* for a menu item determined by dividing the plate cost by the food cost %.
Oven Prepared	The quantity remaining after the raw trims have been removed and the item is oven-ready.
Plate Cost Card	A form used to calculate the cost of one complete menu item.
Portion Cost	Determined by dividing the recipe cost by the number of portions.
Prix-Fixe Menu	Offers a complete meal at a fixed price.
Product Yield Charts	The reference used in order to simplify the procedure when converting purchasing units from weight-to-volume equivalencies and from raw to trimmed food yields, and when determining cooking yields
Raw Trims	Parts that are not usable as an item is being prepared to be cooked, such as fat and additional trimming scraps.
Recipe Cost Card	A form used to calculate the total cost of a specific menu item using a Standardized HACCP Recipe to produce it.
Semi–à la Carte Pricing	Several menu items or selections grouped together for one price.
Spice Factor (SF)	A percentage that is added to every menu item to account for the cost of spices, herbs, seasonings, garnishes, condiments, and waste.

Portion Costing Options

The complexity of the menu, employee skill level, purchasing choices, and management preference will determine the portion costing options that a foodservice operation will use.

LEARNING OBJECTIVE 1
Know the portion costing options that can be used by foodservice operators.

The portion costing options are as follows:

► **Recipe Cost Card:** a form used to calculate the total cost of a specific menu item using a Standardized HACCP Recipe to produce it.

► **Plate Cost Card:** a form used to calculate the cost of one complete menu item as it is served to the customer.

  ▷ The plate cost is determined by adding the total from the Recipe Cost Card to the additional items (side dishes) included with the menu item.

► **Butcher Test:** used to identify the quality and the quantity yield of an item such as beef, pork, lamb, veal, and fish (after cutting and trimming).

  ▷ After the Butcher Test, the items may be portioned, cooked, and served; an item such as prime rib of beef may be roasted first and portioned after cooking.

   NOTE: If the item is portioned after cooking, a Cooking Loss Test would be used to calculate the final portion cost.

► **Cooking Loss Test:** used for menu items that will experience shrinkage during the cooking process.

  ▷ The items are only portioned after cooking.

  ▷ The items may have some additional trimming—**Example:** prime rib of beef.

Recipe Cost Card

LEARNING OBJECTIVE 2
Discuss the application and use of Recipe Cost Cards.

A Recipe Cost Card is a form used to calculate the total cost of a specific menu item using a Standardized HACCP Recipe to produce it. To keep costs current, it is critical to frequently update the pricing on Recipe Cost Cards because prices from suppliers change often.

The information in the Recipe Cost Card (see Figure 2.1 on p. 35) functions as follows:

► **Date:** The date of the most current cost posting to the Recipe Cost Card

► **Recipe Name:** Chicken Noodle Soup (introduced in chapter 1, p. 18.

► **File Code:** Soup-6

► **Yield:** 25 servings

► **Portion:** 10-ounce

► **Spice Factor (SF):** 10% (further explained in the example on p. 32). This is a percentage that is added to every menu item to account for the following:

A POS system that integrates purchasing functions with Recipe Cost Cards may be able to transfer current costs (supplier invoice prices) to Recipe Cost Cards.

1. Spices, herbs, seasonings, oils, and syrups used in quantities that are difficult to identify along with condiments such as mustard, catsup, Tabasco, A-1, Worcestershire sauce, jams, preserves, etc.

2. Garnishes such as pickles, pickle chips, radishes, olives, spiced apple rings, parsley, mint sprigs, powdered sugar, orange slices, etc.

3. Waste, such as small amounts of product left in a can or jar or small amounts spilled or dripped

> NOTE: Menu item recipes that include sub-recipes, such as sauces or fresh pastas—Example: Pomodoro sauce and pasta dough—will include the SF when calculating the cost of the completed menu item recipe, not the sub-recipes.

LEARNING OBJECTIVE 3
Explain how the Spice Factor is determined and calculated.

The SF % represents a proportion percentage of all food items purchased and is determined by:

1. Reviewing recipes and inventory to identify SF items

2. Identifying the frequency and total cost of purchasing the SF items over a period of time, such as by the month and for the year

3. Identifying the total cost for all food purchases for the same period of time—**Example:** for the year

4. Dividing the total cost of the SF items by the total cost of all food items to determine the SF %

$$\frac{\text{Total Cost, Spice Factor Items}}{\text{Total Cost, All Food Items}} = \textbf{Spice Factor \%}$$

A decimal answer is converted to a percentage if multiplied by 100. The decimal point is moved two places to the right. This will pertain to all percentage conversions throughout the text.

Example: If the total cost of all food items purchased for the year was $960,500 and the total cost of all of the SF items was $93,200, the SF would be 10%, calculated as follows:

$$\frac{\$93,200 \text{ (Spice Factor Items)}}{\$960,500 \text{ (All Food Items)}} = 0.097 \times 100 = 9.7\% \text{ rounded up to } \textbf{10\%}$$

> NOTE: The SF percentage will vary according to the complexity of the menu and recipes; fast food would have a lower SF compared to fine dining.

SF is noted in Column E—**Purchasing Cost**—for the bay leaf, parsley, celery salt, and pepper.

▶ **Recipe Cost–AS:** includes the SF and is determined by multiplying the Sum of Ingredient Costs by the SF. (See Figure 2.1 on p. 35 for calculating the Recipe Cost–AS).

> NOTE: **AS** is the acronym for **As** Served: food that has been processed, prepared, cooked, and ready to serve to customers.

Portion costs must be current in order to maintain accurate menu selling prices.

▶ **Portion Cost:** determined by dividing the Recipe Cost by the Number of Portions. (See Figure 2.1 for calculating the Portion Cost.)

▶ **Recipe Contents:** completed by transferring the information directly from the Standardized HACCP Recipe to the following columns on the Recipe Cost Card:

  ▷ **Column A,** the **Quantity**

  ▷ **Column B,** the measuring **Unit**

  ▷ **Column C,** the **Ingredient**

  Example: 1.50 (Quantity), gal (Unit), and Chicken stock (Ingredient)

▶ **Purchasing:** AP is the acronym for **As Purchased**—**Example:** raw food products received from suppliers.

  ▷ **Column D** records the measuring **Unit** in which the ingredient item is purchased—that is, the unit of measure as it appears on the invoice.

  ▷ **Column E** is the actual purchase price, **Cost,** taken directly from current purchasing invoices.

▶ **A POS system that integrates purchasing functions with Recipe Cost Cards** will automatically transfer current costs to the Recipe Cost Cards—and the current ingredient cost would be adjusted on the Recipe Cost Cards. If the Recipe Cost exceeds a predetermined set amount, the system would alert the manager that the Recipe Cost and Menu Selling Price are not in alignment, requiring corrective action.

When converting the recipe unit into the purchasing unit by the use of a calculator, it is essential to know units of measurements: weights and volume measures.

  Example: Chicken Stock, qt (Unit) and $2.20 (Cost). The Chicken Stock is priced per quart.

Chicken Stock may be available in three options:

  1. Produced in-house, therefore a sub-recipe is taken from the recipe stock category that has current cost prices.

  2. Prepared using a stock base.

  3. Purchased in a can or carton.

▶ **Conversion Amounts:**

  ▷ **Column F** is the **Quantity** needed to be purchased for each ingredient—converted from the recipe quantity to the purchasing quantity.

  ▷ **Column G, Unit,** is the unit that the recipe ingredient item is converted (changed) to in order to be purchased—**Example:** cups to pounds).

  ▷ **Column H** shows the converted **Cost**—**Example:** for onions, 50-lb cost is converted to per-pound cost).

  Example: Chicken breast, pound: Purchasing Unit (Column D) and Recipe Unit (Column B) match, therefore the Purchasing Unit just transfers to the Conversion Unit (Column G—lb). The Purchasing Cost (Column E—$4.25 per pound) is transferred to Column H.

> When the recipe unit and the purchasing unit *are not* the same, convert the recipe unit into the purchasing unit.

> When the recipe unit and the purchasing unit *are* the same, just the purchasing cost amount may need to be converted.

Example: Bow-tie egg noodles, purchased in a 10-pound case, which is the Purchasing Unit (Column D), but the recipe unit is by the pound. Therefore the Purchasing Cost ($17.50) is divided by the Purchasing Unit (10 lbs) to determine the Recipe Unit Cost (per lb).

$$\frac{\$17.50 \text{ Purchasing Cost}}{10 \text{ lbs Purchasing Unit}} = \textbf{\$1.75 per lb Unit Cost} \text{ (Column H)}$$

Example: Onions are typically purchased in 50-pound bags and carrots in 25-pound bags, which are the Purchasing Units. Therefore the Purchasing Cost is divided by the Purchasing Unit to determine the Unit Cost (per lb).

Onions:

$$\frac{\$46.00 \text{ Purchasing Cost}}{50 \text{ lbs Purchasing Unit}} = \textbf{\$0.92 per lb Unit Cost} \text{ (Column H)}$$

Carrots:

$$\frac{\$24.00 \text{ Purchasing Cost}}{25 \text{ lbs Purchasing Unit}} = \textbf{\$0.96 per lb Unit Cost} \text{ (Column H)}$$

► **Recipe Cost:**

  ▷ **Column I** is determined by multiplying the Converted Purchasing Quantity (Column F) by the Converted Unit Cost (Column H).

	F		H		I
Chicken stock	6.00	×	2.20	=	$13.20
Chicken breast	2.30	×	4.25	=	$9.78
Bow-tie egg noodles	1.25	×	1.75	=	$2.19
Onion, ¼" dice	0.50	×	0.92	=	$0.46
Carrots, thin slice	0.50	×	0.96	=	$0.48
Sum of Ingredient Costs					**$26.11**

► **Recipe Cost–AS:** the Sum of Ingredient Costs multiplied by 1 plus the Spice Factor. (1 is added to the Spice Factor [1 + .10 = 1.10] to quickly arrive at the recipe cost.)

► **Portion Cost:** the Recipe Cost–AS divided by the Number of Portions.

Determine the Quantities to Purchase

Some foodservice operators will use the acronym EP (Edible Portion) in place of AS; both terms accurately convey the meaning of food being ready to serve to customers.

The recipe ingredients need to be reviewed in order to determine the quantity of each ingredient to purchase. This begins with understanding AP (As Purchased) and AS (As Served) amounts.

► **The AP amount of raw food products is the quantity needed to end up with the AS amount listed in a recipe.** The cost of recipe ingredients must be based on the AP amount of product that will result in the AS amount that the recipe produces.

Figure 2.1   Recipe Cost Card for Chicken Noodle Soup

▶ **Review the Recipe Contents section of Figure 2.1.** Identify the Quantity and Unit amounts that will remain the same and those that will need to be converted because of yield factors.

   ▷ Chicken stock (remain the same)

   ▷ Chicken breast purchased raw*

   ▷ Bow-tie egg noodles (remain the same)

   ▷ Onions purchased raw*

   ▷ Carrots purchased raw*

> Chicken stock and bow-tie egg noodles are listed in amounts that automatically become the AP amounts.

---

* Chicken breast, shredded is listed with a quantity of 2 pounds, but children breasts are purchased raw. Therefore, to produce 2 pounds of cooked chicken breast, 2.30 pounds will need to be purchased. Onions and carrots are listed with quantity unit as cups. The recipe lists 1.50 cups of diced onions and 1.75 cups of sliced carrots. The purchasing units need to be adjusted in order for the yield amounts (from raw to trimmed product yields) to produce the amounts needed (1.50 cups of diced onions and 1.75 cups of sliced carrots).

▷ Bay leaf, celery salt, parsley, and pepper are in the SF category—no conversion necessary

► **Weight and Measure Equivalencies:** When converting purchasing units from weight-to-volume equivalencies, from raw-to-trimmed-food yields, remember that these conversions are approximations and differ depending on the ingredient being measured and will depend on what form the ingredient is converted to, such as peeled, sliced, chopped, diced, or minced.

Example: Onions—1.50 cups diced converted to 0.50 pounds

NOTE: The kitchen-proven method is to actually dice the amount of onions needed to fill 1.50 cups, recording the weight of the onions prior to peeling and trimming.

► **Yield amounts** must be included so that an adequate amount of raw food products can be purchased.

▷ If the difference between the AP ingredient amount and the recipe ingredient amount is minimal, the recipe and the final portion cost (serving) will not be greatly affected for the size of a 25-portion (serving) recipe. This would not be the case if the recipe was changed to 250 or 500 portions; the adjustment would have to be made for accurate purchasing and costing. Therefore, recipe yields have to be determined before purchasing takes place.

► **Produce Yield Charts** are available from different sources, including foodservice distributors such as U.S. Foods as well as various websites and software applications. The charts provide approximate yield percentages for a wide range of products. A yield list of common food products is provided in Figure 2.6 on pp. 53–55. These yield percentages represent raw unprocessed items that have been peeled, trimmed, washed, and cut. The yield percentages will vary according to the product being processed.

LEARNING OBJECTIVE 4
Understand how to calculate product yield amounts when determining ingredient quantities to purchase for menu items.

> **Complete Assignment 3, beginning on p. 46.**

Plate Cost Card

A Plate Cost Card (see Figure 2.2 on p. 38) identifies the cost of one complete menu item. The Plate Cost is determined by adding the total from the Recipe Cost Card to the additional items (potato and vegetable) included with the menu item.

Menu items may be presented as follows:

► **À la Carte:** all menu items priced individually; appetizers, soups, salads, entrées, pastas, and desserts are separately priced; typically associated with higher-priced fine dining restaurants.

► **Semi–à la Carte:** menu items typically include salad, potato or rice, and vegetable for a set price; appetizers, soups, and desserts are separately priced; traditionally offered in most restaurants.

▶ **Prix Fixe:** menu offers a complete meal at a fixed price: appetizer, soup, salad, entrée, potato, vegetable, dessert, and beverage. Popular examples of the prix-fixe menu are New Year's Eve Dinner, Valentine's Dinner, Thanksgiving Dinner, and a Sunday Brunch.

▶ **Buffet:** menu selections may include a variety of soups, salads, entrées, pastas, potatoes, rice, vegetables, desserts, and beverages for a set price. Customers serve themselves and eat as much as they want from the choices presented on the buffet (or salad bar).

NOTE: **Salad bars** are presented buffet style and may be included as an additional item to a semi–à la carte menu item or may be priced as a menu item itself for customers who just want to eat from the salad bar.

> **LEARNING OBJECTIVE 5**
> Demonstrate the application and use of Plate Cost Cards for determining menu pricing.

To prepare a Plate Cost Card for a semi–à la carte menu item do the following:

1. Transfer the Recipe Cost for a single serving from the Recipe Cost Card to the Plate Cost Card.

2. Identify the additional items that will be included with the menu item, such as potato, vegetable, and bread and butter, as shown in the example on p. 38.

   ▷ For pasta entrées, the selection would only include bread and butter.

3. Select the most expensive serving cost items from each category and add up the cost of those items to determine the total cost as shown in the example at the top of the next page (Baked Potato with Sour Cream and Steamed Asparagus).

   ▷ By selecting the most expensive serving cost items from each category, a financial cushion is built into the pricing structure. When a customer chooses the least expensive serving cost items (Garlic Mashed Potatoes and Honey Glazed Carrots) there is a greater profit margin, which helps to offset other potential increased costs.

4. Add the total cost of the additional items to the Recipe Portion Cost to determine the Plate Cost as shown in Figure 2.2 on the next page.

   ▷ **Food Cost Percent** is established by management; in this example it is for menu items at a casual-dining table service restaurant with a medium average Food Cost %.

   Example: 32%, as shown in Figure 2.2.

   NOTE: Typical food cost percentages by foodservice category is explained in Chapter 5, Food Cost, p. 93.

   ▷ **Minimum Menu Price** is the lowest menu price or *minimum selling price* for the menu item and is determined by dividing the Plate Cost by the Food Cost %, as shown in Figure 2.2 on the following page.

Example: Determine the Most Expensive Serving Items

Additional Items:

Prime Rib, 8-oz cut $9.04

Potatoes

Baked Potato with Sour Cream	**0.62**
Garlic Mashed	0.49
Roasted Baby Reds	0.54

Vegetables

Steamed Asparagus	**0.59**
Honey Glazed Carrots	0.44
Peas with Button Mushrooms	0.47

* If the menu pricing were to also include a soup or salad selection with the Prime Rib Entrée, a Plate Card for each of those items would be calculated to determine the final menu selling price.

NOTE: The actual Menu Price would be further rounded to $33.95 or $34.00, perhaps even higher depending upon competitive market conditions.

Plate Cost Card

Menu Item: Prime Rib

Yield: 8-ounce cut

Food Cost Percent: 32%

Date: June 15, 20xx

Plate Cost: $10.86

Minimum Menu Price: $33.94

Recipe Portion Cost: $9.04

Additional Items

Potatoes

Baked with Sour Cream	**0.62**	0.62
Garlic Mashed	0.49	
Roasted Baby Reds	0.54	

Vegetables

Steamed Asparagus	**0.59**	0.59
Honey Glazed Carrots	0.44	
Peas with Button Mushroons	0.47	

Bread and Butter

French Bread, Slice		0.38
Whipped Butter		+ 0.23
	Plate Cost:	**$10.86**

Plate Cost ÷ Food Cost Percent = Minimum Menu Price

$10.86 ÷ 0.32% = **$33.937 (rounded to $33.94)**

Figure 2.2   Plate Cost Card

To prepare a Plate Cost Card for a prix-fixe menu:

1. Transfer the single serving cost for every item on the prix-fixe menu from each item's Recipe Cost Card to the Plate Cost Card.

2. Add the cost of each item to identify the Plate Cost.

Complete Assignment 4 on p. 52.

Menu Pricing

Setting the menu selling prices is determined by what the market will bear, which is the ultimate decision-making factor when establishing actual menu prices. The theoretical selling price can only be achieved when the customer perceives the price–value relationship to be in harmony. Inasmuch as the restaurant exceeds the customer's perceived value in some way, the actual selling price can be set higher than the mathematical minimum. The reverse also holds true—a price–value perceived as poor means the minimum price may not be possible.

Price Rounding Rules: A common rounding rule is that all prices should be just under half and whole dollars. Research has shown that people generally do not perceive much of a difference in price between $8.65 and $9.00. The price selected will depend on competition and the nature of the foodservice operation. If the choice is to round down—from $8.65 to $8.00—then there should be other menu items that have an opportunity to be rounded up. This decision is often based on competitive market prices.

LEARNING OBJECTIVE 6
Prepare a Plate Cost Card for a salad bar or buffet menu.

To Prepare a Plate Cost Card for a buffet or salad bar menu do the following:

1. Transfer the total cost for each item on the buffet or salad bar menu from each item's Recipe Cost Card to the Plate Cost Card for Salad Bar as shown in Figure 2.3 on p. 41.

2. The total cost of all the items presented in a buffet or salad bar is divided by the total number of customers who served themselves to determine the plate cost (that is, the serving portion cost).

   ▷ The amount of food that is consumed and the number of people eating from a buffet or salad bar will often vary by day of the week. Therefore, tracking usage for several consecutive days or for an accounting period (1 week, 2 weeks, etc.) will provide greater accuracy.

   NOTE: An initial estimate of product usage (food consumption) to set up a buffet or salad bar is determined by management until average use can be established and plate cost identified. To identify the plate cost for a typical salad bar, see Figure 2.3, Plate Cost Card for Salad Bar. The same procedure is followed for a buffet.

   ▶ The POS system records the number of customers paying for the salad bar.

   ▷ The example in Figure 2.3 shows that 85 customers paid for the salad bar. If none of the items on the salad bar had to be replenished during the hours of service (11:00 A.M.–2:00 P.M.), the Plate Cost could quickly be determined by dividing the Total Cost of All Items by the Number of Customers.

NOTE: Leftover amounts of food items should be checked for quality and freshness. Reusable items must be safely handled (properly cooled, labeled, and dated) and held at the proper temperature until the next day.

▶ **Since all of the items on a salad bar are not completely consumed,** the kitchen staff must weigh the remaining amounts of reusable items, then subtract those amounts from the initial weight of the items, and then adjust the total cost according to the amounts actually consumed. If items have to be replenished during the hours of service, those items and quantities must be added to the total cost.

▶ The calculation to determine the Minimum Menu Price for the salad bar of a casual-dining table service restaurant with a food cost percent of 32% is calculated as shown in Figure 2.3.

▶ **To determine the plate cost of each individual food item,** the remaining weight is subtracted from the initial weight; the amount used is then multiplied by the unit cost (per pound or per ounce) and divided by the total number of customers.

> **Example:** 5 lb Pasta salad $12.45 ($12.45 ÷ 5 lb = $2.49 per lb unit cost)
> $\underline{- 0.5\ lb}$ Remaining Weight
> 4.5 lb Consumed at the Salad Bar
>
> $2.49 per pound × 4.5 lb = $11.205 rounded to **$11.21**
>
> $11.21 ÷ 85 Customers = $0.131 rounded to **$0.13 Plate Cost**

High-cost food items have to be monitored for usage.

▶ **When determining the items to put on a salad bar or buffet,** it becomes critically important to know the individual plate cost for each food item.

> **Example:** Control is exercised when serving meats by having an experienced cook at a carving station slicing reasonable portions.

> ▷ **A well-managed buffet can be competitively priced for the food items being offered.** Typically, a set price for lunch selections and another set price for dinner selections, which present a good value for customers, are established.

▶ **Daily customer counts** (number of customers per day) are closely examined and are a major component that determines the success of a lunch and/or dinner buffet.

> ▷ Buffets are set up to accommodate a large number of customers who, by serving themselves, allow the service time to be fast and efficient with quick table (seat) turns.

A POS system that integrates purchasing functions with Recipe Cost Cards will automatically transfer current costs to the Recipe Cost Cards and will also update plate cost cards if linked together.

> ▷ To be financially successful the buffet has to attract a significant number of customers. A 175-seat buffet restaurant serving lunch and dinner and operating at peak performance can attract 800 to 1,000+ customers per day.

▶ **Plate Cost Cards** are updated with every price increase from suppliers.

```
┌─────────────────────────────────────────────────────────────────────────┐
│                     Plate Cost Card for Salad Bar                         │
│                                                                           │
│  Menu Item: Salad Bar, 11:00 A.M.–2:00 P.M.          Date: June 15, 20xx │
│                                                                           │
│  Yield: 85 Servings (customer check count)           Plate Cost: $1.08   │
│                                                                           │
│  Food Cost Percent: 32%   ($1.08 plate cost ÷ 0.32 = $3.375)             │
│                                          Minimum Menu Price: $3.38        │
│                                                                           │
│  Recipe Costs:                                                            │
│                                                                           │
│     3 lb   Spring lettuce mix          $10.35                             │
│     5 lb   Pasta salad                  12.45                             │
│     4 lb   Potato salad                 10.12                             │
│     4 lb   Four-bean salad              14.05                             │
│     1 lb   Broccoli                      1.85                             │
│     1 lb   Sliced cucumbers              1.43                             │
│     1 pt   Black olives                  1.89                             │
│     2 pt   Cherry tomatoes               3.15                             │
│     1 pt   Cottage cheese                2.87                             │
│     1 pt   Sliced beets                  2.14                             │
│     1 pt   Red onions                    1.28                             │
│     1 lb   Garlic crouton                3.07                             │
│     1 pt   Blue cheese dressing          6.59                             │
│     1 pt   French dressing               6.05                             │
│     1 pt   Ranch dressing                5.92                             │
│     1 pt   Balsamic vinaigrette          5.87                             │
│     1 lb   Town House crackers         + 2.75                            │
│                              Total:    $91.83                             │
│                                                                           │
│       Total Cost of All Items ÷ Number of Customers = Plate Cost         │
│              $91.83           ÷          85          =    $1.08           │
│                                                                           │
│                          Plate Cost: $1.08                               │
└─────────────────────────────────────────────────────────────────────────┘
```

Figure 2.3 Plate Cost Card for Salad Bar

Butcher Test and Cooking Loss Test

The foodservice operations that conduct Butcher Tests require a skilled staff that can cut, clean, and portion meat and fish products before cooking. Typically, these operations are large enough to justify the added expense. Although certain fine dining restaurants employ chefs that are capable of conducting the tests, the additional cost incurred is reflected in higher menu prices for signature portion cuts that the restaurant may be known for.

The Cooking Loss Test can be used in conjunction with the Butcher Test. That is, following a Butcher Test the product being measured is cooked to determine its final cost per pound and cost per ounce after shrinkage and trimming, as shown in the figure examples on p. 43 and p. 45.

Meat products can be purchased *oven prepared,* from which fat and scrap are already removed. Also, products can be purchased *portion cut* by size and weight. This is simplified by product item numbers established by the North American Meat Institute and detailed in *The Meat Buyer's Guide,* further explained in Chapter 3 Purchasing on p. 64. For example, Item #109, USDA Choice Rib (as shown on the Butcher Test on p. 43), can also be purchased as #109 USDA Choice Rib, Oven Prepared. The Cooking Loss Test is most frequently used to measure product yield and AS (As Served) portion cost for *oven prepared* and *portion cut* items.

Butcher Test

LEARNING OBJECTIVE 7
Understand the purpose of a Butcher Test and know what it identifies.

A Butcher Test (see Figure 2.4 on p. 43) identifies the following:

- ▶ Final amount of usable raw product
- ▶ Per pound cost of the usable raw product
- ▶ Portion cost of usable raw product (for items portioned before cooking)
- ▶ Yield percentages

The Butcher Test is used for food products that can be measured for a set quality standard and quantity yield, such as beef, pork, lamb, veal, and fish. The primary use of a Butcher Test is for meat products, but it is also used in foodservice operations that clean and cut fish, and for items that are portioned before cooking.

The Butcher Test as shown in Figure 2.4 records the following information and contains calculations for determining weights, percentages, and costs:

- ▶ **Date:** Month, Day, and Year of the Test
- ▶ **The Item:** #109 USDA Choice Rib
- ▶ **Prepared By:** The name of the person (Chef Sample) who prepared the test
- ▶ **Purchase Weight:** 26 lb
- ▶ **Purchase Cost (AP) per lb:** $10.45
- ▶ **Oven Prepared Cost per lb:** $12.03
- ▶ **Raw Trims:** Parts that are not usable as the item is being prepared to be cooked, such as **fat** and additional trimming **scrap** (bones).
- ▶ **Oven Prepared Weight:** The quantity remaining after the raw trims have been removed and the item is ready to be placed in the oven.
- ▶ **Adjusted Purchase Cost:** Since fat can be used in other items or for other purposes, the market value price is determined for the trimmed fat and subtracted from the Purchase (invoice) Cost.
- ▶ **Oven Prepared Cost:** Determined **per pound** and **per ounce** (for portion costing).
- ▶ **Yield %:** Knowing the yield percent for the three categories below is important when evaluating identical meat items.
  - ▷ Weight Loss % after Trimming Fat
  - ▷ Weight Loss % after Trimming Scrap
  - ▷ Oven Prepared Weight %

Butcher Test

Item: #109 USDA Choice Rib

Purchase Weight: 26 lb

Purchase Cost (AP) per lb: $10.45

Date: June 15, 20xx

Prepared By: Chef Sample

Oven Prepared Cost per lb: $12.03

RAW TRIMS:

Purchase Weight:	26.0 lb	**Yield:**	**100%**
Weight after Trimming Fat:	− 24.0 lb		
Loss in Trimming Fat:	**2.0 lb**		

▶ **Loss in Trimming Fat ÷ Purchased Weight = Weight Loss Percent after Trimming Fat**

2.0 lb	÷	26.0	=	$0.0769 \approx 7.7\%$

Weight Loss % after Trimming Fat—Yield %:   −7.7%

Weight after Trimming Fat:	24.0 lb
Weight after Trimming Scrap:	− 22.5 lb
Loss in Trimming Scrap:	**1.5 lb**

▶ **Loss in Trimming Scrap ÷ Purchased Weight = Weight Loss Percent after Trimming Scrap**

1.5 lb	÷	26.0	=	$0.0576 \approx 5.8\%$

Weight Loss % after Trimming Scrap—Yield %:   −5.8%

OVEN PREPARED WEIGHT:

Purchase Weight:	26.0 lb	
Weight of Raw Trims:	− 3.5 lb	(2 lb Fat + 1.5 lb Scrap)
Oven Prepared Weight:	**22.5 lb**	

▶ **Oven Prepared Weight ÷ Purchased Weight = Oven Prepared Weight Percent**

22.5 lb	÷	26.0	=	$0.8653 \approx 86.5\%$

Oven Prepared Weight %—Yield %:   86.5%

ADJUSTED PURCHASE COST:

▶ **Quantity   Unit   ×   Unit Cost   =   Purchase (Invoice) Cost**

Quantity	Unit		Unit Cost		Purchase (Invoice) Cost	
26.0	lb	×	$10.45	=	$271.70	
2.0	lb	×	.50	=	− 1.00	(2 lb Fat @ .50 per lb)
					$270.70	**Adjusted Purchase Cost**

OVEN PREPARED COST:

▶ **Adjusted Purchase Cost ÷ Oven Prepared Weight = Oven Prepared Cost per lb**

270.70	÷	22.5 lb	=	$12.031 \approx $12.03

Oven Prepared Cost per lb: $12.03

$$\frac{\$12.03 \text{ per pound}}{16 \text{ ounces per pound}} = 0.751$$

Oven Prepared Cost per oz: $0.75
(for portion costing)

Figure 2.4   Butcher Test

Cooking Loss Test

When an item such as prime rib of beef (#109 USDA Choice Rib) is portioned after cooking, a Cooking Loss Test (see Figure 2.5) is used to calculate the final portion cost (AS cost per oz) and contains the following information:

▶ **Item:** #109 USDA Choice Rib, oven prepared

▶ **Date:** Month, Day, and Year of the Test

▶ **Prepared By:** The name of the person (Chef Sample) who prepared the test

▶ **Cooking Procedure—should be according to a Standardized HACCP Recipe:** The cooking objective is to control the cooking process so there is minimal shrinkage and moisture loss during cooking.

> NOTE: Many commercial kitchens are equipped with *slow cooking ovens* that cook meat at a lower temperature over a longer period of time, resulting in considerably less shrinkage after cooking.

▶ **Weight Loss after Cooking:** The amount of weight lost due to shrinkage from the cooking process. When the meat is removed from the oven, it is weighed, and that weight is subtracted from the Oven Prepared Weight to identify the Weight Loss after Cooking.

▶ **Weight Loss after Trimming:** The weight of remaining fat and scrap necessary for cooking, trimmed from the item after cooking.

▶ **Servable Weight—AS:** Identifies the final servable weight as a percentage of the Oven Prepared Weight.

▶ **Adjusted Purchase Cost (from Butcher Test):** Since fat can be used in other items or for other purposes, the market value price is determined for the trimmed fat and subtracted from the Purchased (Invoice) Cost to arrive at the Adjusted Purchase Cost.

▶ **AS (As Served) Cost:** Determines cost **per pound** and **per ounce** (for portion costing).

▶ **Yield %:** Knowing the yield percent for the three categories below is important when evaluating identical meat items.
Weight Loss % after Cooking
Weight Loss % after Trimming
Servable Weight–AS (As Served) %

> NOTE: **Portion cost** can be determined for such items as prime rib of beef (#109 USDA Choice Rib, oven prepared) following a Cooking Loss Test that determines the AS cost per pound by converting to cost per ounce.

Knowing the exact portion cost for such high-cost items as prime rib allows food-service operators to be competitive in menu pricing. For example, the 8-ounce portion of prime rib could be reduced to a 6-ounce portion ($1.13 per ounce × 6 ounces = $6.78 portion cost)—further reducing the menu selling price. Refer to Restaurant Reality, p. 58.

Cooking Loss Test

Item: #109 USDA Choice Rib, Oven Prepared

Date: June 15, 20xx

Prepared By: Chef Sample

COOKING PROCEDURE: Oven temperature 350°F, bone side down, moisture added to roasting pan; approximately 3½ hours cooking time.

Oven Prepared Weight: **22.5 lb**

WEIGHT LOSS AFTER COOKING:

Oven Prepared Weight:	22.5 lb	(taken from Butcher Test)	**100%**
Weight after Cooking:	− 17.0 lb		
Loss after Cooking:	**5.5 lb**	(shrinkage)	

▶ **Loss after Cooking ÷ Oven Prepared Weight = Weight Loss Percent after Cooking**

$$5.5 \text{ lb} \div 22.5 \text{ lb} = 0.244 = 24.4\%$$

Weight Loss % after Cooking—Yield %:   **−24.4%**

WEIGHT LOSS AFTER TRIMMING:

Weight after Cooking:	17.0 lb	
Weight after Trimming:	− 15.0 lb	(Servable Weight)
Loss after Trimming:	**2.0 lb**	

▶ **Loss after Trimming ÷ Oven Prepared Weight = Weight Loss Percent after Trimming**

$$2.0 \text{ lb} \div 22.5 \text{ lb} = 0.088 \approx 8.9\%$$

Weight Loss % after Trimming—Yield %:   **−8.9%**

SERVABLE WEIGHT–AS (AS SERVED):

▶ **Servable Weight ÷ Oven Prepared Weight = Servable Weight Percent**

$$15.0 \text{ lb} \div 22.5 \text{ lb} = 0.666 \approx 66.7\%$$

Servable Weight—Yield %:   **66.7%**

ADJUSTED PURCHASE COST:

▶ **Quantity   Unit   ×   Unit Cost   =   Purchase (Invoice) Cost**

Quantity	Unit		Unit Cost		Purchase (Invoice) Cost	
26.0	lb	×	$10.45	=	$271.70	
2.0	lb	×	.50	=	− 1.00	(2 lb Fat @ .50 per lb)
					$270.70	**Adjusted Purchase Cost**

AS (AS SERVED) COST:

▶ **Adjusted Purchase Cost ÷ Servable Weight = Oven Prepared Cost per lb**

$$270.70 \div 15.0 \text{ lb} = 18.046 \approx \$18.05$$

AS (As Served) Cost per lb: **$18.05**

$$\frac{\$18.05 \text{ per pound}}{16 \text{ ounces per pound}} = 1.128$$

AS Cost per oz: **$1.13**
(for portion costing)

Figure 2.5   Cooking Loss Test

Assignment 3

Refer to Chapter 1, pp. 14–15, Figure 1.1, Standardized HACCP Recipe for Farfalle Arrabbiata, which includes sub-recipes for Bow-tie Pasta and Pomodoro Sauce. Then complete the Recipe Cost Cards that appear below and on pp. 47–48. (The "Spice Factor" percentage is not included in sub-recipes.)

NOTE: Calculate to 3 digits past the decimal point then round to 2 digits.

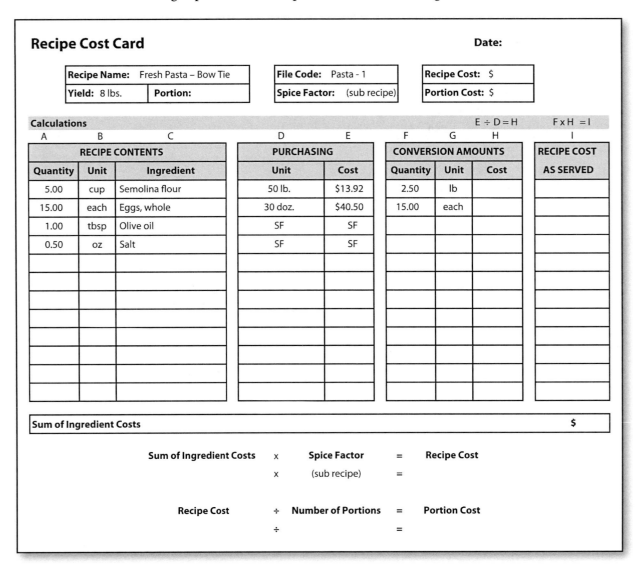

Recipe Cost Card   Date:

| Recipe Name: Fresh Pasta – Bow Tie | File Code: Pasta - 1 | Recipe Cost: $ |
| Yield: 8 lbs.   Portion: | Spice Factor: (sub recipe) | Portion Cost: $ |

Calculations   E ÷ D = H   F x H = I

A	B	C	D	E	F	G	H	I
RECIPE CONTENTS			PURCHASING		CONVERSION AMOUNTS			RECIPE COST
Quantity	Unit	Ingredient	Unit	Cost	Quantity	Unit	Cost	AS SERVED
5.00	cup	Semolina flour	50 lb.	$13.92	2.50	lb		
15.00	each	Eggs, whole	30 doz.	$40.50	15.00	each		
1.00	tbsp	Olive oil	SF	SF				
0.50	oz	Salt	SF	SF				

Sum of Ingredient Costs $

Sum of Ingredient Costs	x	Spice Factor	=	Recipe Cost
	x	(sub recipe)	=	
Recipe Cost	÷	Number of Portions	=	Portion Cost
	÷		=	

Assignment 3, continued

Recipe Cost Card   Date: **month/day/year**

| **Recipe Name:** Pomodoro Sauce | **File Code:** Sauces - 15 | **Recipe Cost:** $ |
| **Yield:** 1.5 gal. | **Portion:** | **Spice Factor:** (sub recipe) | **Portion Cost:** $ |

Calculations   E ÷ D = H   F x H = I

A	B	C	D	E	F	G	H	I
RECIPE CONTENTS			**PURCHASING**		**CONVERSION AMOUNTS**			**RECIPE COST**
Quantity	**Unit**	**Ingredient**	**Unit**	**Cost**	**Quantity**	**Unit**	**Cost**	**AS SERVED**
10.00	lb.	Roma tomatoes	10 lb.	$14.98	10.00	lb		
1.00	cup	Brown stock	1 gal	$1.50	8.00	oz		
1.00	cup	White wine	25 oz	$4.75	8.00	oz		
2.00	tbsp	Garlic oil	SF	SF				
1.00	head	Garlic, fresh	SF	SF				
1.50	tsp	Salt	SF	SF				
1.50	tsp	Pepper, black	SF	SF				
3.00	each	Bay leaf	SF	SF				
1.00	tbsp	Basil, fresh	SF	SF				
0.33	oz	Chili flakes	SF	SF				
2.00	tbsp	Parsley, fresh	SF	SF				

| **Sum of Ingredient Costs** | $ |

Sum of Ingredient Costs	x	**Spice Factor**	=	**Recipe Cost**
	x	(sub recipe)	=	
Recipe Cost	÷	**Number of Portions**	=	**Portion Cost**
	÷	1.5	=	

Assignment 3, continued

NOTE: Calculate to 3 digits past the decimal point then round to 2 digits.

Recipe Cost Card

Date: January 12, 20xx

Recipe Name:	Farfalle Arrabbiata
Yield: 20 servings	Portion: 14-ounce

File Code:	Entrée - 8
Spice Factor:	10%

Recipe Cost:	
Portion Cost:	

Calculations   E ÷ D = H   F x H = I

A	B	C	D	E	F	G	H	I
RECIPE CONTENTS			**PURCHASING**		**CONVERSION AMOUNTS**			**RECIPE COST**
Quantity	Unit	Ingredient	Unit	Cost	Quantity	Unit	Cost	
5.50	lb	Bow-tie pasta (sub-recipe)	1 lb		5.50	lb		
1.50	gal	Pomodoro sauce (sub-recipe)	1 gal		1.50	gal		
8.50	cup	Peppers, red sliced	11 lb	$29.85	1.75	lb		
8.50	cup	Peppers, green sliced	22 lb	$31.50	1.75	lb		
12.00	oz	Calamata olives	9 lb	$40.32	0.75	lb		
12.00	cup	Button mushrooms, whole	10 lb	$17.50	2.50	lb		
100.00	each	Shrimp, 16/20 count	50 lb	$412.50	6.25	lb		
1.50	cup	Parmesan cheese	10 lb	$45.40	5.50	oz		
40.00	each	Bread sticks, thin 7.5"	10 bags (200/bg)	$120.00	40.00	each		
1.25	cup	Parsley, chopped	SF	SF				
2.50	cup	Olive oil	SF	SF				

Sum of Ingredient Costs	$

Sum of Ingredient Costs   x   Spice Factor   =   Recipe Cost

   x   =

Recipe Cost   ÷   Number of Portions   =   Portion Cost

   ÷   =

Assignment 3, answers

Compare your answers with the correctly completed recipe cost cards below and on pp. 50–51.

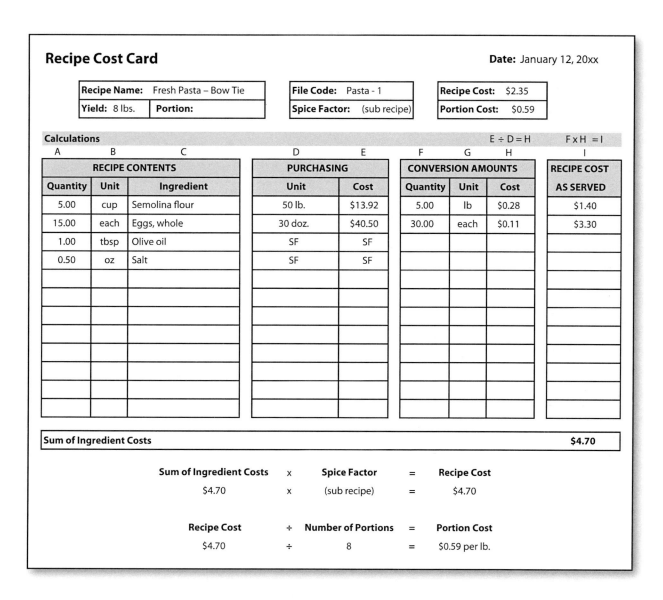

Recipe Cost Card   **Date:** January 12, 20xx

| Recipe Name: | Fresh Pasta – Bow Tie | File Code: | Pasta - 1 | Recipe Cost: | $2.35 |
| Yield: 8 lbs. | Portion: | Spice Factor: | (sub recipe) | Portion Cost: | $0.59 |

Calculations   E ÷ D = H   F x H = I

A	B	C	D	E	F	G	H	I
RECIPE CONTENTS			**PURCHASING**		**CONVERSION AMOUNTS**			**RECIPE COST**
Quantity	Unit	Ingredient	Unit	Cost	Quantity	Unit	Cost	**AS SERVED**
5.00	cup	Semolina flour	50 lb.	$13.92	5.00	lb	$0.28	$1.40
15.00	each	Eggs, whole	30 doz.	$40.50	30.00	each	$0.11	$3.30
1.00	tbsp	Olive oil	SF	SF				
0.50	oz	Salt	SF	SF				

| Sum of Ingredient Costs | $4.70 |

Sum of Ingredient Costs	x	Spice Factor	=	Recipe Cost
$4.70	x	(sub recipe)	=	$4.70

Recipe Cost	÷	Number of Portions	=	Portion Cost
$4.70	÷	8	=	$0.59 per lb.

Assignment 3, answers

Recipe Cost Card

Date: January 12, 20xx

Recipe Name:	Pomodoro Sauce
Yield: 1.5 gal.	Portion:

File Code:	Sauces - 15
Spice Factor:	(sub recipe)

Recipe Cost:	$16.60
Portion Cost:	$11.07

Calculations

E ÷ D = H   F x H = I

A	B	C	D	E	F	G	H	I
RECIPE CONTENTS			PURCHASING		CONVERSION AMOUNTS			RECIPE COST
Quantity	Unit	Ingredient	Unit	Cost	Quantity	Unit	Cost	AS SERVED
10.00	lb.	Roma tomatoes	10 lb.	$14.98	10.00	lb	$1.50	$15.00
1.00	cup	Brown stock	1 gal	$1.50	8.00	oz	$0.01	$0.08
1.00	cup	White wine	25 oz	$4.75	8.00	oz	$0.19	$1.52
2.00	tbsp	Garlic oil	SF	SF				
1.00	head	Garlic, fresh	SF	SF				
1.50	tsp	Salt	SF	SF				
1.50	tsp	Pepper, black	SF	SF				
3.00	each	Bay leaf	SF	SF				
1.00	tbsp	Basil, fresh	SF	SF				
0.33	oz	Chili flakes	SF	SF				
2.00	tbsp	Parsley, fresh	SF	SF				

Sum of Ingredient Costs	$16.60

Sum of Ingredient Costs	x	Spice Factor	=	Recipe Cost
$16.60	x	(sub recipe)	=	$16.60

Recipe Cost	÷	Number of Portions	=	Portion Cost
$16.60	÷	1.5	=	$11.07 per gal

Assignment 3, answers

Recipe Cost Card   **Date:** January 12, 20xx

Recipe Name: Farfalle Arrabbiata	**File Code:** Entrée - 8	**Recipe Cost:** $99.37
Yield: 20 servings	**Portion:** 14-ounce	**Spice Factor:** 10%	**Portion Cost:** $4.97

| Calculations | | | | | | | E ÷ D = H | F x H = I |

A	B	C	D	E	F	G	H	I
RECIPE CONTENTS			**PURCHASING**		**CONVERSION AMOUNTS**			**RECIPE COST**
Quantity	Unit	Ingredient	Unit	Cost	Quantity	Unit	Cost	AS SERVED
5.50	lb	Bow-tie pasta (sub-recipe)	1 lb		5.50	lb	$0.59	$3.25
1.50	gal	Pomodoro sauce (sub-recipe)	1 gal		1.50	gal	$11.07	$16.61
8.50	cup	Peppers, red sliced	11 lb	$29.85	1.75	lb	$2.71	$4.74
8.50	cup	Peppers, green sliced	22 lb	$31.50	1.75	lb	$1.43	$2.50
12.00	oz	Calamata olives	9 lb	$40.32	0.75	lb	$4.48	$3.36
12.00	cup	Button mushrooms, whole	10 lb	$17.50	2.50	lb	$1.75	$4.38
100.00	each	Shrimp, 16/20 count	50 lb	$412.50	6.25	lb	$8.25	$51.56
1.50	cup	Parmesan cheese	10 lb	$45.40	5.50	oz	$0.28	$1.54
40.00	each	Bread sticks, thin 7.5"	10 bags (200/bg)	$120.00	40.00	each	$0.06	$2.40
1.25	cup	Parsley, chopped	SF	SF				
2.50	cup	Olive oil	SF	SF				

Sum of Ingredient Costs	**$90.34**

Sum of Ingredient Costs	x	**Spice Factor**	=	**Recipe Cost**
$90.34	x	1.10	=	$99.37

Recipe Cost	÷	**Number of Portions**	=	**Portion Cost**
$99.37	÷	20	=	$4.97

Assignment 4

Complete the Plate Cost Card for Farfalle Arrabbiata.

Plate Cost Card Additional Items

Menu Item: Farfalle Arrabbiata (Bow-tie Pasta)   **Date:** January 12, 20xx

Yield: 1 Serving   **Portion:** 14-ounce   **Plate Cost:** $ _____

Food Cost Percent: 32%   **Minimum Menu Price:** $ _____

Recipe Portion Cost: $ _____

Additional Items

Bread and Butter
Focaccia Bread   0.46
Herbed Butter   +   0.34

Plate Cost: $ _____

Plate Cost	÷	Food Cost Percent	=	Minimum Menu Price
_____	÷	_____	=	_____

Average Yield Percentages for Common Products

The following product items are typically purchased raw and unprocessed. The yield percentage for each item represents a composite average from generally accepted product yield guides. The most accurate yield amounts are determined after the items have been processed, prepared, and measured for weight or volume in the kitchen.

VEGETABLES			FRUITS		
Artichokes	trimmed	90%	Apples	cored, peeled	75%
Asparagus	trimmed	75%	Avocado	pitted, peeled	80%
Beans, green	trimmed, cut	90%	Bananas	peeled, sliced	80%
Beets, whole	trimmed, cut	70%	Blackberries		95%
Broccoli, bunch	trimmed, cut	65%	Blueberries		90%
Brussels Sprouts	trimmed	90%	Cherries	pitted, stemmed	90%
Cabbage, green/red	cored, chopped	80%	Coconut (whole)	cracked, cored	60%
Carrots	sliced, diced	90%	Dates (whole)	pitted	90%
Cauliflower	cored, cut	65%	Figs		98%
Celery	trimmed	70%	Grapefruit	sectioned	65%
Chicory / Curly Endive	trimmed	85%	Grapes, green	stemmed	95%
Cilantro	trimmed, cut	90%	Grapes, red	stemmed	95%
Corn (cob)	cut	35%	Lemons	juiced	40%
Cucumber	peeled, sliced	90%	Limes	juiced	45%
Eggplant	peeled, sliced	80%	Mangos	pitted, peeled	70%
Endive, Belgian	cored	85%	Melons:	seeded, cut	60%
Fennel, stemmed	sliced	60%	Canteloupe	seeded, cut	65%
Garlic, cloves	peeled	85%	Watermelon	seeded, cut	70%
Kale	cored, chopped	70%	Nectarines	pitted, sliced	75%
Leeks	trimmed	55%	Oranges	peeled, sliced	80%
Lettuce/Iceberg	cored, trimmed	75%	Papayas	seeded, peeled	70%
Lettuce/Romain	cored, trimmed	80%	Peaches	pitted, sliced	75%
Mushrooms	trimmed	90%	Pears	cored, peeled	80%
Onions	peeled, sliced	90%	Pineapple	cored, peeled, cut	45%
Peppers	cored, seeded	80%	Plantains	peeled, sliced	75%
Potatoes	peeled, cut	85%	Plums	pitted, sliced	90%
Shallots	peeled, diced	80%	Pomegranates	seeded	50%
Spinach	trimmed	75%	Raspberries		95%
Squash	peeled, cut	80%	Strawberries	stemmed	90%
Zucchini	peeled, sliced	90%	Tomatoes	cored, cut	95%

Figure 2.6 Common Product Yields

Average Yield Percentages
for Common Products

MEATS

BEEF

Bottom Round	75%
Flank Steak	85%
Prime Rib	65%
Strip Loin (NY)	80%
T– Bone Steak	75%
Tenderloin, whole	60%
Top Round	75%
Top Sirloin Butt	70%

VEAL

Breast	80%
Cutlets	75%

MEATS

LAMB

Leg, boned	70%
Rack, double	65%
Rib, chops	75%
Shoulder, boned	70%

PORK

Loin, boneless	75%
Loin Chops, center cut	70%
Ham, short shank	60%
Tenderloins	85%

Figure 2.6 Common Product Yields (continued)

Average Yield Percentages
for Common Products

POULTRY

CHICKEN

Breast	80%
Breast, boneless/skinless	95%
Legs	60%
Thighs	65%
Wings	40%

TURKEY

Whole, dressed	85%
Breast, boneless	90%
Legs and Thighs	55%
Wings	40%

DUCK

Whole, dressed	90%
Breast	75%

SEAFOOD

Ahi Tuna	65%
Bass, Sea	55%
Cod	55%
Halibut	65%
Lobster	30%
Mahi Mahi	75%
Salmon	70%
Snapper	55%
Swordfish	65%
Tilapia	60%
Trout	65%

Figure 2.6   Common Product Yields (continued)

Summary

A commitment by management to focus on controlling portion costs begins with preparing Recipe Cost Cards, which are forms used to calculate the cost of each menu item using a Standardized HACCP Recipe to produce it. To complete these forms with accuracy requires management to determine the appropriate Spice Factor Percentage for the foodservice operation. The Spice Factor includes all of the products that go into producing and serving the menu items but are difficult to individually track.

The purchasing quantities of food products that are uncooked, raw and unprocessed must be determined. This begins by referring to Product Yield Charts that are available from various sources along with software applications. The charts provide approximate yield percentages for a wide range of products. By calculating the product yield amounts for the recipe ingredients, a determination can be made for purchasing the correct quantities of products to prepare menu items.

A Plate Cost Card identifies the cost of one complete menu item, and is prepared for every menu item on an à la carte, semi-à la carte, or prix-fixe menu; for a salad bar or buffet, the total cost for each item on the salad bar or buffet would be transferred from each item's Recipe Cost Card to the Plate Cost Card. To determine the plate cost of a salad bar or buffet, divide the total cost of all the items presented by the total number of customers who served themselves.

The Butcher Test is used for food products that can be measured for a set quality standard and quantity yield, such as beef, pork, lamb, veal, and fish. This is used primarily in foodservice operations that have a skilled staff trained in performing the cutting and trimming functions.

The purpose of the Cooking Loss Test is to measure the shrinkage and trimming loss after cooking a high-cost item such as prime rib. Cooking loss can be attributed to a number of factors having to do with the quality of the item being tested and the procedure that is used to cook the product.

Portion costing is essential to menu pricing and being able to control quality standards and product purchasing costs. It also allows the restaurant operator to maintain a competitive edge in the market place.

Discussion Questions

1. What determines the portion costing options that a foodservice operation will use?
2. Discuss the purpose of a Recipe Cost Card and why it is important to the restaurant operation.
3. Why is the Spice Factor added to every menu item?
4. List 10 examples of product categories that would be considered Spice Factor items.
5. How is the Spice Factor calculated?
6. Explain what the acronyms AS and AP represent.
7. How are product yield amounts calculated when determining ingredient quantities to purchase for menu items?
8. Explain the procedure for determining purchasing quantities for a specific menu item.
9. How is Plate Cost determined?
10. Discuss the differences between à la carte, semi–à la carte, prix–fixe, and buffet menus.
11. Explain how a Plate Cost Card functions when calculating additional plate items such as potatoes and vegetables.
12. How is the Minimum Menu Price calculated?
13. When preparing a Plate Cost Card for a salad bar or buffet menu, why is it important to know exactly how many customers served themselves from that salad bar or buffet? And, how would the restaurant manager find that exact number of customers?
14. Explain the purpose of a Butcher Test and what it specifically identifies.
15. Why is the Cooking Loss Test so important for high-cost items such as prime rib? Explain what is determined by using a Cooking Loss Test?

Project Exercises

(Continued from Chapter 1)

The following Exercises are to begin with the information taken from the Chapter 1 Exercises, and can be successfully completed after a thorough understanding of Chapters 3, 4 and 5.

1. **Prepare Recipe Cost Cards** *using 10% as the Spice Factor* for each of the Standardized HACCP Recipes that were created from the Project Exercise in Chapter 1. To identify the Recipe Ingredient Purchasing Unit size and Cost will require doing some research, which will be provided in the Project Exercises for Chapter 3, Purchasing Functions.

    NOTE: Each Recipe Cost Card must be typed and submitted on the Recipe Cost Card form that is available in Excel format for this text / work book.

    Reminder: The Spice Factor is not included in sub-recipes.

2. After the Recipe Cost Cards are completed, **Prepare Plate Cost Cards** *using 32% as the Food Cost Percentage* for each of the menu items: Soup, Salad, Entrée (with the sides), Additional Items, and Dessert. Food Cost Percentage will be explained in Chapter 5, Food Cost.

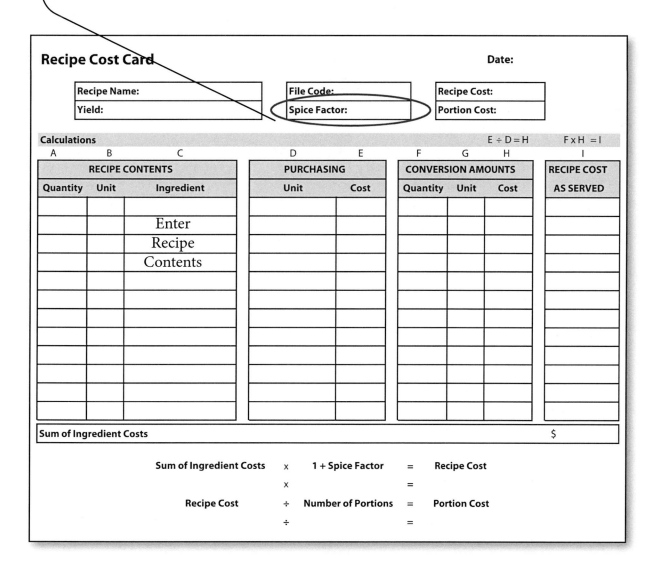

**Menu
Cost Control**

Restaurant Reality

Adjust the portion size and menu price to compete for banquet business

The manager of a fine dining restaurant with an adjoining banquet room successfully operates the business by controlling costs with constant updates to recipe cost cards and plate cost cards. The chef regularly does butcher tests to ensure product quality standards are met and to verify product yields, which are frequently measured by cooking loss tests. This enables the manager to have up-to-date portion costs, which is helpful when having to compete for banquet business.

A wedding rehearsal prime rib dinner for 46 was being planned, and the family hosting the dinner met with the manager to review the banquet menu. The menu price for prime rib slightly exceeded their budget, so they inquired about other menu items; however, the restaurant manager recognized that their hearts were set on prime rib for this special occasion. So the manager suggested the following option for their consideration: although the portion size of the prime rib on the banquet menu was 8 ounces, it could be adjusted to 6 ounces, placed over a thin slice of French bread, and served with au jus sauce. This option presented a good value and was gladly accepted by the customer.

Refer to pages 44–45, Cooking Loss Test example, Item: #109 USDA Choice Rib (Prime Rib), which shows the AS (As Served) Cost per ounce to be $1.13. Keep in mind that the 8-ounce portion on the restaurant banquet menu would cost $9.04 ($1.13 per ounce × 8 ounces = $9.04 portion cost). By adjusting to the 6-ounce portion, the menu item would cost $6.78 ($1.13 per ounce × 6 ounces = $6.78 portion cost).

Knowing the exact cost per ounce enabled the manager to quickly adjust the portion size and menu price to an acceptable level for his client. Otherwise, he may have lost the banquet business for the wedding rehearsal dinner for 46 to a competitor restaurant.

Purchasing Cost Control

3 Purchasing Functions
4 Receiving, Storing, and Issuing Products and Processing Invoices
5 Food Cost

Once the menu selection is set and the recipes are standardized, the next task becomes purchasing. The purchasing objective is to select the right products, in the right quantities, from the right distributors/suppliers, at the right prices.

The responsibility of the buyer is to ensure that the foodservice operation has all of the necessary food, beverage, supplies, and services required to adequately meet the needs of the business. Large hospitality organizations with multiple units, chain restaurants, hotels, and resorts may have several buyers, each specializing in certain product and service categories. The buying function for the small to mid-size foodservice operation is typically the responsibility of the manager, chef, or owner.

A formal procedure to receive, store, and issue products further assures accountability from the time products and services are received until invoice payment is approved. Through the use of requisitions and transfers, products are accounted for and tracked according to usage.

The foodservice operator who effectively controls food cost understands how to manage inventory and how to prepare inventory sheets, inventory turnover reports, and food cost reports on a consistent basis for every accounting period.

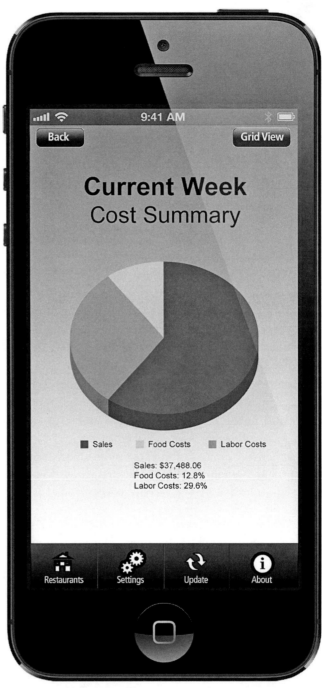

Courtesy of Action Systems, Inc.

3

Purchasing Functions

Introduction

Identifying **what to buy** depends on the buyer's ability to define precisely the qualities of the product. In order to accomplish this, specifications or "specs" are developed for each product that needs to be purchased. Without specifications, there is no guarantee that what was ordered is, in fact, the correct product for the menu item.

Finding **where to buy** requires the buyer to research local foodservice distributors and wholesale foodservice suppliers that can fulfill the product needs of the foodservice operation at the most competitive prices.

Determining **how much to buy** requires the buyer to identify the correct amount of products to order that will meet the needs of production from one delivery date to the next. A system is needed to avoid over—or under—ordering.

This begins with finding the proper order levels by referring to accurate sales records and standard portion sizes established in the recipes.

Learning Objectives

Upon successfully completing this chapter, readers will be able to:

1. Determine what to purchase in meeting the needs of a foodservice operation.
2. Explain the procedure involved in writing a product specification.
3. Understand the benefits that convenience products offer.
4. Know the advantages of product outsourcing for foodservice chains.
5. Recognize and explain the various services offered by foodservice distributors and wholesale foodservice suppliers.
6. Understand how to do business with foodservice distributors.
7. Recognize timely information provided by newsletters and market reports.
8. Discuss the role of foodservice brokers
9. Know the correct amounts to buy with a thorough understanding of inventory management.
10. Understand how to determine inventory par stock amounts.

11. Determine order quantities using par stock amounts.
12. Explain how order sheets are efficiently arranged.
13. Know the purpose of standing orders.
14. Understand competitive pricing by using bid sheets.
15. Discuss the use of purchase orders.
16. Understand contract services.

Chapter Outline

Product Specifications	Order Sheets
Convenience Products	Standing Orders
Product Outsourcing	Bid Sheets
Foodservice Distributors	Purchase Orders
Wholesale Foodservice Suppliers	Contract Services
Newsletters and Market Reports	Summary
Foodservice Brokers	Discussion Questions
Inventory Management	Project Exercises
Par Stock	

Key Terms and Definitions

Begin by first reading the key terms and their definitions. An advance understanding of the terms will be helpful prior to reading the chapter.

Bid Sheet	A form that itemizes each product for competing distributors and is used to compare prices between the different distributors.
Broadline Distributors	Carry food, nonfood, smallwares, kitchen equipment, dining room furnishings and equipment, and bar supplies; may offer a variety of services that include training seminars, facility design, and consulting.
Convenience Products	Can range from partially processed or prepared items to completely finished products that are ready-to-use or serve.
FIFO (First In, First Out)	As items are added to inventory, the items already in stock should be used before the newer items. This process is referred to as "First In, First Out."
Foodservice Brokers	Independent marketing companies that promote food manufacturers' products through the foodservice distribution system in local and regional markets.
Foodservice Distributors	Companies that provide food and nonfood products to foodservice operations: restaurants, hotels, resorts, healthcare facilities, schools, delis, fast-food (quick-service) restaurants, cafeterias, buffets, and convenience stores.
Inventory Management	The process of keeping enough products on hand so that the needs of the foodservice operation are met, without spending more money than necessary.

Market Reports	Inform foodservice operators about conditions that may affect prices.
The Meat Buyer's Guide	Recommends that products be specified by corresponding NAMI (North American Meat Institute) item number, product name, and weight range to be purchased.
Newsletters	Introduce new products and services along with announcing cost-saving specials for certain products. Also contain the dates, along with relevant details, for upcoming trade shows and culinary demonstrations.
Order Sheet	Provides a systematic approach to ordering correct quantities from foodservice distributors.
Par Stock	The minimum amount of every inventory item needed to carry production between delivery days.
Product Specifications	Detailed descriptions of products, which assist the foodservice operator when ordering from a foodservice distributor/supplier. Commonly referred to as "specs."
Purchase Order	A numbered form that identifies the item or items—by specs or stock number, the quantity ordered, the unit price, the total, any special instructions or information, the date issued, and the authorization signature from the buyer or accounting office.
The Seafood Handbook	A comprehensive source directory for specific information for all types of seafood.
Specialty Foodservice Distributors	Specialize in a limited line of specialty products, which may range from bakery items made fresh daily, to ethnic foods such as Asian to imported food items such as Italian cheeses.
Standardized Recipes	Allow for a comprehensive inventory list of all ingredients that need to be purchased—as well as preparation methods and the right amounts.
Standing Orders	When a use pattern has been established for certain items that are frequently delivered, a specific quantity order can be in place.
System Distributors	Are used by large national chains and multi-unit restaurants to supply products to individual stores. Also referred to as commissaries.
Wholesale Foodservice Suppliers	Require customer membership and are in the category of the warehouse big-box stores such as Costco and Sam's Club.

What to Buy

All foodservice operations should strive to offer the highest quality menu items at a price that is appropriate for the quality and amount of food being served. Simply stated, the food offered should be as high a quality as possible in relationship to the menu price of the food. Therefore, standardized recipes with ingredient (product) specifications are essential.

Standardized recipes create a comprehensive inventory list of all ingredients that need to be purchased—as well as preparation methods and the right amounts.

▶ Begin by referring to the standardized recipes to develop the inventory list.

▶ The inventory list then becomes the "shopping list."

Product Specifications

Product specifications commonly referred to as "specs" are detailed descriptions of products that assist the foodservice operator when ordering from a foodservice distributor/supplier.

The product is not necessarily the most expensive or the least expensive. It is simply the best fit, given the parameters of the menu and standardized recipe.

Writing specs involves thoroughly researching all the possible choices in the quest to select the best product. This can lead to products that can be cross-utilized (used with more than one recipe) or products that are partially processed or prepared—convenience products—which may be more cost effective.

The following are examples of specifications for products in the major categories of meats, poultry, seafood, dairy, bakery, grocery, and produce.

Meats

Purchasing the correct meat products is critical from a cost and customer satisfaction perspective.

▶ Meat specifications for beef, lamb, veal, pork, and other meat products are described in *The Meat Buyer's Guide* published by (NAMI) North American Meat Institute (www.meatinstitute.org).

▶ *The Meat Buyer's Guide* recommends that products be specified by the corresponding item number, product name, and weight range to be purchased.

Examples: Item #109—Beef Rib, Roast Ready, Weight Range 14 to 16 lbs.
Item #136*—Ground Beef, Weight in pounds.
*The fat percentage content in Ground Beef is defined by Item #136.

▶ Foodservice distributors, such as Sysco, will have their own particular method of specifying meat with various codes for tracking and ordering items.

Poultry

The Meat Buyer's Guide has a poultry section that provides specific information for all types of poultry—chicken, turkey, duckling, quail, pheasant, and others.

▶ Poultry can be purchased fresh or frozen and cut according to foodservice specifications.

Examples: Chicken Breast B/S (Boneless/Skinless), 5 ounce
Chicken Tenders, 4 ounce

▶ Poultry can also be specified by brand names such as, Perdue, Tyson, or by foodservice distributor, such as Sysco.

Seafood

The Seafood Handbook is a comprehensive source directory for specific information for all types of seafood (www.seafoodsource.com/seafood-handbook).

▶ Fish and shellfish can be purchased fresh daily packed on ice or purchased fresh frozen.

▶ Fish and shellfish can be purchased by specification.

Examples: Salmon (Sockeye), 6 oz. skinless fillet
Shrimp, 16/20 count,* peeled and deveined, tails-on
*16 to 20 refers to the number of shrimp per pound

Dairy

Product information is available from producers and manufacturers of dairy foods and from the International Dairy Foods Association (www.idfa.org).

▶ Dairy products are purchased by specifications that include product form (such as cheese: wheels, blocks, cubes, sliced, shredded, grated) and packaging size and by brand name.

Examples: Cream Cheese, 3-lb block, Kraft
Sour Cream, 5-lb tub, Sysco

Bakery

Most bakery items are purchased fresh with early-morning deliveries to foodservice operations, often on a daily basis.

▶ Pastries, croissants, muffins, cupcakes, doughnuts, bagels, rolls, specialty breads, cookies, pies, and cakes are consistently in demand.

▶ Purchasing specifications may include certain recipe ingredients and product size.

Examples: Dutch Apple Pie, 10 inch
Chocolate Cake, 8 inch round, 3 layers
Flourless Chocolate Torte, Ganache Topping,
Gluten-Free, 10 inch

Grocery

Grocery items are the primary products used in the kitchen to prepare the foods that are on the menu and being served to customers.

> ► Grocery items are purchased in sizes and quantities large enough to adequately meet the needs of the business for a certain number of days.

> ► Grocery items are replenished according to delivery schedules and in amounts that allow for proper inventory rotation.

> ► Brand names identify many of the products being purchased.

> **Examples:** Tomatoes—Diced, Contadina
> Egg Noodles, La Bella
> Olive Oil, Colavita

Produce

Fresh produce is typically available throughout the year with seasonal peak times having the greatest abundance of products to offer.

> ► The United States Department of Agriculture (USDA), Agricultural Marketing Service, is a resource to consult for fresh produce quality-grade specifications. The USDA also provides quality-grade specifications for dairy, poultry, and meat (www.ams.usda.gov).

> ► The price of fresh fruits and vegetables will fluctuate according to market conditions and seasonal availability.

> ► Foodservice distributors/suppliers provide USDA quality-graded produce to assure cost value: USDA #1

> **Examples:** Lettuce, Romaine
> Potatoes, Russet, Burbank
> Onions, Spanish

Convenience Products

Convenience products can range from partially processed or prepared items to completely finished products that are ready-to-use or serve.

> **Examples:** Cheese—cubed, sliced, shredded, grated
> Carrots—carrot sticks, baby peeled, shredded
> Salads—fresh green salad mixes, potato salads,
> macaroni salads
> Puddings—chocolate, rice, tapioca
> Bakery—cakes, pies, cupcakes, cheesecakes,
> gluten-free desserts (e.g., www.sweetstreet.com)

The use of convenience products can offer the following benefits:

- ▶ Reduced labor cost
- ▶ Reduced workload on existing kitchen equipment
- ▶ Reduced inventory cost
- ▶ Reduced waste with typically 100% product yield
- ▶ Opportunity to offer menu items that could not be prepared with existing kitchen equipment
- ▶ Replacement of menu items in need of improvement

The use of convenience products could also be:

- ▶ At a cost greater than preparing from scratch
- ▶ Inconvenient with foodservice distributor delivery schedule

The decision to use a ready-to-serve convenience product is based on the following:

1. Final portion cost including labor
2. Availability of the product
3. Customer satisfaction

Complete Assignment 5 on p. 77.

> **LEARNING OBJECTIVE 3**
> Understand the benefits that convenience products offer.

Product Outsourcing

There are food manufacturing firms that have the capability to produce customized food products according to a foodservice operator's recipe specifications.

- ▶ Foodservice chains and multi-unit operators will often outsource production for popular menu item products.

  Example: Chicken parts that may be cut, seasoned, precooked, and packaged according to recipe specifications

- ▶ Outsourcing the production of certain products can be cost effective with savings in kitchen space, in storage space, and in the use of skilled labor.

> **LEARNING OBJECTIVE 4**
> Know the advantages of product outsourcing for foodservice chains.

Where to Buy

Foodservice distributors and wholesale foodservice suppliers are where the majority of products are offered to and purchased by foodservice operators.

Foodservice Distributors

Foodservice distributors are companies that provide food and nonfood products to foodservice operations: restaurants, hotels, resorts, healthcare facilities, schools, delis, fast-food (quick-service) restaurants, cafeterias, buffets, and convenience stores.

LEARNING OBJECTIVE 5
Recognize and explain the various services offered by foodservice distributors and wholesale foodservice suppliers.

▶ **Foodservice distributors** function as intermediaries between food manufacturers and foodservice operators.

▷ Foodservice distributors purchase bulk quantities direct from food manufactures.

▷ Foodservice distributors inventory the products until orders are received from foodservice operators requesting delivery.

▶ **Broadline distributors** carry food, nonfood, smallwares, kitchen equipment, dining room furnishings and equipment, and bar supplies; they may offer a variety of services that include training seminars, facility design, and consulting.

Examples: Sysco: www.sysco.com
US Foods: www.USFoods.com

▶ **Specialty foodservice distributors** specialize in a limited line of specialty products, which may range from bakery items made fresh daily, to ethnic foods such as Asian and to imported food items such as Italian cheeses.

▶ **System distributors, also referred to as commissaries,** are used by large national chains and multi-unit restaurants to supply products to individual stores.

▷ Warehouses and plants are regionally located and service stores in a specific area.

▷ Commissaries may purchase raw product and create finished goods in kitchens, using company recipes, or purchase already processed goods for distribution.

LEARNING OBJECTIVE 6
Understand how to do business with foodservice distributors.

Online billing and payment is rapidly becoming the preferred method.

Doing business with foodservice distributors requires an understanding of the following:

1. **Credit amount and payment terms.** A credit amount is established at the time a foodservice operator opens an account with a foodservice distributor.

   ▷ The credit amount represents the dollar limit worth of products that the distributor is willing to extend to the operator for deliveries during a set period of time—for example within 10 to 30 days.

   ▷ The payment terms may include a discount for prompt payment. A delayed payment—a payment made beyond the required payment date—may result in lowering the credit amount previously granted.

2. **Lead time for placing orders.** When processing orders for next-day deliveries, the foodservice distributor may require foodservice operators to place their orders by a certain time—for example by 2:00 P.M. the previous day.

   ▷ Foodservice distributors have established a specific lead time for placing orders, often referred to as "the cut-off time," which allows enough time to process the orders and load the trucks for deliveries.

3. **Online ordering.** The ability to place orders online further adds to the speed and efficiency of the order being placed. Although some smaller foodservice operations may prefer to call in or fax their orders, these procedures are quickly giving way to online ordering.

4. **Minimum order amount.** The costs associated with processing an order, loading the ordered products onto the truck, and scheduling the truck for a delivery stop requires the order to be at a set minimum dollar amount—for example $500 or $1,000.

> NOTE: Wholesale foodservice suppliers do not have minimum order amounts; no minimum purchase quantities are required because there are no delivery costs. The foodservice operator arranges for the pick-up and transportation costs.

5. **Delivery schedules.** A foodservice distributor's delivery schedule by days of the week and times during certain days is generally established to accommodate foodservice operators in the most efficient way possible, giving consideration to peak business periods and highway traffic flows. When weather conditions, traffic congestion, or unexpected emergencies cause delivery delays, foodservice operators are informed and given a revised delivery time.

Wholesale Foodservice Suppliers

Wholesale foodservice suppliers serve the needs of independent foodservice operators, caterers, clubs, pizza restaurants, bars and taverns, and nonprofit foodservice organizations. Wholesale foodservice suppliers provide a variety of products and services, including food, beverages, nonfood items, smallwares, kitchen equipment, dining room furnishings and equipment, and a variety of value-added service partners that offer restaurant website and menu design, payroll and accounting services, etc.

Wholesale foodservice suppliers:

► Require customer membership and are in the category of the warehouse big-box stores such as Costco and Sam's Club. Applicants for membership are required to submit proof of a business license and tax permit (identification number).

► Contract with food manufacturers and suppliers to obtain the lowest possible pricing for their customers.

► Don't require minimum purchase quantities; customers may purchase a single item or items by the case. In-store product specials are continually being offered at low prices.

► Are set up so customers push store carts through the warehouse aisles, selecting the products they want; when finished shopping, they pay at the checkout and then load the merchandise into their own vehicle (truck, van, etc.). The wholesale foodservice supplier does not deliver.

► Are able to meet the complete needs of most foodservice operators; wine and spirits are sold where state liquor laws allow (customer required to show proof of state liquor license).

Example: Restaurant Depot: www.restaurantdepot.com

► Continue to grow in the number of new warehouse locations being opened annually.

LEARNING
OBJECTIVE 7
Recognize timely
information provided by
newsletters and
market reports.

Newsletters and Market Reports

Foodservice distributors and wholesale foodservice suppliers offer their customers *online access to newsletters and market reports* that provide timely information.

- ▶ **Newsletters** introduce new products and services along with announcing cost-saving specials for certain products; and provide the dates, along with relevant details, for upcoming trade shows and culinary demonstrations.

- ▶ **Market reports** inform foodservice operators about conditions that may alter product availability and affect prices, such as weather conditions (heavy rains, droughts, and freezes). When anticipating increased costs for products in the categories of meat, poultry, seafood, dairy, and produce, foodservice operators can take the appropriate action. Example: www.USFoods.Com/farmersreport

Foodservice brokers
are a good source
to learn about new
products along with
new applications for
existing products.

Foodservice Brokers

Foodservice brokers are independent marketing companies that promote food manufacturers' products through the foodservice distribution system in local and regional markets.

LEARNING
OBJECTIVE 8
Discuss the role of
foodservice brokers.

Foodservice brokers:

- ▶ Are hired by a manufacturer to help sell its products to foodservice operators, which includes promoting existing products and introducing new items.

- ▶ Range in size from very small businesses specializing in limited product types to large firms, complete with test kitchens and many sales representatives.

- ▶ May also be responsible for getting foodservice distributors and wholesale foodservice suppliers to stock the manufacturer's products.

- ▶ Receive a sales commission from the manufacturer based on the amount of products sold within a designated period of time.

- ▶ Promote the product lines they represent at foodservice distributor trade shows by providing product samples and cost information.

LEARNING
OBJECTIVE 9
Know the correct amounts
to buy with a thorough
understanding of inventory
management.

How Much to Buy

Knowing the correct amounts to buy begins with a thorough understanding of inventory management, which is to identify the optimum inventory level for the foodservice operation, simply stated as follows:

- ▶ Large enough to avoid running out of products during peak business times

- ▶ Small enough to be properly rotated

Inventory Management

Inventory management is the process of keeping enough products on hand so that the needs of the foodservice operation are met, without spending more money than necessary. The financial investment in both food and nonfood items can range from a thousand dollars for a small food and beverage quick-service operation to tens of thousands of dollars for a large foodservice operation.

▶ An important part of managing inventory is to maintain organized storage areas: dry storage (storeroom), refrigerator, and freezer.

▶ The products in each storage area should be arranged according to categories and alphabetized as much as possible.

Example: Dry storage (storeroom) the category of canned tomato products, alphabetized (cans arranged) in the following order—Tomatoes–Diced, Tomato Paste, Tomato Puree

▷ Wherever possible, the shelves under the items should be labeled with the name of each item to avoid any confusion or the misplacement of products.

▷ The items listed on the **inventory sheets** and the **order sheets** should be printed in the same product categories and alphabetical order. This procedure maximizes efficiency, speed, convenience, and accuracy when taking inventory and preparing orders.

▶ The appropriate inventory level is directly related to product usage. Some inventory products will be used more and others less.

▶ Rotating the inventory means that most of the items on the shelves should be used within 1 to 28 days. As items are added to inventory, the items already in stock should be used before the newer items. This process is referred to as FIFO, an acronym for "First In, First Out."

A well-planned **inventory balance** is critical in order to avoid the negative effects of too little or too much inventory, summarized in the box below:

Low inventory levels can result in:	High inventory levels can result in:
Running out of menu items, causing customer dissatisfaction	Unnecessary product spoilage or deterioration
Frustration for kitchen staff and servers	Too much money invested in inventory
Additional trips to a wholesale supplier to purchase needed products	Increased opportunity for product waste and theft
Increased cost caused by purchasing smaller quantities	Additional storage space required
Increased food cost	Increased food cost

The key to determining correct inventory amounts is knowing how much of any given item should be on hand in inventory. Therefore a par stock (amount) is set for all inventory items. Recommended inventory levels are shown in the box on the next page.

Inventory Items	Recommended Inventory Levels
Bakery items	1- to 2-day supply
Fresh meats, poultry, seafood, dairy, produce	2- to 3-day supply
Frozen products	1-week supply
Canned and dry goods	1- to 2-week supply
Paper goods	2- to 4-week supply
Cleaning supplies	2- to 4-week supply

LEARNING OBJECTIVE 10
Understand how to determine inventory par stock amounts.

Par Stock

Par stock is the minimum amount of every inventory item needed to carry production between delivery days.

Par stock amounts are used to:

▶ Provide an adequate supply of items to meet the expected product demand—and can be frequently adjusted in response to menu changes and increasing or decreasing customer counts.

▶ Reduce the possibility of spoilage through good inventory rotation.

▶ Control the dollar investment in inventory.

The **par stock amount** level between deliveries depends on how often deliveries take place. If deliveries occur twice a week (*Tuesday and Friday*), then the par amount that needs to be on the shelf is the maximum number of items used per day multiplied by the number of days between deliveries—from *Friday to Tuesday is 4 days* between deliveries.

Example: Tomatoes–Diced (purchased in #10 cans) is an ingredient for several recipes, and on average 3 to 4 cans are used every day, and some days up to 6 cans may be used. Therefore, to be certain that an adequate number of cans is in inventory, the maximum number of cans used per day would be 6, resulting in a par stock amount of 24 (#10 cans), calculated as follows:

$$\text{Maximum Number of Items Used per Day} \times \text{Number of Days Between Deliveries} = \textbf{Par Stock Amount}$$

$$6\ (\#10\ \text{cans}) \qquad \times \qquad 4 \qquad = \qquad \textbf{24 (\#10 cans)}$$

LEARNING OBJECTIVE 11
Determine order quantities using par stock amounts.

A par stock amount of 24 cans means that the foodservice operation should have a minimum of 24 cans of tomatoes–diced on the shelf on the day after the delivery. Since #10 cans are packed 6 to a case, the par stock amount may be adjusted to accommodate for how the product is packed. Determining how many cases of tomatoes–diced to order at any given time will depend on the number of cans currently on the shelf.

Example: If there are only 4 cans on the shelf and delivery is expected the following morning, the amount to be ordered would be determined as follows: 24 – 4 = 20; this would be rounded up to 4 cases (6 #10 cans to a case)—refer to Tomatoes–Diced under Grocery items in Figure 3.1, Order Sheets with Par Stock Amounts, on p. 74.

The box below provides useful information to help foodservice operators identify volume amounts contained in certain size cans and the number of cans contained in a case.

Popular Can Sizes	Approximate Equivalency in Volume	Number of Cans per Case	Product Examples
#300	1.7 cups/14 fluid oz.	24	Fruits
#303	2 cups/16 fluid oz.	24	Vegetables, Fruits
#2	2.5 cups/20 fluid oz.	24	Juices, Fruits, Soups
#2½	3.5 cups/28 fluid oz.	24	Fruits, Vegetables
#3 tall	5.7 cups/46 fluid oz.	12	Vegetable Juices
#5	7 cups/56 fluid oz.	12	Canned Seafood, Potatoes
#10	13 cups/104 fluid oz.	6	Fruits, Vegetables

Order Sheets

Order sheets with par stock amounts for every inventory item provide a systematic approach to ordering correct quantities from foodservice distributors.

> ► Order sheets are arranged according to product categories, such as: meats, poultry, seafood, dairy, bakery, grocery, produce, and nonfood items (paper goods/cleaning supplies)—with several pages for each category according to the size of the inventory. Under each product category is the list of current inventory items with product specs, purchasing unit, par stock amount, and on-hand amount, followed by the need and order quantity.
>
> ► The inventory items would be listed in the same order (category and alphabetized) as they appear on the shelves in the storage areas—dry storage (storeroom), refrigerator, and freezer.
>
> > ▷ **Figure 3.1 on p. 74 is an abbreviated version of the typical order sheets.** Using printed order sheets or a hand-held tablet, the buyer enters the *On-Hand* amount and subtracts that amount from the *Par* to determine the *Order Quantity*. Some software applications may automatically calculate the order once the on-hand amount is entered.
>
> ► Placing the orders directly to distributors using the Internet allows the ordering process to be timely and efficient for the foodservice operator and the distributor.

LEARNING OBJECTIVE 12
Explain how order sheets are effectively arranged.

Standing Orders

A standing order is a specific quantity to be delivered—for example 6 dozen croissants daily. When a use pattern has been established for certain items that are frequently delivered, such as croissants (bakery), a standing order can be in place.

LEARNING OBJECTIVE 13
Know the purpose of standing orders.

Order Sheets

Date: January 11, 20xx

Calculation [C – D = E]

A	B	C	D	E
Product Categories	**Purchasing Unit**	**Par**	**On-Hand**	**NEED/ORDER**
Meats				
Rib Roast #109	14–16 lb	60 lb	15 lb	45 lb (14–16 lb each—3 Rib Roast)
Ground Beef #136	Random lb weight	80 lb	13 lb	67 lb (round up to 70 lb)
Poultry				
Chicken Breast–B/S 5 oz	10 lb/case	40 lb	5 lb	35 lb (round up to 4 case)
ChickenTenders, 4 oz.	10 lb/case	30 lb	4 lb	26 lb (round up to 3 case)
Seafood				
Salmon/Sockeye, 6 oz.	10 lb/case	20 lb	2 lb	18 lb (round up to 2 case)
Shrimp, 16/20 count	50 lb/case	50 lb	15 lb	35 lb (round up to 1 case)
Dairy				
Cream Cheese	4/3-lb block/case	12 lb	1½ lb	11 lb (round up to 1 case)
Sour Cream	6/5-lb tub/case	1 case	2¼ tub	4 tub (round up to 1 case)
Bakery				
Dutch Apple Pie	10 inch	4 pie	1½ pie	3 pie
Chocolate Cake	8 inch, 3 layer	2 cake	1 cake	1 cake
Flrless Choc Torte	10 inch	1 torte	½ torte	1 torte
Grocery				
Tomatoes, Diced,	6/#10 can/case	24 can	4 can	20 can (round up to 4 case)
Egg Noodles	2/5-lb bag/case	30 lb	7 lb	23 lb (round up to 3 case)
Olive Oil	6/1 gal/case	6 gal	2 gal	4 gal (round up to 1 case)
Produce				
Lettuce, Romaine	24 heads/case	1 case	4 heads	20 heads (round up to 1 case)
Potatoes, Russet	70 count/case	2 case	¼ case	2 case
Onions, Spanish	50 lb/mesh bag	1 bag	¼ bag	1 bag
Paper Goods				
Napkins, white	3,000 ct/case	4 case	1½ case	3 case
Cups, 12 oz.	2,500 ct/case	2 case	¾ case	1 case
Lids for 12 oz.	1,000 ct/case	5 case	1 case	4 case

Figure 3.1   Order Sheets with Par Stock Amounts

Getting the Best Price from Foodservice Distributors

LEARNING OBJECTIVE 14
Understand competitive pricing by using bid sheets.

Foodservice operators are usually in a position to negotiate price with foodservice distributors that are competing for business. This begins with a request for price quotes—*bid prices* for the items that are currently being purchased or planned to be purchased. The competing distributors are given a *bid sheet* with a list of the items, specs, and purchasing unit for each item. The distributors may not have all of the exact items, but items that are almost identical—perhaps only being differentiated by brand name or purchasing-unit size. When this occurs, the distributor may explain the difference on the bid sheet next to the bid price for the item.

Bid Sheet

Food Service Distributor: Major Broadline Distributor   **Date:** January 11, 20xx

Product Categories	Purchasing Unit	Bid Price
Meats		
Rib Roast #19	14–16 lb.	$12.5 lb
Ground Beef #136	Random lb. weight	$2.89 lb (#181/15) Distr Brand
Poultry		
Chicken Breast–B/S 5 oz	10 lb./case	$48.10 case
ChickenTenders, 4 oz.	10 lb./case	$32.65 case
Seafood		
Salmon/Sockeye, 6 oz.	10 lb./case	$61.10 case
Shrimp, 16/20 count	50 lb./case	$34.85 case (30 lb./case) Distr case weight
Dairy		
Cream Cheese, Kraft	4/3-lb. block/case	$38.40 case Distr Brand
Sour Cream	6/5-lb. tub/case	$87.40 case
Grocery		
Tomatoes, Diced, Contadina	6/#10 can/case	$19.20 Distr Brand
Egg Noodles, La Bella	2/5-lb. bag/case	$11.25
Vegetable Oil, Wesson	6/1 gal./case	$28.85 Distr Brand
Produce		
Lettuce, Romaine	24 heads/case	$24.50
Potatoes, Russet	70 count/case	$37.80
Onions, Spanish	50 lb./mesh bag	$46.00
Paper Goods		
Napkins, white	3,000 ct/case	$68.55
Cups, 12 oz.	2,500 ct/case	$122.15
Lids for 12 oz.	1,000 ct/case	$19.80

Figure 3.2   Bid Sheet

▶ **Bid sheets** can be prepared by transferring product-item specs with the purchasing units from the order sheets. Figure 3.2 is an abbreviated example of a bid sheet.

The key to competitive and fair pricing is in developing a professional working relationship with the distributor of choice: from online ordering to on-time deliveries that are complete with the items and quantities ordered—followed by payment on or before the required due date according to the established credit and payment terms.

Purchase Orders

Purchase orders are commonly used by large organizations as a method of tracking purchases and further validating all the terms and conditions of a sales agreement.

LEARNING OBJECTIVE 15
Discuss the use of purchase orders.

A purchase order is a numbered form that identifies the item or items—by specs or stock number, quantity ordered, unit price, total, any special instructions or information, date issued, and authorization signature from the buyer or accounting office. It creates a legally binding contract when prepared and signed by the buyer and received by the supplier.

The purchase order number is given to the supplier when the order is placed.

Purchase Orders:

> ▶ Document the products, quantity, price, and delivery date of the items ordered or services to be performed.

> ▶ Include special instructions for the supplier.

> ▶ Clarify for the receiving department exactly what deliveries are expected each day—exactly what has been ordered (according to specs), and exactly how much should be received.

> ▶ Clarify the exact terms and conditions of the sale.

> ▶ Include an authorized signature—assuring the invoice will be paid when verification that the products have been received or services performed according to the terms and conditions of the purchase order agreement (contract).

Contract Services

> **LEARNING OBJECTIVE 16**
> Understand contract services.

Foodservice operations require a variety of necessary services that are essential to allow the business to function properly. Similar to purchase orders, contract agreements between the foodservice operation and the companies providing the services set forth the specific terms and conditions for those services to be performed. Some of those services may include the following:

> ▶ Trash removal and recycling service

> ▶ Landscape maintenance and snow removal

> ▶ Parking lot maintenance

> ▶ Electric and gas equipment service and maintenance

> ▶ POS system service, maintenance, and upgrades

> ▶ Maintenance and service of fire systems (vents and ducks) and extinguishers

> ▶ Pest control service

> ▶ Deep cleaning services: carpets, drapes, upholstery

> ▶ Laundry and linen service

> ▶ Business insurance

> ▶ Payroll, financial services

> ▶ Advertising services

Assignment 5
Make or Buy Decision

Currently, German Potato Salad is made in-house, and is a popular side dish. The business has increased, and right now the kitchen equipment and space are at capacity. You are considering convenience food products but know that it is important to justify the increased purchasing cost. The test sample of German Potato Salad from your foodservice distributor proved to be comparable to your in-house recipe, so it is time to calculate the cost.

The foodservice distributor price per case is $61.50 for 30 lbs packed in 5-lb tubs, 6 tubs per case. Your in-house cost to make it is as follows: Recipe Cost: $18.60 that yields 15 lbs. Labor Cost: $16. So, it is decision time.

Analysis Calculations and Recommendation:

Summary

Purchasing for any foodservice operation begins with understanding what to buy. This requires a comprehensive inventory list of all the ingredients that need to be purchased which is obtained from standardized recipes that include product specifications, commonly referred to as "specs"—detailed descriptions of products.

The use of convenience products can range from partially processed or prepared items to completely finished products that are ready-to-use or serve. These products offer several cost-saving benefits and should be frequently evaluated.

Foodservice chains often outsource production for certain products to food manufacturing firms, such as chicken parts that may be cut, seasoned, precooked, and packaged according to recipe specifications. This can result in cost-effective savings in kitchen space, storage, and skilled labor.

The second step in the purchasing process is finding where to buy. The foodservice operation can review the products, pricing, and services offered by broadline distributors, specialty foodservice distributors, and wholesale foodservice suppliers. Newsletters and market reports that are offered by the distributors and wholesales provide timely information regarding new products and conditions that may affect product pricing. Also, foodservice brokers, the independent marketing companies that represent the food manufacturers' products are excellent sources for new and existing product information.

The third step in the purchasing process is determining how much to buy. This begins with a thorough understanding of inventory management. By establishing par stock amounts, a well-planned inventory balance can be maintained through the use of efficiently organized order sheets. When standing orders are in place, specific quantities are set forth according to scheduled deliveries.

Foodservice operations are able to solicit competitive pricing from foodservice distributors by requesting the distributors to prepare bid sheets for products that the foodservice operation uses. A large foodservice operation may use purchase orders as a method of tracking certain purchases, along with including specific instructions, terms, and conditions for the supplier. Finally, contract services are necessary and essential to allow the foodservice business to function properly, and can include a wide range of various services.

Discussion Questions

1. Explain where the inventory list of items to purchase originates.
2. What are product specifications?
3. Discuss the procedure involved in determining and writing a product specification.
4. List five examples of product specifications.
5. Discuss the benefits of using convenience products.
6. What are the issues to consider when making the decision to use ready-to-serve convenience products?
7. What type of foodservice operations typically outsource production for popular menu items, and what is the advantage for these operations?
8. Explain the function of foodservice distributors.
9. What are the services offered by broadline distributors?
10. Give two examples of specialty foodservice distributors.
11. System distributors, also known as commissaries, serve what functions for large chains and multi-unit restaurants?
12. Discuss the essential factors to know and understand when doing business with foodservice distributors.
13. Contrast the difference between a wholesale foodservice supplier and a broadline distributor.

14. Discuss the type of information that is provided in newsletters and market reports.

15. What is the function of foodservice brokers?

16. Explain the importance of a well-planned inventory balance and summarize the effects of low inventory levels contrasted with high inventory levels.

17. How are inventory par stock amounts established?

18. List several popular can sizes that are used in foodservice operations.

19. How many #10 cans are packed per case?

20. What is the most efficient way that order sheets can be arranged?

21. What are standing orders?

22. Discuss the procedure for preparing competitive bid sheets for foodservice distributors.

23. Explain how purchase orders function.

24. List five typical contract services that are necessary and essential for a foodservice operation.

Project Exercises

(Continued from Chapter 2)

1. Prepare a list of specialty foodservice distributors, broadline distributors, and wholesale foodservice suppliers that service your city or community. Begin by searching the Internet and visiting company websites. Write a brief description for each company, detailing the products and services offered by those companies.

2. Begin to research the Purchasing Unit size and Cost of the Recipe Ingredients that were listed on your Recipe Cost Cards from the Project Exercise in Chapter 2.

**Purchasing
Cost Control**

Restaurant Reality

Control the increased cost of a much-used operating supply item

The director of foodservices for a community school district was confronted with the possibility of having to do away with the use of plastic trash can bag liners in all of its kitchens and dining areas. A final decision would be made within the next twelve months. The school district leadership felt that with the increasing public concern over the use of all non-recyclable plastic bags, they wanted to be prepared with an alternative solution. The cost would definitely have to remain within the annual operating budget.

A scheduled meeting was set by the director of foodservices and the foodservice managers for each school. After the situation was clearly explained, a direct question was asked by one of the young foodservice managers: "What did the kitchens use before plastic trash can bag liners were invented?" The answer is simple, said another manager: "Nothing!" The trash cans were taken out and emptied into a large dumpster adjacent to each school's loading and receiving dock. A utility worker (janitor) with a high-pressure hose would then wash out and sanitize each trash can and place it upside down on a rack to dry.

The decision was made to identify the cost of the additional number of trash cans that would be needed for the washing exchange at each school along with the cost of drying racks to be placed in a covered area near the dumpsters. A clean dry trash can would always be in place while the others were drying out. The foodservice managers were also asked to prepare a budget for the estimated additional labor hours that would be required to handle and wash the trash cans.

Upon further analysis, it was documented that the cost of plastic trash bag liners had been slightly increasing every year. Therefore, although convenient to use, it revealed that returning to the previous method of high-pressure washing and sanitizing trash cans may be within the operating budget. Once the costs of the additional trash cans, drying racks, required amount of additional labor hours were all computed and totaled, a cost comparison could be made and presented to the school district leadership.

When the possibility that an operating procedure may change, foodservice managers quickly respond by identifying an alternative operating procedure and the costs associated with it.

4

Receiving, Storing, and Issuing Products and Processing Invoices

Introduction

The receiving, storing, and issuing of products along with correctly processing invoices are important management functions requiring attention to every detail. A strict procedure that verifies accuracy and accountability must be in place and properly documented—from the moment products and services are received until payment is approved.

Learning Objectives

Upon successfully completing this chapter, readers will be able to:

1. Know the basic requirements to properly receive products.
2. Explain the receiving process.
3. Understand how to deal with a short order, credit memo, and pick-up slip.
4. Explain when a Receiving Form may be used.
5. Define purchases that are Directs and Stores.
6. Discuss proper storage procedures.
7. Explain the use of a Requisition for issuing products.
8. Understand the purpose and function of Transfers.
9. Explain the procedure for processing and paying invoices.

Chapter Outline

Key Terms and Definitions

Begin by first reading the key terms and their definitions. An advance understanding of the terms will be helpful prior to reading the chapter.

Approved Payee List	A list of companies that have been selected by the foodservice operation as the companies it will do business with.
Billing Statement	A list of invoices for the period, which will include the dates and billed amounts that appear on the invoices and any credits on the account.
Credit Memo	A form listing the unacceptable or short item, the quantity amount unacceptable or short, and the price.
Directs	Purchases that go directly into production.
Invoice	A form that typically accompanies the products that are delivered and provides an itemized list of what was delivered. It also can serve as a bill for payment.
Invoice Payment Schedule	A form used to document all purchases during an accounting period and to ensure that suppliers are paid in a timely fashion.
Received Stamp	A stamp with an imprinted form to be stamped on the invoice and filled out by the receiving person, which ensures the receiver checked for quantity, quality, and price so that invoice payments can move forward.
Receiving Equipment	Scales, temperature probes, knives, carts, dollies, and hand trucks.
Receiving Form	A form used to classify incoming food products into one of two cost categories: directs or stores.
Requisition	A written order to obtain products from the storeroom, refrigerators, and freezers.
Short Order	When a different quantity amount for an item appears on the invoice than was actually delivered.
Stores	Refers to the storeroom and is used for purchases that will be placed into storage areas (storeroom, refrigerators, and freezers).
Transfer	A document that tracks the movement of products from one department to another to provide an accurate record of costs.

Receiving Basics

LEARNING
OBJECTIVE 1
Know the basic
requirements to properly
receive products.

The basic requirements to properly receive products are as follows:

▶ **Designated receiving area** that can be secured when not in use and restricted to authorized employees and delivery people.

▷ Adequate amount of space with good lighting to be able to examine, count, and weigh products and test for HACCP (Hazard Analysis Critical Control Point) safety temperatures.

▷ An office or desk to process paperwork.

▶ **Standard receiving equipment** that includes the following:

▷ Scales—heavy-duty pound scales, accurate to a fraction of a pound and scales able to weigh to a fraction of an ounce, for portion controlled products

▷ Temperature probes (properly calibrated), as well as food handler gloves

▷ Knives to cut product to spot-check for quality (primarily used for produce)

▷ Carts, dollies, and hand trucks to efficiently move products into storage areas

▷ Stainless steel work tables (if applicable), on which to place products for inspection

Obviously, the exact equipment needed to receive products will vary by size and type of foodservice operation. Smaller operations will manage with a minimum amount of equipment; larger operations may require pallet jacks, forklifts, and skilled drivers.

▶ **Qualified person** assigned to receive food, beverage, and nonfood products. This person needs to be knowledgeable and experienced, particularly with meat, poultry, and seafood items, and able to properly handle and store the items. Qualifications include:

▷ The ability to recognize that the quality of the products delivered is consistent with what was ordered. For example, it would be extremely awkward and difficult to have someone who has little knowledge of fat content, marbling, color, and so on, receiving, inspecting, and checking in fresh and frozen meat products. Although most distributors try their best to deliver the exact products that have been ordered, errors do occur, and at times products not meeting specs may be delivered.

▷ The complexity of the receiver's job is determined by the size of the foodservice operation, the extensiveness of the menu selection, and the type of food production.

Receiving Process

LEARNING
OBJECTIVE 2
Explain the receiving
process.

When a truck arrives to deliver an order, the driver will transport the products from the truck to the designated receiving area. *An invoice* with an itemized list of the products being delivered accompanies the order. The person receiving the products checks each delivered item quantity amount against the invoice quantity amount. Then, using *a copy of the order sheets* or *purchase order* (if one is used), the receiver reads the list of the items and the quantities ordered, confirming by a case or item count that the quantity amount is, in fact, present. As an item is verified, a checkmark is made next to that item. If there are any missing or broken items or if incorrect quantities were delivered, the situation is noted and resolved.

The receiver then checks the products for quality, verifies weights, and tests for HACCP safety temperatures.

As soon as the order has been checked in, the receiver signs the invoice. There are always two copies of an invoice: the original and a duplicate. The original copy goes back with the driver making the delivery and the duplicate remains with the receiving person. Then the receiver will stamp the invoice with a **received stamp** that includes the information in the example below:

The receiving person or the accounting office will verify that the invoice prices are correct and will recalculate quantity amount totals and invoice totals to verify accuracy.

Dealing with Potential Problems in Receiving

LEARNING OBJECTIVE 3
Understand how to deal with a short order, credit memo, and pick-up slip

▶ **Short Order:** A short order is when a different quantity amount for an item appears on the invoice than was actually delivered. A correction should be made immediately by the driver making the delivery. The incorrect item quantity amount should be crossed off, and the quantity amount actually delivered should be recorded, followed by the driver's initials, thereby noting the change. The invoice total will be reduced.

Some distributors prefer that the driver issue a credit memo for the difference instead of making any changes on the original invoice.

▶ **Credit Memo:** A form used for listing an item that is short—the quantity amount short, and the price—or an item that is not acceptable (and is sent back with the driver) because of quality, breakage or damage, improper HACCP temperature at the time of delivery, or the wrong product.

The credit memo is signed by the driver, with a duplicate copy given to the receiver. The credit memo goes to the accounting office where it can be reconciled with the invoice at the end of the billing period.

▶ **Pick-up Slip:** A form that lists a product(s) to be returned. If a product is delivered, accepted, and later found to be incorrect, the product is usually picked up by the driver with the next delivery and a credit is issued for the product. The driver will have a pick-up slip listing the product to be returned.

The pick-up slip requires the signatures of the driver and the receiver. Similar to the credit memo, the pick-up slip will go to the accounting office where it can be reconciled with the invoice at the end of the billing period.

Some distributors may not accept the return of a frozen or refrigerated product for safety reasons if it cannot be verified that the product was handled properly at all times.

Receiving Form

A Receiving Form (Figure 4.1) may be used to classify the incoming food products into one of two cost categories: **directs** or **stores**. The direct items and their cost can be entered on the Receiving Form as follows:

> **LEARNING OBJECTIVE 4**
> Explain when a Receiving Form may be used.

Receiving Form

Directs—to—Department: Café

Date: January 12, 20xx
Time: 6:20 A.M.

Bakery Items	Purchasing Unit	Quantity	Price	Extension
Dutch Apple Pie	10 inch	3 pie	Price and extension are completed
Chocolate Cake	8 inch, 3 layer	1 cake	by accounting office and calculated
Flourless Choc Torte	10 inch	1 torte	by software application

Figure 4.1   Receiving Form

▶ **Directs** stands for direct purchases—purchases that go directly into production. These items are charged to daily food cost as soon as received, since they are used immediately. The **item price** and **extension** (*item quantity × price*) is recorded by the accounting office.

▶ **Stores** refers to the storeroom and is used for purchases that will be placed into storage areas (storeroom, refrigerators, and freezers). These items will be used gradually and issued with Requisitions.

> **LEARNING OBJECTIVE 5**
> Define purchases that are Directs and Stores.

Directs	Stores
Used immediately	Drawn out of storage areas as needed
Charged to food cost	Charged to food cost only when issued
Invoice is the tracking form	Requisition is the tracking form that identifies costs
Type of products: Bakery, Dairy, Produce	Type of Products: Meats, Poultry, Seafood, Grocery, Frozen Foods and Nonfood Items*

* Nonfood Items include paper goods, cleaning supplies, smallwares, etc. These items are accounted for under the expense category of direct operating expenses on the income statement.

LEARNING
OBJECTIVE 6
Discuss proper storage
procedures.

Storage

Once the products have been checked in, they should be quickly moved to the appropriate storage areas to reduce the chances of spoilage or theft. The products are moved into one of the following areas:

- ► Refrigeration units (41°F or below)
- ► Freezer units (–10°F to 0°F)
- ► Dry storage/storeroom (50°F to 70°F)
- ► Cleaning supplies storage area (50°F to 70°F)

All storage areas should be secured with locks. Some operations may have video surveillance in place to monitor storage areas.

- ► **Refrigeration and freezer units** must meet the simple criteria of maintaining products at safe temperatures (monitored and frequently checked)—and operating as follows:

  - ▷ Appropriate shelving, which allows for proper circulation of air; shelving 6 inches from the walls and the lowest shelf 6 inches from the floor—nothing is ever stored on the floor

  - ▷ Raw foods separated from cooked foods; raw foods on shelves below cooked foods

  - ▷ Products properly labeled, dated, and rotated

- ► **Dry storage/storeroom** equipped with shelving 6 inches from the walls and the lowest shelf 6 inches from the floor—nothing is ever stored on the floor; products are properly labeled and rotated.

- ► **Cleaning supplies** must be stored away from food products—never in the same storage areas.

  - ▷ Material Safety Data Sheets (MSDS) provided by manufacturers of chemical-based cleaning products must be posted in a conspicuous place, so employees have access to the information.

Issuing

Requisitions

LEARNING
OBJECTIVE 7
Explain the use of a
Requisition for issuing
products.

- ► Requisitions are used to request and issue products, and to charge the cost of those products to the ordering department.

  - ▷ As a security measure, products are only issued to Requisitions with authorized signatures.

  - ▷ When the products are delivered to the ordering department, a person from the department will check each product quantity amount against the Requisition quantity amount. Once the amounts are verified, the person accepting the products will sign the Requisition.

- ► Requisitions are a means of tracking the movement of products from the storage areas to production areas. As products are issued, the costs of those products are then charged to the requisitioning department. This system is primarily used in large foodservice operations with multiple revenue centers—such as a café, dining room, cocktail lounge–bar, and catering departments operating within a large hotel. An example of a Requisition is shown in Figure 4.2.

NOTE: Requisitions may include "par stock" and "on hand" amounts for product items that are used and ordered on a daily basis.

Requisition

Storeroom—to—Department: Café

Date: January 12, 20xx
Time: 6:30 A.M.

Items	Purchasing Unit	Quantity	Price	Extension
Mangoes	each	2	$1.88	$3.76
Pineapples	each	6	$2.29	$13.74
Soy Milk	half-gallon	1	$3.65	$3.65

Price and extension are completed by accounting office and calculated by software application

---

Figure 4.2   Requisition

The Requisition Procedure:

1. A Requisition is prepared by the department needing products, for example, a café within a large hotel.

2. The Requisition is sent to the storeroom; it may be handwritten and given to the storeroom manager, or electronically sent, using a software application via a POS terminal within the department.

3. The food items are put on a service cart and delivered to the requisitioning department.

4. The department receives the products.

5. The costs of the products are charged to the requisitioning department.

6. Requisitions are quickly recorded in the accounting office.

Transfers

▶ Transfers track the movement of products from one department to another, documenting an accurate record of costs. Transfers keep track of products that have already been accounted for by a Requisition.

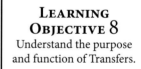

LEARNING OBJECTIVE 8
Understand the purpose and function of Transfers.

Transfer

Kiosk—to—Café

Date: January 12, 20xx
Time: 9:15 A.M.

Items	Purchasing Unit	Quantity	Price	Extension
Croissant	each	5	Price and extension are completed	
Cherry Danish	each	3	by accounting office and calculated	
Blueberry Muffin	each	2	by software application	

Figure 4.3   Transfer

Example: A kiosk (food cart) located in a hotel lobby may offer fresh-baked croissants, pastries, and muffins daily until 9:00 A.M. The items remaining beyond that time could be transferred to the café, therefore providing an effective method in maintaining quality and freshness, minimizing waste, and controlling cost.

The accounting office will subtract the cost of the bakery items from the kiosk (**Transfer-Out**) and add the cost of the items to the café (**Transfer-In**). Figure 4.3 on the previous page provides an example of a Transfer.

Processing Invoices

LEARNING OBJECTIVE 9
Explain the procedure for processing and paying invoices.

Processing invoices can be an efficient task when a basic procedure is established and followed—from the time products are received or services rendered to final payments. The procedure should ensure that products ordered at designated prices and quantities are actually what were delivered to the foodservice operation, and that contract services were rendered according to the approved agreements.

Food and Nonfood Products

▸ The receiving person delivers the stamped invoices to the accounting office for payment, along with copies of accompanying purchase orders (if used) and any credit memos or pick-up slips.

▸ The received stamp (see p. 84) ensures that the receiver checked for quantity, quality, and price so that invoice payments can move forward.

▸ The receiving person or the accounting office will verify that the invoice prices are correct and will recalculate quantity amount totals and invoice totals to verify accuracy.

Contract Services

The foodservice manager or accounting office will validate that the work or service was completed according to the terms, conditions, and scheduled frequency set forth in the contract agreement. These services include trash removal and recycling service, landscape maintenance, snow removal, pest control service, laundry and linen service, and so on.

Paying Invoices

The simplest way to pay invoices is to list them on an **invoice payment schedule.** This is a formal way of documenting all purchases during a given period of time. The invoices are grouped by company and are listed in chronological order. The payment schedule is determined by the terms of agreement established with each distributor/supplier and service provider. Their terms may range from requiring payment on receipt to payment being due within 10 to 30 days from the date of the invoice. Checks or online payments are issued as needed, such as every Friday for the 10-day accounts and on the 15th and 25th of the month for the 30-day accounts.

A foodservice distributor, at the end of a billing period, will send a **billing statement** to the foodservice operator. The billing statement will list the invoices for the period, which will include *the dates and amounts of those invoices, and any credits on the account.* The accounts payable person (accounting office) will reconcile the statement with the invoices and any credit memos or pick-up slips on file before payment is approved.

Many foodservice operations develop an **approved payee list** of distributors, suppliers, and service providers. This represents a list of companies that have been selected by the foodservice operation as the companies it will do business with. As an approved payee, any properly received stamped invoice is paid. Invoices received in the accounting office from companies that are not on the approved payee list are automatically reviewed.

Assignment 6

List 3 types of products that would be considered "directs" and 6 types of products that would go into "stores."

Directs: 1. _____

2. _____

3. _____

Stores: 1. _____

2. _____

3. _____

4. _____

5. _____

6. _____

Summary

To properly receive products, a foodservice operation should have a designated receiving area that can be secured and offer restricted access to only authorized employees and delivery people. The area also should include proper receiving equipment such as scales, temperature probes, carts, and hand trucks, and be staffed by a qualified person assigned to receive the products.

The receiving process begins with an invoice that itemizes all of the products being delivered, and the receiving person, with a copy of the order sheets or purchase order (if one is used), confirms by count that the products and quantity amounts are correct. If an item is missing or damaged, the situation is noted and resolved.

Potential problems in receiving include a "short order"—when less than what was ordered is delivered; a "credit memo"—signed by the delivery driver and the receiving person acknowledging an item missing, damaged, improper HACCP temperature, or the wrong product being returned with the driver; a "pick-up-slip" for an incorrect product that was accepted by mistake and is to be returned with the next delivery.

The Receiving Form may be used to classify products being received that are either "Directs"—products going directly into production (bakery, dairy, produce) or "Stores"—products that will be placed in storage areas until ready for use. Proper temperatures must be maintained in refrigerator, freezer, and dry storage areas.

Requisitions are used to request and issue products, and to charge the cost of those products to the ordering department. Transfers track the movement of products from one department to another.

An invoice payment schedule is a formal way of processing invoices by documenting all purchases during a given period of time. The payment schedule is determined by the terms of agreement established by each distributor/supplier and service provider.

Discussion Questions

1. What are the basic requirements to properly receive products?
2. Discuss the normal procedures that occur during the "receiving process," starting from the time a truck arrives to deliver an order.
3. Explain what is meant by a "short order."
4. When is a "credit memo" used, and how does it work?
5. What is a "pick-up slip" and how is it used?
6. A Receiving Form can classify products into what categories?
7. Explain the different between "Directs" and "Stores" and list several product examples for each.
8. What are the specified storage temperatures for the following: refrigeration units _____ freezer units _____ dry storage/storeroom _____ and cleaning supplies storage _____?
9. Discuss the reasons for using Requisitions.
10. Explain the Requisition procedure.
11. What is the purpose of a Transfer?
12. Explain the difference between a "Transfer-Out" and a "Transfer-In".
13. The simplest way to pay invoices is to list them on an invoice payment schedule. Explain that process.
14. After receiving a foodservice distributor's billing statement, what is the procedure for making payment?

Project Exercises

(Continued from Chapters 2 and 3)

1. Prepare a Requisition for all of the Recipe Ingredients that were listed on the Recipe Cost Cards from your Project Exercise in Chapter 2. The research that you have completed for the Project Exercises in Chapter 3 will be helpful for this Exercise.

   NOTE: Each Requisition, if more than one is used, must be typed and submitted on the Requisition form that is available in Excel format for this text / work book.

2. After all of the Recipe Ingredient Purchasing Unit Size and Cost numbers are listed on the Requisitions, **that information can be inserted in the Purchasing column on the Recipe Cost Cards** presented in the Chapter 2 Project Exercises.

3. The next step is to **complete the Conversion Amounts column on the Recipe Cost Cards,** then finalize completion of each Recipe Cost Card.

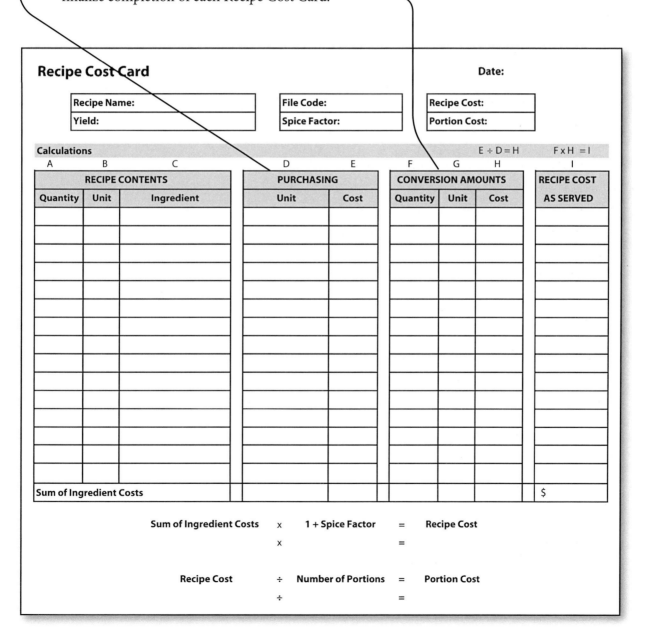

5

Food Cost

Introduction

Food cost is the total dollar amount spent on food in a foodservice operation. When foodservice managers talk about food cost, they are usually referring to the cost as a percentage. A foodservice manager who effectively controls food cost understands purchasing and proper receiving procedures; how to manage inventory by using Inventory Sheets, Inventory Turnover Reports, and Requisitions and Transfers; as well as how to process invoices.

Learning Objectives

1. Know how to calculate a Food Cost Percentage.
2. Recognize the typical food cost percentages for various foodservice categories.
3. Explain the possible circumstances that can contribute to increasing or fluctuating food costs.
4. Demonstrate how to prepare a Food Cost Report.
5. Know the information required to prepare a Department Food Cost Report.
6. Explain when a Physical Inventory is taken and the correct way to conduct the inventory.
7. Understand the importance of comparing inventory book value to actual value.
8. Explain and demonstrate how to calculate Inventory Turnover Rate.

Chapter Outline

Food Cost Percentages

Food Cost Report

Department Food Cost Report

Physical Inventory

Inventory Book Value

Inventory Turnover Rate

Summary

Discussion Questions

Project Exercises

Key Terms and Definitions

Begin by first reading the key terms and their definitions. An advance understanding of the terms will be helpful prior to reading the chapter.

Accounting Period	A standard period of time (day, week, month [4-week period]) between the tabulation of accounting records.
Book Value	The value of the inventory calculated from invoices minus what was used during the accounting period.
Closing Inventory	A physical count of the inventory at the ending of an accounting period.
Complimentary Meals	Meals given away (no charge) by the owner or manager to accommodate a dissatisfied customer, as a promotional gift, to entertain professional associates, or as menu item samples for potential catering customers.
Employee Meal Credit	The amount charged for employee meals.
Extension	The dollar value of inventory, determined by multiplying the price by the quantity.
Food Cost	The total dollar amount spent on food in a foodservice operation.
Food Cost Percentage	Determined by dividing the cost of food sold by the total food sales.
Food Cost Report	A form used to calculate food cost percentage.
Inventory	The physical quantity of food and nonfood products used in a foodservice operation.
Inventory Sheet	Lists the food and nonfood products by categories, purchasing unit, quantity, price, and location within the foodservice operation.
Inventory Turnover Rate	The number of times that the total inventory is used during a given accounting period.
Menu Mix	The number of each menu item sold in relationship to the other items sold.
Opening Inventory	A physical count of the inventory at the beginning of an accounting period.
Total Food Sales	The sum total of all food sales for an accounting period.

Food Cost Percentage

Food cost is the actual cost of purchasing the raw food products and related ingredients that are used to generate sales. These costs are measured and expressed in terms of a percentage, which is referred to as the **food cost percentage** and simply calculated as follows:

Food Cost ÷ Food Sales = **Food Cost Percentage**

Each foodservice category has a food cost percentage range (low, medium, high) that is normal for that particular type of foodservice operation. Generally, three factors shape the food cost percentage:

1. Type of foodservice establishment—ethnic foods, steak house, and so on.

2. Type, quality, and theme of food served—French bistro, western barbecue, etc.

3. Style of service—formal fine dining to self-service.

The box below shows typical food cost percentages for the various foodservice categories, which is a composite of averages from foodservice industry professional associations.

Foodservice Category	Low %	Medium %	High %
Fine Dining Table Service	25	27	34
Casual-Dining Table Service	27	32	36
Fast Casual	28	30	35
Quick Service (Fast Food)	30	34	38
Mobile (Food Truck/Trailer)	28	34	40
Catering Full Service	24	26	30
Cafeteria	33	35	37
Buffet	35	40	45

> **LEARNING OBJECTIVE 1**
> Know how to calculate a Food Cost Percentage.

> **LEARNING OBJECTIVE 2**
> Recognize the typical food cost percentages for various foodservice categories.

It is important to recognize that each foodservice category has a specific operating formula that distinguishes one category from the next and is the basis for understanding how each makes a profit in the competitive foodservice marketplace.

When a foodservice operation runs a high food cost percentage, the labor cost percentage* should be lower. Such is the case with quick service (fast-food) restaurants compared to fine dining restaurants that employ skilled chefs and a professional service staff. Refer to the comparison in the box below:

Quick Service (Fast Food)	Fine Dining Table Service
Higher food cost percentage (34%)	Lower food cost percentage (27%)
Lower labor cost percentage (24%)*	Higher labor cost percentage (36%)*
Lower guest check average	Higher guest check average
Higher customer count	Lower customer count

*Refer to Chapter 8, Typical Payroll Cost Percentages, on p. 155.

Food Cost Report

The food cost percentage is an important indicator of how well management is functioning in controlling food cost.

A Food Cost Report is used to accurately identify the food cost (cost of food sold) and the food cost percentage. The Food Cost Report indicates the actual cost percentage of food used for all food sales for any given period of time, such as by the day, week, or month (4-week period).

Preparing a Food Cost Report on a weekly basis provides for tight control of costs. This frequency allows management adequate time to react intelligently to increasing or fluctuating food costs.

Learning Objective 3
Explain the possible circumstances that can contribute to increasing or fluctuating food costs.

Increasing or fluctuating food costs can usually be attributed to one or more of the following circumstances:

1. **Standardized recipes not being followed.** This practice can result in inaccurate recipe yields, as well as inconsistent products with increased food costs.

2. **Serving incorrect portion sizes.** Too much or too little being served to customers skews the predictability of food costs.

3. **Employees not properly trained.** Poorly trained employees make costly errors in just about every area of a foodservice operation.

4. **Product spoilage or waste.** If any food items spoil or are not fresh due to improper handling or incorrect product rotation, they cannot be served to the customer. Waste occurs when items are only partially used, then thrown away.

5. **Theft of products or cash.** Foodservice operations are always vulnerable to theft by employees, unscrupulous delivery people, and sometimes even customers.

6. **Product cost increases.** Unexpected price increases due to sudden shift in product availability can hamper cost control.

7. **Owner or manager on vacation or on sick leave.** The owner or manager usually is the person supervising the operation to ensure that employees are trained and following standard operating procedures. If the owner or manager is not present in the operation, this function goes unattended, which means that costs could increase.

8. **Product receiving, storing, and issuing procedures not followed.** When product accountability procedures are not strictly followed, product quality and usage are compromised in a way that increases food cost.

9. **Mathematical mistakes or incorrect counts on inventory.** Arithmetic errors may dramatically increase or decrease the reported cost.

10. **Invoices are not recorded on an invoice payment schedule.** This means there is less food recorded as being purchased than was actually purchased.

11. **Employee meal credit, complimentary or promotional meals not being properly recorded.** All of these free or reduced-cost meals cost money, and if they are not recorded, the Food Cost Report will not include all the food costs of the operation.

12. **Menu mix is out of balance.** The menu mix is the number of each menu item sold in relationship to the other menu items sold. If standardized

recipes are followed and suppliers' prices are constant, each menu item has a fixed cost for its ingredients. Some menu items cost more to produce than other items. If more of the high-cost menu items are sold, the food cost would increase more than was expected.

Preparing a Food Cost Report

The following is a discussion of Figure 5.1 on p. 99, which is an example of a Food Cost Report (one-week period) prepared for a casual-dining table service restaurant.

LEARNING OBJECTIVE 4
Demonstrate how to prepare a Food Cost Report.

▶ **Debits:** Debit is an accounting term used to indicate an **inflow** into an account.

  ▷ **Opening Inventory:** The Opening Inventory is the value of the previous week's Closing Inventory. Every Closing Inventory becomes the Opening Inventory for the following week, because this product is still on the shelves the first day of the new operating period (week).

   ◆ The Opening Inventory for the week (period) ending 01/11/20xx is $14,870, which was the Closing Inventory for the previous week (period) ending 01/04/20xx.

  ▷ **Food Purchases:** This Debit category represents all of the food items purchased for the one-week period ($17,650). Food purchases are easily tracked using the invoice payment schedule. The amount is added to the Opening Inventory because it was available for sale during the week.

   ◆ Careful attention must be given to the invoice payment schedule because only the value of the products that have been used in production and counted as inventory should be included.

   ◆ Products that have not been used or counted as inventory will be listed on the following week's payment schedule, the value of which will count for the next week's food cost.

  ▷ **Sum of the Inflows:** Sum of the Inflows ($32,520) represents all of the dollars spent on food for the one-week period.

▶ **Credits:** A credit is an accounting term used to indicate an **outflow** from the food cost account. In other words, a credit is an adjustment to the cost of food available for sale for products purchased but not used to generate sales. Credit adjustments decrease the cost of food available for sale, allowing management to determine just how much money was actually spent to generate sales.

  ▷ **Closing Inventory:** The Closing Inventory is the dollar value of the inventory taken the last day of the accounting period.

   ◆ The Closing Inventory for the week (period) ending 01/11/20xx is $15,350, which will become the Opening Inventory for the following week (period) ending 01/18/20xx.

   ◆ A standard operating procedure for taking and valuing inventory must be followed. Errors in the inventory count or valuing translates into an error in the cost of food sold.

When to take inventory and how to take inventory are explained in detail in the Physical Inventory section on p. 101.

▷ **Employee Meal Credit:** The employee meal credit is the amount charged for employee meals. It is usually taken from the payroll report, which identifies the days of the week and number of hours worked by each employee, together with the amount charged per day for each employee meal.

♦ This food, too, was received on invoice and is included in food purchases listed under Debits. The food served to employees did not generate sales, so a credit adjustment is made and it becomes part of the outflows.

♦ Employee Meals are charged at $5.00 for each employee working a shift over 4 hours. The value of these meals is accumulated for the week (operating period) and calculated as follows:

$$\begin{array}{ccccc} \text{Number of} & & \text{Amount} & & \textbf{Employee} \\ \text{Employee Meals Served} & \times & \text{per Meal} & = & \textbf{Meal Credit} \\ 136\ \text{Meals} & \times & \$5.00 & = & \$680 \end{array}$$

♦ Employee Meals may be provided as follows:

▫ Predetermined menu items offered in an employees' cafeteria. This would occur in a large foodservice operation, hotel, resort, or casino.

▫ Selected menu items prepared each day for employees. This may occur in a large restaurant, or in a healthcare or school foodservice operation.

▫ Employees allowed to select certain food and beverage items from the restaurant menu. This is accounted for by being issued a guest check for the items each employee selects, a common procedure in many restaurant operations.

NOTE: The amount charged for the employee meal is the cost of the meal not the menu selling price. For example, a $5.00 amount would represent an average cost of designated menu items (selected for employee meals) that may have a menu price range up to $18.00 on the menu or a combination of items totaling that amount.

♦ Employee meal allowances will vary according to the amount the foodservice operation establishes.

▷ **Complimentary Meals:** Meals given away (not charged for) by the owner or manager for various reasons, such as: to accommodate a dissatisfied customer, as a promotional gift certificate, to entertain professional associates, or as menu item samples for potential catering customers. In Figure 5.1, $160 is attributed to Complimentary Meals.

♦ Complimentary meals are charged for the cost of the meals not the menu selling prices. Because these meals do not

Food Cost Report

Period Ending: January 11, 20xx

Debits

Opening Inventory	$14,870	
Food Purchases	+ 17,650	
Sum of Inflows	$32,520	$32,520

Credits

Closing Inventory	$15,350	
Employee Meal Credit	680	
Complimentary Meals	+ 160	
Sum of Outflows	$16,190	– 16,190
Cost of Food Sold		**$16,330**

Total Food Sales (Sum of Customer Guest Checks)   **$50,975**

Food Cost Percentage   **32%**

Calculated as follows:

Cost of Food Sold ÷ Total Food Sales = **Food Cost Percentage**

$16,330   ÷ $50,950   = 0.3202 rounded to **32%**

Figure 5.1   Food Cost Report

have a sales value, their cost must be subtracted from the food cost. The amount would be charged as a promotional expense on the business income statement.

> ▷ **Sum of Outflows:** The Sum of the Outflows ($16,190) represents the dollars that did not generate sales.

> ▷ **Cost of Food Sold:** The Cost of Food Sold is calculated by subtracting the Sum of Outflows from the Sum of Inflows:

▶ **Total Food Sales:** The Total Food Sales for the one-week period is the Sum of All Customer Guest Checks. In Figure 5.1, the Total Food Sales are $50,975. The POS system can record and total the food sales for each day with a cumulative total for the one-week period.

▶ **Food Cost Percentage:** The Food Cost Percentage is then calculated by dividing the Cost of Food Sold by the Total Food Sales as shown in Figure 5.1.

Complete Assignment 7 on p. 107.

Preparing a Department Food Cost Report

Each department must be considered as a separate entity, therefore the Department Food Cost Report has the same function as the Food Cost Report. The only difference is that it focuses on a specific department within a foodservice operation, if more than one exists. The goal is to arrive at an accurate cost of food sold and the food cost percentage for the department.

Normal food costs can be identified within each department, such as those that may exist within a large hotel. For example: 25 to 34 percent for a fine dining–table service restaurant, 27 to 36 percent for a casual-dining table service restaurant, 24 to 30 percent for catering, and 30 to 38 percent for a quick service kiosk (food cart). Refer to typical food cost percentages listed by foodservice category on p. 95.

The importance of departmentalizing is to be able to determine the actual costs for each department, allowing for greater financial control. It removes the possibility of a problem going undetected within a department.

Figure 5.2 is an example of a Department Food Cost Report (one-week period) prepared for a casual-dining table service restaurant (*Hotel Café*) located within a large hotel.

- ▶ **Opening Inventory and Closing Inventory:** The Opening Inventory ($2,540) and the Closing Inventory ($2,490) represent the items inventoried within the department.

- ▶ **Requisitions:** Requisitions ($7,770) are all of the food items requisitioned from the storeroom for the one-week period. The cost of those products is charged to the department.

- ▶ **Directs (purchases):** Directs ($345) are the bakery, dairy, and produce items that go directly into production and immediate use when received from delivering suppliers. The cost of those products is recorded on a daily receiving form and charged to the department.

- ▶ **Transfers-In and Transfers-Out:** Transfers-In ($90) and Transfers-Out ($35) track the movement of products from one department to another, documenting an accurate record of costs.

  Example: Transfers-In may represent bakery items sent from the kiosk (food cart) to the café; Transfers-Out may represent beverage items (juice, coffee, tea) sent from the café to the kiosk.

- ▶ **Employee Meal Credit and Complimentary Meals:** Employee Meal Credit ($280) and Complimentary Meals ($20) are costs that are tracked and recorded for the department.

- ▶ **Total Food Sales:** The Total Food Sales for the one-week period is the sum of customer guest checks ($25,975).

- ▶ **Food Cost Percentage:** The Food Cost Percentage is calculated as shown in Figure 5.2.

Department Food Cost Report
> Hotel Café <

Period Ending: January 11, 20xx

Debits

Opening Inventory	$2,540	
Requisitions	7,770	
Directs (purchases)	345	
Transfers-In	+ 90	
Sum of Inflows	$10,745	$10,745

Credits

Closing Inventory	$2,490	
Employee Meal Credit	280	
Complimentary Meals	20	
Transfers-Out	+ 35	
Sum of Outflows	$2,825	– $2,825
Cost of Food Sold		**$7,920**

Total Food Sales (Sum of Customer Guest Checks) $25,975

Food Cost Percentage   30.5%

Calculated as follows:

Cost of Food Sold ÷ Total Food Sales = **Food Cost Percentage**

$7,920   ÷ $25,975   = 0.3049 rounded to **30.5%**

Figure 5.2   Department Food Cost Report

Physical Inventory

A physical inventory has to be taken, and then valued the last day of the accounting period.

- ► An accounting period can be one day, one week, or a month (4-week period).

- ► Taking inventory means taking an actual hands-on count of every item stored in the foodservice operation. The task should follow an established procedure.

- ► After the physical inventory is taken, the dollar value of the inventory must be established.

When to Take Inventory

Inventory should be taken during a practical time. Many foodservice operators take inventory when the foodservice operation is closed. This may be either in the late evening or in the early morning. Although that certainly is a good time,

> **LEARNING OBJECTIVE 6**
> Explain when a Physical Inventory is taken and the correct way to conduct the inventory.

it may not be the most practical. Taking inventory after the foodservice operation closes may require paying overtime wages and inconveniencing employees. Also, it may not be possible for a 7-day-a-week, 24-hour-a-day business to close just to take inventory. Therefore, many operators prefer to take inventory during slow periods of the business day. Slow periods may be times between 9:00 and 11:00 A.M. or between 1:30 and 4:30 P.M.

When inventory is taken during the business day (hours of operation), it is important to remember three critical points:

1. **Establish a consistent day and time that the inventory is to be taken within the accounting period.** For example, inventory is taken every Monday at 10:00 A.M., if done weekly.

   ▷ Doing this will ensure consistent reporting of calculated food cost percentages. It creates a standard period of time so that inventory information can be accurately measured and compared.

   ▷ If a manager decided to take inventory on another day, or perhaps on the same day but at 3:00 P.M. instead of 10:00 A.M., the inventory amount reported (although accurate) would not be consistent. There would be additional sales and perhaps additional products to consider. Doing this would make the inventory information not exactly comparable with that of the previous week (period), resulting in a fluctuation in the food cost percentages.

2. **Do not schedule or accept deliveries during the time that the inventory is being taken.** Products arriving while inventory is being taken can make the inventorying process more difficult and create confusion.

3. **Inventory the food in actual production.** Food that is in production is called **in-process inventory**—*food that is in the process of getting ready to be sold.*

   An accurate dollar value must be assigned to the following:

   ▷ Food that is being prepared in the kitchen

   ▷ All prepared food held in refrigeration

   ▷ Food on the steam table

   ▷ All open stock being used in day-to-day production

   ▷ Difficult items to count, such as spices, must be assigned a fixed dollar value. For example, all opened spices may have cost $360 unopened. The manager may assume that all of the spice containers will average being half full. Thus, an average of $180 will be assigned as the dollar value for all opened spices. This dollar amount will be used until the manager believes that significant price increases have occurred or until the number of spices being used has changed.

> Consistent information must be used to properly analyze what is going on in the foodservice operation.

How to Take Inventory

Using an Inventory Sheet or a hand-held tablet, inventory is best taken by two people. One person conducts the hands-on count and calls out the quantity and product name. The other person records the quantity numbers on the **Inventory Sheet** or enters the numbers on a **hand-held tablet** that contains the inventory file.

▶ Inventory Sheets are arranged according to product categories, such as: grocery, bakery (storeroom), dairy, produce (refrigerator), meats, poultry, seafood (refrigerator–freezer), and nonfood items, such as paper goods/cleaning supplies (dry storage)—with several pages for each category according to the size of the inventory.

▶ The inventory items are listed in the same order (category and alphabetized) as they appear on the shelves in the storage areas—storeroom, refrigerator, freezer, and dry storage.

This procedure maximizes efficiency, speed, convenience, and accuracy. Figure 5.3 on p. 104 is an abbreviated version of a typical Inventory Sheet.

▶ **Location:** Storeroom

▶ **Grocery**

    ▷ **Canned Items**—Items are listed and cans arranged in alphabetical order by category and individual item: Beets: Beets, Pickled, Beets, Sliced; Tomatoes: Tomatoes, Diced, Tomato Paste, and Tomato Puree.

    ▷ Next to each item is the item's Purchasing Unit, Quantity, Price, and Extension.

▶ **Purchasing Unit:** Identifies the sizes of the individual items, such as #10 cans, pounds, cases, or any unit of measurement. The Purchasing Units on the Inventory Sheets correspond with the purchasing units on the invoices.

▶ **Quantity:** Lists the physical count of items that make up the inventory.

    NOTE: Occasionally, purchasing unit size and quantity may be confused; cake flour, for example, is normally listed by pounds instead of bags. The person counting may say "four," meaning four 25-pound bags of cake flour, instead of "one hundred," the number of pounds of flour. The inventory would be short (understated) by 96 pounds.

▶ **Price:** Shows the individual price of each item. For example, the purchasing unit price for a #10 can of Beets, Pickled is $7.15—packed 6/#10 cans to the case priced at $42.90 (case price) from the supplier. Therefore, $42.90 ÷ 6 = $7.15 per #10 can, the price of the purchasing unit listed on the Inventory Sheet.

▶ **Extension:** The inventory dollar value of each item listed calculated by multiplying the quantity by the price.

Quantity × Price = Extension

Example: Beets, Pickled   2   × $7.15 = $14.30

When the inventory has been completed, the accounting office may input the item prices, calculate the extensions, and total the inventory, or a software application may automatically do the calculations.

Inventory Sheet

Period Ending: 1/11/20xx

Date: January 11, 20xx　　**Taken by:** Storeroom Manager　　**Page:** 1 of 40

Time: 10:00 A.M.　　**Recorded by:** Assistant Manager　　**Location:** Storeroom

Grocery	Purchasing Unit	Quantity	Price	Extension
Canned Items				
Beets				
Beets, Pickled	#10 can	2	$7.15	$14.30
Beets, Sliced	#10 can	3	4.80	14.40
Tomatoes				
Tomatoes, Diced	#10 can	4	3.20	12.80
Tomato Paste	#10 can	2	5.10	10.20
Tomato Puree	#10 can	3	2.90	8.70

Figure 5.3　Inventory Sheet

Inventory Book Value versus Actual Value

LEARNING OBJECTIVE 7
Understand the importance of comparing inventory book value to actual value.

A method for double-checking the value of inventory is to compare the **inventory book value** (perpetual inventory) with the **actual physical inventory value** (periodic count value). The book value is the value of the inventory calculated from adding the value of the Closing Inventory to the invoices paid during the accounting period and subtracting what was used during the accounting period. Products used are tracked and accounted for when Requisitions are recorded. Software applications have made the calculation of book value easy to accomplish.

The book value typically is larger because the amount on the books does not account for some of the small losses due to human error and losses during the processing of food products.

The book inventory value is determined as follows:

Opening Inventory	$15,125	(Closing Inventory from the previous accounting period)
Purchases	+ 17,650	(Invoices paid during the accounting period)
Subtotal	**$32,775**	
Requisitions	– 17,220	(Products used during the accounting period)
Inventory Book Value	**$15,555**	**(Closing Inventory from the current accounting period)**
Physical Inventory Value	– 15,350	(Actual physical count value from current accounting period)
Difference	**$ 205**	**(Less dollars) (1.3%)** ($205 ÷ $15,555 = 0.013) Acceptable difference

A wider than acceptable difference (as determined by management) between inventory book value and physical inventory value can usually be attributed to one or more of the following reasons:

► Mathematical mistakes or incorrect counts

► Products issued without Requisitions (not being accounted for when used)

► Spoiled or wasted products tossed out (not counted)

► Theft

Inventory Turnover Rate

An optimum inventory turnover rate that provides for operational efficiency can be established, monitored, and maintained. This is accomplished by initially calculating the inventory turnover rate of a well-planned inventory. Once that rate is established it can be monitored for every accounting period. An increase or decrease in the rate will alert management that inventory adjustments may need to occur.

An average foodservice operation turns over its inventory within a one- to two-week period. This is based on the dollar valuation of the inventory, noting that certain products will turn over in a day or within a few days, while others may be within 7 to 28 days.

Calculating Inventory Turnover Rate

There are three steps to calculating the inventory turnover rate:

1. **Determine the average inventory value.** This is done by adding the total dollar amount of the Opening Inventory to the total dollar amount of the Closing Inventory for an accounting period and then dividing by 2.

   NOTE: The accounting period in the following example is one week.

   The Opening Inventory for the week beginning January 11, 20xx, is $14,870. The Closing Inventory for the week beginning January 11, 20xx, is $15,350.

Opening Inventory	+	Closing Inventory	=	(total)	÷ 2 =	Average Inventory Value
$14,870	+	$15,350	=	$30,220	÷ 2 =	**$15,110**

2. **Determine the cost of goods sold.** This is done by adding the Opening Inventory ($14,870) to the food purchases ($17,650) for the week of January 11, 20xx (= $32,520); then subtracting the Closing Inventory ($15,350).

Opening Inventory	+	Food Purchases	=	(total)	−	Closing Inventory	=	Cost of Goods Sold
$14,870	+	$17,650	=	$32,520	−	$15,350	=	**$17,170**

LEARNING OBJECTIVE 8
Explain and demonstrate how to calculate Inventory Turnover Rate.

3. **Calculate the inventory turnover rate.** This is done by dividing the cost of goods sold for the week of January 11, 20xx ($17,170), by the average inventory value ($15,110).

Cost of Goods Sold	÷	Average Inventory Value	=	**Inventory Turnover Rate**
$17,170	÷	$15,110	=	1.136 rounded up to **1.14**

The inventory turnover rate for the one-week accounting period is 1.14 times.

> **Complete Assignment 8 on p. 110.**

Assignment 7

1. Prepare the **Food Cost Report** for *All American*, a Casual-Dining Restaurant.

The following information is provided:

Period Ending:	January 18, 20xx
Opening Inventory:	$15,350
Closing Inventory:	18,220
Food Purchases:	15,730
Employee Meal Credit:	710
Complimentary Meals:	120
Total Food Sales:	$52,245

Food Cost Report

Period End: _____

Debits

_____

_____

   Sum of Inflows: _____

Credits

_____

_____

_____

   Sum of Outflows: _____

Cost of Food Sold: _____

Food Cost Percentage: _____

2. Prepare a **Food Cost Report** for *Top of the Town*, a Fine Dining Restaurant.

The following information is provided:

Period Ending:	March 6, 20xx
Opening Inventory:	$21,652
Closing Inventory:	20,937
Food Purchases:	24,828
Employee Meal Credit:	840
Complimentary Meals:	193
Total Food Sales:	$97,975

Food Cost Report

Period End: _____

Debits

_____

_____

   Sum of Inflows: _____

Credits

_____

_____

_____

   Sum of Outflows: _____

Cost of Food Sold: _____

Food Cost Percentage: _____

3. Prepare a **Food Cost Report** for *All Events*, a Foodservice Catering Company.

The following information is provided:

Period Ending:	June 12, 20xx
Opening Inventory:	$16,763
Closing Inventory:	18,561
Food Purchases:	31,092
Employee Meal Credit:	790
Complimentary Meals:	215
Total Food Sales:	$108,152

Food Cost Report

Period End: _____

Debits

_____

_____

   Sum of Inflows: _____

Credits

_____

_____

_____

   Sum of Outflows: _____

Cost of Food Sold: _____

Food Cost Percentage: _____

4. Prepare a **Food Cost Report** for *Fresh Today*, a Soup, Salad, and Sandwich Fast Casual Restaurant.

The following information is provided:

Period Ending:	April 17, 20xx
Opening Inventory:	$8,716
Closing Inventory:	9,098
Food Purchases:	19,209
Employee Meal Credit:	655
Complimentary Meals:	78
Total Food Sales:	$59,978

Food Cost Report

Period End: _____

Debits

_____

_____

   Sum of Inflows: _____

Credits

_____

_____

_____

   Sum of Outflows: _____

Cost of Food Sold: _____

Food Cost Percentage: _____

5. Prepare a **Department Food Cost Report** for *Grand Buffet*, a Buffet Restaurant within a Casino.

The following information is provided:

Period Ending:	July 24, 20xx
Opening Inventory:	$6,952
Closing Inventory:	7,237
Direct Purchases:	2,875
Requisitions:	17,990
Transfers-In	588
Transfers-Out	1,022
Employee Meal Credit:	710
Complimentary Meals:	68
Total Food Sales:	$49,875

Department Food Cost Report

Period End: _____

Debits

_____

_____

_____

_____

   Sum of Inflows: _____

Credits

_____

_____

_____

_____

   Sum of Outflows: _____

Cost of Food Sold: _____

Food Cost Percentage: _____

6. Prepare a **Department Food Cost Report** for *On-the-Fly*, a Quick Service Restaurant within a Resort Property.

The following information is provided:

Period Ending:	May 8, 20xx
Opening Inventory:	$4,718
Closing Inventory:	4,633
Direct Purchases:	3,740
Requisitions:	15,835
Transfers-In	190
Transfers-Out	672
Employee Meal Credit:	435
Complimentary Meals:	16
Total Food Sales:	$54,890

Department Food Cost Report

Period End: _____

Debits

_____

_____

_____

_____

   Sum of Inflows: _____

Credits

_____

_____

_____

_____

   Sum of Outflows: _____

Cost of Food Sold: _____

Food Cost Percentage: _____

Assignment 8

1. Calculate the **Inventory Turnover Rate** for *All American*, a Casual-Dining Restaurant.

The following information is provided:

Period Ending: January 18, 20xx

Opening Inventory: $15,350

Closing Inventory: 15,710

Food Purchases: 18,220

Inventory Turnover Rate

Period End: _____

1. Average Inventory:

_____

_____

2. Cost of Goods Sold:

_____

_____

3. Inventory Turnover Rate:

_____

---

2. Calculate the **Inventory Turnover Rate** for *Top of the Town*, a Fine Dining Restaurant.

The following information is provided:

Period Ending: March 6, 20xx

Opening Inventory: $21,652

Closing Inventory: 20,937

Food Purchases: 24,828

Inventory Turnover Rate

Period End: _____

1. Average Inventory:

_____

_____

2. Cost of Goods Sold:

_____

_____

3. Inventory Turnover Rate:

_____

3. Calculate the **Inventory Turnover Rate** for *All Events*, a Foodservice Catering Company.

The following information is provided:

Period Ending:	June 12, 20xx
Opening Inventory:	$16,763
Closing Inventory:	18,561
Food Purchases:	31,092

Inventory Turnover Rate

Period End: _____

1. Average Inventory:

_____

_____

2. Cost of Goods Sold:

_____

_____

3. Inventory Turnover Rate:

_____

4. Calculate the **Inventory Turnover Rate** for *Fresh Today*, a Soup, Salad, and Sandwich Fast Casual Restaurant.

The following information is provided:

Period Ending:	April 17, 20xx
Opening Inventory:	$8,716
Closing Inventory:	9,098
Food Purchases:	19,209

Inventory Turnover Rate

Period End: _____

1. Average Inventory:

_____

_____

2. Cost of Goods Sold:

_____

_____

3. Inventory Turnover Rate:

_____

Summary

Food cost is the actual cost of purchasing all of the food products that are used to generate sales. These costs are measured and expressed in terms of the **food cost percentage**, calculated as follows:

Food Cost ÷ Food Sales = Food Cost Percentage.

Each foodservice category has a food cost percentage range that is normal for that particular type of foodservice operation—ranging from fine dining, casual dining, fast casual, quick service, catering, cafeteria, and buffet.

A Food Cost Report is used to accurately identify food cost (cost of food sold) and the food cost percentage for the accounting period (day, week, or a 4-week month). It is important to recognized that food costs can increase and fluctuate between accounting periods due to circumstances. Therefore, careful attention must be given to the following: standardized recipes being followed, serving correct portion sizes, employees being properly trained, controlling product spoilage or waste, guarding against theft, monitoring product cost increases, following receiving, storing and issuing procedures, incorrect inventory counts, invoices not properly recorded, employee meal credit or promotional meals not being properly recorded, and the possibility of the menu mix being out of balance.

When preparing a Department Food Cost Report, it is important to include the requisitions, directs, and transfers-in for the sum of the inflows, as well as the employee meal credit, complementary meals, and transfers-out for the sum of the outflows.

The Physical Inventory is taken on the last day of the accounting period. When taken during the business day (hours of operation) it is important to remember three critical points: (1) establish a consistent day and time that the inventory is to be taken, (2) do not schedule or accept deliveries during the time the inventory is to be taken, (3) inventory the food in actual production. Also, when comparing Inventory Book Value to the Actual Physical Inventory Value, the book value typically is larger because the amount on the books does not account for small losses due to human error and the losses that occur during the processing of food products.

An optimum Inventory Turnover Rate for a foodservice operation should be established, then carefully monitored and maintained. An average foodservice operation turns over its inventory within a one-to two-week period. To calculate the Inventory Turnover Rate, determine the Average Inventory Value, determine the cost of goods sold, and then calculate the Inventory Turnover Rate.

Discussion Questions

1. How is the Food Cost Percentage calculated?
2. Why would a Quick Service (fast food restaurant) have a higher food cost percentage compared to a Fine Dining Table Service restaurant?
3. List the possible reasons for increasing or fluctuating food costs.
4. How is the "opening inventory" determined when preparing a Food Cost Report?
5. Explain how "food purchases" are tracked.
6. What does the "closing inventory" represent?
7. Why is "employee meal credit" included in the Food Cost Report?
8. What are the typical ways that employee meals can be provided?
9. Complimentary Meals are charged with the cost of the meals not the menu selling prices. Why?
10. How is the Cost of Food Sold determined?
11. Why is it necessary to prepare a Department Food Cost Report?

12. When preparing a Department Food Cost Report, explain what would be listed under Debits (Inflows) and what would be listed under Credits (Outflows).

13. When is the Physical Inventory taken?

14. When inventory is taken during the business day (hours of operation), what are the three critical points to remember?

15. Explain Inventory Book Value and how it is determined.

16. Describe the three steps to calculating the Inventory Turnover Rate.

Project Exercise

(Continued from Chapters 1, 2, 3, and 4)

1. **Prepare Plate Cost Cards** *using 32% as the food cost percentage* **for each of the menu items:** Soup, Salad, Entrée (with sides), Additional Items (if any), and Dessert.

   NOTE: Each Plate Cost Card must be typed and submitted on the Plate Cost Card form that is available in Excel format for this text / work book.

Plate Cost Card

Menu Item: _____   Date: _____

Yield: _____   Portion: _____   Plate Cost: $ _____

Food Cost Percent: _____   Minimum Menu Price: $ _____

Recipe Portion Cost: $ _____

Additional Items

Plate Cost: $ _____

Plate Cost	÷	Food Cost Percent	=	Minimum Menu Price
_____	÷	_____	=	_____

Congratulations! You have experienced creating a menu, placing the menu recipes on Standardized HACCP Recipe forms, completed Requisitions for the food product items required for the recipes, completed Recipe Cost Cards and Plate Cost Cards, and accurately determined the cost of your menu items. Now you can insert the menu item selling prices on the menu that you created.

NOTE: A review of Menu Pricing p. 39 may be helpful.

Food Production Cost Control

S e c t i o n 3

The preparation of food to be sold to customers is a basic manufacturing process—and the kitchen is the production plant. Raw and prepared products are ordered and received, stored and inventoried, and then assembled into products that are resold to customers. Thus, the kitchen is the factory for a foodservice operation.

Controlling exactly how much and what is to be prepared is the responsibility of the foodservice manager and/or chef. The task should never be left to guesswork or hunches. To effectively control food production, managers use menu item sales and popularity indexes to establish sales forecasts that determine food production schedules—thereby assuring adequate quantities of each menu item are prepared for the expected level of sales. In doing this, over-production and waste are kept to a minimum—it also avoids under-production and running out of popular menu items. Then it becomes an ongoing process to review each menu item's profitability.

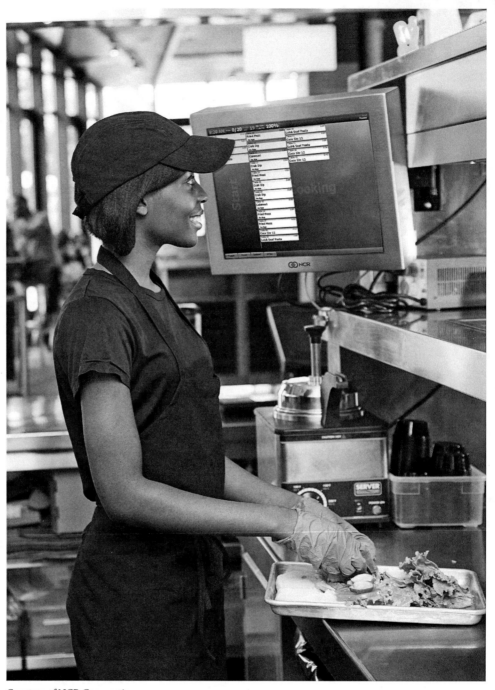

Courtesy of NCR Corporation.

6

Controlling Food Production

Introduction

Controlling food production is essential to controlling food cost. There are operational procedures needed to direct food production and reconcile daily production to daily sales. Once production levels are set and food preparation begins, other records monitor sales and assist with reconciling prepared food portions with ordered and served food portions.

Learning Objectives

Upon successfully completing this chapter, readers will be able to:

1. Explain when Food Production can begin.
2. Discuss the type of information recorded in a Sales History.
3. Understand how to prepare a Sales Forecast.
4. Recognize the importance of Customer Counts.
5. Understand that Menu Item Sales and Popularity Percentages track customers' menu preferences.
6. Demonstrate preparing a Menu Item Sales Report and Menu Item Sales Forecast.
7. Describe the purpose and function of a Food Production Schedule.
8. Discuss portion serving control, tracking portions, and the function of a Portion Control Report.
9. Explain the importance of a Food Mishap/Void Orders Report.

Chapter Outline

Food Production
Sales History
Sales Forecast
Customer Counts
Menu Item Sales and
    Popularity Percentages
Menu Item Sales Report

Menu Item Sales Forecast
Food Production Schedule
Portion Control Report
Food Mishap/Void Orders
Summary
Discussion Questions

Key Terms and Definitions

Begin by first reading the key terms and their definitions. An advance understanding of the terms will be helpful prior to reading the chapter.

Customer Count	The number of customers that eat during a designated period of time, such as a meal period, day, week, month, or year.
Dish-up	The process of putting food on the plate.
Food Mishap/Void Orders	Accounts for wasted food portions when balancing with a Portion Control Report.
Food Production Schedule	A schedule that informs cooks and chefs how much food to prepare.
Menu Item Sales Report	Records the number of each menu item sold.
Menu Popularity Percentage	The frequency with which each menu item is selected as it competes with other menu items.
Over-portioning	Placing more food on the plate by not following the Standardized HACCP Recipe.
Over-production	Producing more food than is needed, which can result in higher than planned food cost.
Portion Control Report	A report used to verify that the number of portions that should be served were actually served.
Sales Forecast	An estimate of the foodservice operation's sales based on the number of expected customers along with the menu items that will be ordered by those customers.
Sales History	A record of the "business history" of the foodservice operation.
Under-portioning	Placing less food on the plate by not following the Standardized HACCP Recipe.
Under-production	Producing less food than is needed, possibly causing customer dissatisfaction, frustrated employees, and an effect on sales.

Food Production

Food production can begin when the following two questions have been answered:

1. How many customers are expected?

2. How many portions of each menu item (and size of each) should be prepared?

To begin to answer these two questions management needs to review the **sales history** for each meal period (breakfast, lunch, dinner). Then a **sales forecast** (prediction) can be made based on the sales history.

Sales History

A sales history records the "business history" of a foodservice operation. Each time a guest order is entered into a POS system, a detailed record of the day's business is recorded within the system software. All the details accumulated together create a story line that includes the **number of customers served** and the **menu items they selected.**

▶ The number of each food and beverage menu item ordered by meal period (breakfast, lunch, dinner), and the menu items in order of popularity—the most sold to the least sold within each menu category, such as appetizers, soups, salads, sandwiches, entrées, desserts, and beverages—are all recorded.

▶ Events that have affected sales are an important component of any sales history and are recorded daily, such as the following:

▷ Weather conditions—snow storm, heavy rain, hurricane, etc.

▷ Competition from other restaurants—new restaurant openings, coupons, etc.

▷ Neighborhood or community events—street fair, bicycle races, etc.

▷ Meeting or convention business—club meeting, association annual convention, etc.

▷ A supplier delivery may be late—weather conditions or traffic delays a scheduled delivery time.

▷ A power outage or equipment breakdown—ice machine leaks, dish-machine jammed, etc.

▷ Holidays—Mother's Day, Father's Day, Valentine's Day, St. Patrick's Day, Cinco de Mayo.

NOTE: If Valentine's Day, February 14th; St. Patrick's Day, March 17th; or Cinco de Mayo, May 5th falls on a Friday or Saturday, sales will be increased versus earlier days of the week, such as Monday or Tuesday.

▶ Managers read and analyze the "business story line" through reports that can be printed at the end of every shift and/or day's business. The information is used for the tasks of scheduling kitchen production and adjusting employee work schedules for the level of business anticipated. The information provided includes the following:

▷ Customer Counts

▷ Menu Item Sales Report

▷ Portion Control Report

▷ Food Mishap/Void Orders

► A well-documented **sales history** becomes a critical factor in allowing the foodservice operator to review what had occurred during the same time (month, week, days) the previous year in order to anticipate and plan for the current month, week, and days when preparing a **sales forecast**.

Sales Forecast

<table>
<tr><td>

LEARNING OBJECTIVE 3

Understand how to prepare a Sales Forecast.

</td></tr>
</table>

A sales forecast is developed from the sales history that includes customer counts and menu item sales and popularity percentages for all of the menu items. The forecast **predicts how many customers are expected along with the menu items that will be ordered by those customers.**

With a sales forecast, the foodservice operator is able to determine product order quantities, schedule kitchen production, and establish employee work schedules to adequately meet the needs of the anticipated business.

Customer Counts

<table>
<tr><td>

LEARNING OBJECTIVE 4

Recognize the importance of Customer Counts.

</td></tr>
</table>

The following restaurant example is used to illustrate customer counts:

► A 125-seat casual-dining table service restaurant that does $4.2 million in annual sales with an average customer guest check of $15 for lunch and $28 for dinner had served 205,500 customers the past year.

► The restaurant is open daily from 11:00 A.M. to 10:00 P.M.:
Lunch—11:00 A.M. to 2:00 P.M., a 3-hour period—and
Dinner—5:00 P.M. to 10:00 P.M., a 5-hour period.

Customer counts can be recorded by the hour, meal period, day, week, month—and by the year. The frequency of recording customer counts is determined by management in order to meet the information needs of the foodservice operation, ranging from quick service (fast food) to fine-dining table service, and buffet.

The annual customer counts and weekly customer counts provide the foodservice operator with the information data that is an important component to operational decision making.

► The **annual customer counts** by the month and meal period (lunch and dinner) reflect the sales patterns for the year, as shown in Figure 6.1. This provides an overview for management that is helpful when scheduling employee vacation time, new-hire and staff training sessions, kitchen deep-cleaning (exhaust vents, etc.), equipment upgrades and replacements, dining room deep-cleaning (carpet, window coverings, etc.), chairs, tables and booth repairs, as well any remodeling or POS system changes or upgrades. The slower months of February (14,998) and October (15,098) would be ideal months for such activities.

	Jan	Feb	Mar	Apr	May	Jun	Jul	Aug	Sep	Oct	Nov	Dec	Totals
Lunch	6,118	4,749	5,606	5,821	5,705	5,945	6,084	5,651	5,298	4,982	5,652	6,202	67,813
Dinner	10,418	10,249	11,436	11,854	13,007	12,069	12,351	11,473	10,727	10,116	11,398	12,589	137,687
Totals	16,536	14,998	17,042	17,675	18,712	18,014	18,435	17,124	16,025	15,098	17,050	18,791	205,500

Annual Customer Counts

Year: 20xx

Figure 6.1   Annual Customer Counts by Month and Meal Period

▷ The example also shows that May (18,712), June (18,014), July (18,435), and December (18,791) are the busiest months for the restaurant—times when additional staff and work hours are needed to adequately handle the increased business. These are the months when the restaurant should be operating at peak efficiently—kitchen and dining room equipment and facilities running smoothly, inventory at optimum levels, and trained staff working in harmony.

▶ The **weekly customer counts** by day and meal period, shown in Figure 6.2 on p. 122, reflect current sales patterns that can be used to guide management in effectively planning for the needs of the business.

The **sales patterns** will determine the number of employees to schedule and the food and beverage quantities needed. The example shows an increase in business on Friday, Saturday, and peaking on Sunday—the busiest days of the week.

▶ The weekly customer counts provide the information that the foodservice operator needs in order to quickly respond to an increase or decrease in business. When business is trending upward, a pattern will emerge, which can be factored into immediate future planning.

▷ For example: if the weekly customer count is 4,124 as shown in Figure 6.2, and the previous week's total was 3,793—that would be an 8.7 % increase over the previous week, calculated as follows:

Current Count − Previous Count = **Number of Increase**

4,124   −   3,793   = **331** more customers

Number of Increase ÷ Previous Count =   **Percent Increase**

331   ÷   3,793   = .0872 rounded to **8.7%**

▷ The **8.7 % increase** could be used to forecast next week's customer count, calculated as follows:

Current Count × (1 + Percent Increase) =   **Forecasted Count**

4,124   ×   1.087*   = 4,482.7 rounded up to **4,483**

* 1 is added to the decimal percentage to quickly arrive at the Forecasted Count.

Weekly Customer Counts								
						Week of: 1/11/20xx		
	Monday	**Tuesday**	**Wednesday**	**Thursday**	**Friday**	**Saturday**	**Sunday**	**Total**
Lunch 11 A.M.–2 P.M.	184	189	196	204	262	246	258	1,539
Dinner 5 P.M.–10 P.M.	296	311	322	341	415	438	462	2,585
Totals	480	500	518	545	677	684	720	4,124

Figure 6.2   Weekly Customer Counts by Day and Meal Period

▷ If a **decrease** in business occurred, the percentage change would be a minus. For example, if the previous week's total was 4,310—that would be a 4.3% decrease over the previous week, calculated as follows:

Previous Count − Current Count = **Number of Decrease**

4,310   −   4,124   = **186** less customers

Number of Decrease ÷ Previous Count =   **Percent Decrease**

186   ÷   4,310   = .0431 rounded to **4.3%**

▷ The 4.3 decrease could be used to forecast next week's customer count, calculated as follows:

Whole Number − Percent Decrease = **Forecasted Percentage**

1.00   −   .043   =   .957 (or **95.7%**)

Current Count × Forecasted Percentage =   **Forecasted Count**

4,124   ×   .957   = 3,946.6 rounded to **3,947**

▶ The foodservice operator analyzes the increase and decrease in customer counts by day and meal period (lunch and dinner) in order to further identify what may have affected the changes and also reviews the number of reservations for each day and meal period and the source of those reservations—telephone call-in, restaurant website, OpenTable (www.opentable.com), etc.

▶ Well-documented customer counts become a critical factor in allowing the foodservice operator to review what had occurred during the same time (month, week, days) the previous year in order to anticipate and plan for the current month, week, and days when preparing a sales forecast.

▶ The goal of every successful foodservice operator is to attract new customers along with encouraging existing customers to return more frequently.

Menu Item Sales and Popularity Percentages

LEARNING OBJECTIVE 5
Understand that Menu Item Sales and Popularity Percentages track customers' menu preferences.

Menu item sales and popularity percentages track customers' menu preferences, which are the menu items that customers select ranked by popularity. It is reasonable to conclude that the same proportion (percentage) of customers who normally order a particular item will continue to do so unless there is an unforeseen circumstance that changes the preference pattern. The proportion percentage is known as the **popularity percentage.**

The popularity percentage is defined as the frequency with which each menu item is selected as it competes with other menu items. As long as the selection pattern shown via the sales history is stable, it is logical to use the popularity percentage to:

► Determine menu item counts

► Determine kitchen production quantities

Computing Popularity Percentages

The popularity percentages for the restaurant's soup selections—shown in Figure 6.3—shows the sales data for the week of January 11, 20xx. Popularity percentages can be computed using sales information for a day, a week, a month, or any other time period. The exact length of time to use is established by management. It should be a period of time that reflects the most current customer selection pattern.

To calculate the popularity percentage, divide each item's total number sold by the total number of items sold, rounding up or down to the next whole number. The percentages should add up to 100%. Figure 6.3 shows the total number sold for each soup by the day and for the week, and the combined total of all soups sold for the week is 817. The Chicken Noodle's week's total is 327. (Note that the popularity percentage for Minestrone has been rounded up to 25%.)

With a POS system software application this example could easily be turned into a rolling popularity percentage by simply inserting the most current day's sales information into the appropriate day's spot; by removing the old information, the popularity percentage would reflect the most current sales information for the period identified.

It is also important to recognize that popularity percentages will fluctuate with any of the following:

► Seasons—demand for menu items such as soups will fluctuate by season

► Weather conditions

► Food trends

► Menu changes

► Special events

Menu Item Sales Report (with Popularity Percentages)

Menu Category: Soups | | | | | | | | **Week of:** January 11, 20xx |

Items	Mon	Tues	Wed	Thurs	Fri	Sat	Sun	Total	Popularity %
Chicken Noodle	48	37	41	49	54	55	43	327 ÷ 817 =	40%
Clam Chowder	32	40	36	39	48	44	49	288 ÷ 817 =	35%
Minestrone	26	29	28	32	30	28	29	202 ÷ 817 =	25%
Total Soups	106	106	105	120	132	127	121	817	100%

Figure 6.3   Menu Item Sales Report (with Popularity Percentages)

Popularity percentages are often used to help identify customer preferences for specific types of foods, such as poultry, seafood, beef, and so on. This information can then be used to develop menu selections that cross-utilize these products, which can lead to reduced purchasing costs and increased customer satisfaction.

Complete Assignment 9 on p. 130.

Using Popularity Percentages and Sales History to Forecast Menu Item Sales

Once the popularity percentages are known, the task of forecasting can begin. The Menu Item Sales Forecast for soups in Figure 6.4 demonstrates how the process functions.

Although the total number of soups sold the week of January 11, 20xx, was 817, the forecast for the week of January 18, 20xx, as determined by the foodservice manager, is 865. The increased amount over the 817 is based on an anticipated increase in the number of customers as reported for the same week of the previous year—business increases during the third and fourth weeks of January.

Therefore, when 865 servings of soup are forecasted, calculating by the popularity percentages will determine the forecasted number of orders for each kind of soup for that week, as shown in Figure 6.4.

Menu Item Sales Forecast

Menu Category: Soups   **Week of:** January 18, 20xx

Items	Popularity %	Forecast: 865 Servings	Total
Chicken Noodle	40%	(865 × .40 = 346)	346
Clam Chowder	35%	(865 × .35 = 302.75) rounded up	303
Minestrone	25%	(865 × .25 = 216.25) rounded down	216
Total	100%		865

Figure 6.4   Menu Item Sales Forecast

Complete Assignment 10 on p. 131.

Using a Menu Item Sales Forecast to Determine Food Production Quantities

The quantity of food to be prepared should be determined as accurately as possible using portion forecasts derived from popularity percentages and a sales forecast.

- ▶ If too much is prepared—**over-production,** the result may be higher than planned for food costs because of food wasted and not sold.

- ▶ If too little is prepared—**under-production,** menu items will run out, which can cause customer dissatisfaction, frustrated employees, and lost sales.

Menu Item Sales Forecast	is used to prepare the	Food Production Schedule
Records the forecasted number of orders for each menu item of the week and by day.		Provides set production quantities / par amounts with start and finish times.

Once the forecasted number of orders for each menu item for the week is determined, then a daily forecast can be calculated. The daily forecast is stated as a par amount on the Food Production Schedule as shown in Figure 6.5.

Food Production Schedule

The Food Production Schedule establishes the **par amount** to be prepared for each food item. The remaining food at the end of the previous shift or day is recorded as **on-hand** amounts (food that can be used the following shift or day). The on-hand amounts are subtracted from the par amounts to determine the amounts to **prepare**, calculated in Figure 6.5.

The amounts to prepare are often rounded up or down by a small margin to simplify recipe conversions, as determined by the foodservice manager or chef. The resulting **total amounts** should be within an acceptable range of the par amounts, as shown in Figure 6.5, that is, a very small amount above the par amount. This is closely monitored by the chef on a daily basis.

LEARNING OBJECTIVE 7
Describe the purpose and function of a Food Production Schedule.

► The food item par amounts are typically increased toward the end of the week (Friday, Saturday, and Sunday) with increased customer counts and greater sales.

► A production **start** and **finish** time is determined by the foodservice manager or chef so that food production is kept on schedule. If the restaurant opens for lunch at 11:00 A.M., then the soups should be prepared and ready to be served prior to opening.

Food Production Schedule

Date: January 18, 20xx   **Day:** Monday

Soups	Par Amount		On-Hand		Prepare		Total Amt.	Start Time	Finish Time
Chicken Noodle	5 gal	–	1.6 gal	+	3.5 gal	=	5.1 gal	7:30 A.M.	10:45 A.M.
Clam Chowder	4 gal	–	0.2 gal	+	4.0 gal	=	4.2 gal	7:30 A.M.	10:45 A.M.
Minestrone	3 gal	–	0.7 gal	+	2.5 gal	=	3.2 gal	7:30 A.M.	10:45 A.M.

Figure 6.5   Food Production Schedule

Portion Control and Presentation

After the food is prepared, the challenge is to serve the correct amount in the correct way to each customer. The process is typically referred to as **dishing up the food**. The process of putting food on the plate is frequently called the **dish-up**. Usually food is portioned and sold according to weight and volume. Therefore, portion scales should be conveniently placed near the serving line along with the correct size serving utensils to ensure that the portion dish-up is done properly.

LEARNING OBJECTIVE 8
Discuss portion serving control, tracking portions, and the function of a Portion Control Report.

Kitchen
Essentials
Portion Control:
For serving
utensils by size,
see p. 27.

The following is a list of procedures to ensure the proper dish-up:

1. If the food is in small pieces (peas, corn, and so on), use the correct-size slotted spoon or spoodle for dish-up. If it is in a liquid form (gravies, sauces, and soups), use the correct-size ladle for dish-up. Portion control is assured when using the correct-size serving utensil.

   Example: When serving a 5-ounce cup of soup, a 5-ounce ladle would be used; for a 10-ounce bowl of soup, a 10-ounce ladle.

2. If the food is in a semisolid form (mashed potatoes, ice cream, and so on), use the correct scoop for dish-up. Examples of slotted spoons, spoodles, ladles, and scoops in various sizes can be seen by going to www.vollrath.com.

3. If the item is solid, sold by the ounce, then the item will need to be cut into the portion size required. Prime rib and roasts are examples of this type of dish-up. After the item is cut, it should be weighed on a portion scale. A meat slicer may be used to regulate the size of the cut. After an initial adjustment, a meat slicer may slice cooked meat into the exact number of ounces required.

4. Purchase pre-portioned items when possible—for example, 8-ounce steaks.

5. Portion pies and cakes by using a pie or cake marker prior to cutting.

The presentation is made consistent by using the following processes:

1. Follow the Standardized HACCP Recipe without exception. The recipe describes how the food is to be prepared and portioned.

2. Refer to a picture of the final plate presentation. If a picture has not been included with the Standardized HACCP Recipe, then take the picture so that it can be easily accessed on a nearby system screen or tablet.

3. In many fine-dining restaurants, an expediter will often check the food and compare the dished-up plate to a mental picture of the correct plate. The dining room manager in some restaurants is often the expediter.

Tracking Portions

To control usage, a Portion Control Report, Figure 6.6, is prepared on a daily basis. The report begins with the total amount prepared for each food item, which is taken directly from the Food Production Schedule, Figure 6.5 on p. 125. The portion size to be served follows along with the total possible servings.

The soups are served by the bowl as a 10-ounce portion, and on customer request, are available in a 5-ounce portion by the cup. To calculate the possible number of servings, the total amount prepared is converted to ounces and then divided by the largest portion size (10 oz.) as follows:

Chicken Noodle   5.1 gal × 128 oz per gal = 652.8 rounded down to **652 oz***

	Total Amount Prepared	÷	Portion Size	=	**Possible Servings**
Chicken Noodle	5.1 gal / 652 oz	÷	10 oz	=	65
Clam Chowder	4.2 gal / 537 oz	÷	10 oz	=	53
Minestrone	3.2 gal / 409 oz	÷	10 oz	=	40

* Liquids (soup) held at 135°F on a serving line will have some evaporation. Therefore, always round down when calculating ounces and possible serving portions.

Portion Control Report

Date: January 18, 20xx   **Day:** Monday

Soups	Total Amt. Prepared	Portion Size	Possible Servings	Amt. Sold	Mishap Void	Amount On-Hand	+ or – Difference
Chicken Noodle	5.1 gal / 652 oz	10 oz	65	46	1	1.3 gal / 166 oz (16)*	–2
Clam Chowder	4.2 gal / 537 oz	10 oz	53	38		1.1 gal / 140 oz (14)*	–1
Minestrone	3.2 gal / 409 0z	10 oz	40	31		0.7 gal / 89 oz (8)*	–1

*Remaining Servings

Figure 6.6   Portion Control Report

The amounts sold are obtained from that day's Menu Item Sales Report, in which those amounts have been totaled from customer guest checks. Food mishap/void orders are recorded from the Food Mishap/Void Orders Report (see Figure 6.7 on p. 128).

The amounts of food left are weighed and measured at the close of either the shift or the day's business and then recorded in the amount on-hand column and converted to ounces. The ounces are divided by the portion size to determine the number of remaining servings as follows:

Chicken Noodle   1.3 gal × 128 oz per gal = 166.4 round to **166 oz**

Amount On-Hand ÷ Portion Size = **Remaining Servings**

Chicken Noodle	1.3 gal / 166 oz	÷	10 oz	= 16.6 round to **16**
Clam Chowder	1.1 gal / 140 oz	÷	10 oz	= **14**
Minestrone	0.7 gal / 89 oz	÷	10 oz	= 8.9 round to **8**

NOTE: The amount on-hand will also be recorded on the Food Production Schedule for the following shift or day.

The difference column is determined by adding the amount sold (plus any mishap-void orders) to the on-hand remaining servings and then subtracting that total from the possible servings as follows:

	Amt Sold	(Mishap -Void)		Remaining Servings		Possible Servings		+ or – Difference
Chicken Noodle	46	1	+	16	= **63**	65 (− **63**) =		−2
Clam Chowder	38		+	14	= **52**	53 (− **52**) =		−1
Minestrone	31		+	8	= **39**	40 (− **39**) =		−1

The difference could be plus or minus, which will indicate **under-portioning (a plus difference)** or **over-portioning (a minus difference)** when dishing up the food item, or due to possible waste which is tracked through the Food Mishap/Void Orders Report (see Figure 6.7).

Soup sales continue to advance with coffee houses, delis, and fast casual restaurants offering a variety of soups on take-out menus. Take-out paper cups and plastic containers used for soups typically range in size—8, 12, and 16 ounces.

LEARNING OBJECTIVE 9

Explain the importance of a Food Mishap/Void Orders Report.

Management will determine if there is an acceptable difference variance. If the food items are in the category of soups, a small minus difference may be acceptable.

NOTE: A plus difference may exist if on any given shift or day there are more customers requesting a 5-ounce cup serving versus the 10-ounce bowl serving—although an advanced POS system application could accurately account for the different sizes and balance the quantities.

There would not be an acceptable difference variance with high-cost food items such as steaks, lobster tails, etc.

Food Mishap/Void Orders

Mistakes and mishaps are often made as a result of human errors. As much as perfection is the goal, it is quite likely that a plate will be sent back from the dining room or a mistake will be made on the serving line, making an item unacceptable to the customer. Whatever the circumstances, the wasted products need to be accounted for and recorded as Food Mishap/Void Orders. Any food portions ready for service that did not generate sales are contributing to increased food cost. To track these items, a Food Mishap/Void Orders Report is used for two significant functions:

1. To account for wasted food portions when balancing with the Portion Control Report
2. To identify responsibility and accountability within the production and service staff

The Food Mishap/Void Orders Report should be placed on a conveniently located clipboard with a pencil or provided as a system (or tablet) software function to be used immediately following the mishap. The food mishaps are reviewed by management at the end of the shift. Figure 6.7 reflects some typical examples of situations that often occur.

The main reasons an item is recorded as a mishap is as follows:

▶ Serving error

▶ Cooking error

Food Mishap/Void Orders Report

Food Mishaps: Dinner Shift   **Date:** January 18, 20xx

Item Description	Mishap	Time	Name
Chicken Noodle Soup	Spilled	6:10 P.M.	Server Sample
Rack of Lamb	Overcooked	7:20 P.M.	Chef Sample
Spinach Salad	Order Error	7:50 P.M.	Server Sample
Veal Parmesan	Soggy and Cold	8:05 P.M.	Cook Sample
Tiramisu	Dropped	8:35 P.M.	Server Sample

Figure 6.7 Food Mishap/Void Orders Report

- ▶ Ordering error

- ▶ Customer dissatisfaction with some aspect of the item

- ▶ The item has been dropped, spilled, spoiled, or is otherwise compromised and cannot be sold

When an item is prepared but not sold, the reason(s) should immediately be investigated.

The foodservice operator can use the Food Mishap/Void Orders Report to:

- ▶ Identify production problems

- ▶ Evaluate employee performance—especially new employees

- ▶ Single out employees in need of retraining

- ▶ Develop standards to minimize mishaps for both the front-of-house and back-of-house employees

- ▶ To avoid theft—collusion between employees

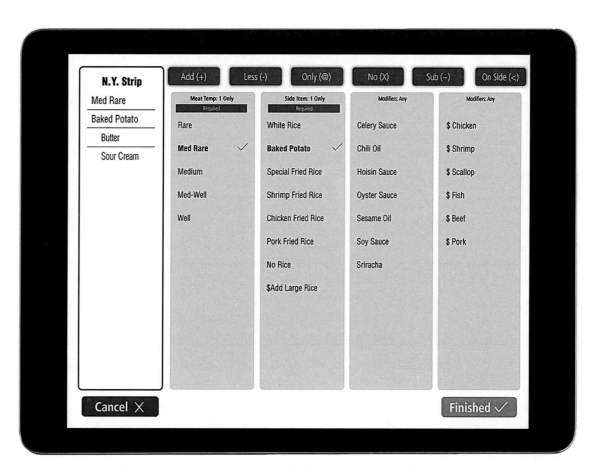

Menu item modifiers on a handheld tablet / cloud POS system can further assure accuracy in placing guest orders. Courtesy of Action Systems, Inc.

Assignment 9

Calculate the **Popularity Percentages** for the following **Menu Item Sales Reports.**

Menu Item Sales Report (with Popularity Percentages)

Menu Category: Appetizers

Week of: Current Week

Items	Mon	Tues	Wed	Thurs	Fri	Sat	Sun	Total		Popularity %
Bruschetta	42	36	32	34	51	63	47	____	=	____
Antipasti	28	25	24	20	34	46	39	____	=	____
Grilled Eggplant	14	12	15	17	21	28	26	____	=	____
TOTAL APPETIZERS	____	____	____	____	____	____	____	____		____

Menu Item Sales Report (with Popularity Percentages)

Menu Category: Entrées

Week of: Current Week

Item	Mon	Tues	Wed	Thurs	Fri	Sat	Sun	Total		Popularity %
Cioppino	8	11	9	13	21	26	20	____	=	____
Scaloppine di Vitello	5	8	16	14	18	29	26	____	=	____
Salmone alla Griglia	14	12	18	23	24	34	29	____	=	____
Bistecca	6	14	9	18	16	19	21	____	=	____
Filetto di Maiale	4	8	12	19	20	18	19	____	=	____
Pollo con Carciofini	13	11	14	22	26	33	27	____	=	____
TOTAL ENTRÉES:	____	____	____	____	____	____	____	____		____

Menu Item Sales Report (with Popularity Percentages)

Menu Category: Desserts

Week of: Current Week

Item	Mon	Tues	Wed	Thurs	Fri	Sat	Sun	Total		Popularity %
Crema Fritta	3	2	4	5	7	11	10	____	=	____
Tiramisu	5	4	6	6	14	21	9	____	=	____
Gelato	6	8	7	11	16	19	22	____	=	____
Fresh Fruit of the Day	9	12	12	15	26	24	21	____	=	____
Chocolate Mousse Cake	13	9	14	16	31	28	22	____	=	____
Flourless Chocolate Torte	8	10	9	12	25	27	19	____	=	____
TOTAL DESSERTS:	____	____	____	____	____	____	____	____		____

Assignment 10

Complete the **Menu Item Sales Forecasts** by using the popularity percentages from Assignment 9.

Menu Item Sales Forecast

Menu Category: Appetizers   **Week of:** Following Week

Items	Popularity %	Forecast: 685 Servings	Total
Bruschetta	_____	_____	_____
Antipasti	_____	_____	_____
Grilled Eggplant	_____	_____	_____
Total:	100%		685

Menu Item Sales Forecast

Menu Category: Entrées   **Week of:** Following Week

Items	Popularity %	Forecast: 950 Servings	Total
Cioppino	_____	_____	_____
Scaloppine di Vitello	_____	_____	_____
Salmone alla Griglia	_____	_____	_____
Bistecca	_____	_____	_____
Filetto di Maiale	_____	_____	_____
Pollo con Carciofini	_____	_____	_____
Total:	100%		950

Menu Item Sales Forecast

Menu Category: Desserts   **Week of:** Following Week

Items	Popularity %	Forecast: 525 Servings	Total
Crema Fritta	_____	_____	_____
Tiramisu	_____	_____	_____
Gelato	_____	_____	_____
Fresh Fruit of the Day	_____	_____	_____
Chocolate Mousse Cake	_____	_____	_____
Flourless Chocolate Torte	_____	_____	_____
Total:	100%		525

Summary

Food production can begin when the number of customers that are expected, along with the number of portions of each menu item to be prepared are identified. Therefore, management needs to review the **Sales History** in order to be able to prepare a **Sales Forecast.**

The **Sales Forecast** can be determined by reviewing the **Customer Counts,** which reflects current sales patterns, followed by the **Menu Item Sales** and **Popularity Percentages** that have been recorded and computed.

The **Food Production Schedule** establishes the "par amounts" to be prepared for each menu item. Then the on-hand amounts are subtracted from the par amounts for each menu item to determine the amounts to prepare, along with start and finish times.

The **Portion Control Report** tracks usage, beginning with the total amount prepared for each menu item, portion size, possible servings, amount sold, mishap/void orders, and amount on-hand (remaining portion servings).

The **Food Mishap/Void Orders Report** tracks mistakes and errors, which can account for wasted portions and identify responsibilities of personnel, as well as establish accountability within the production and service staff.

Discussion Questions

1. What two questions have to be answered before Food Production can begin?
2. List the type of information that should be recorded in a Sales History.
3. Explain how a Sales Forecast is developed.
4. When Customer Counts are recorded annually by the month and meal period, how can that information by used by management?
5. Weekly Customer Counts reflect sales patterns that can be effectively used by management—specifically, in what ways?
6. Why is it important for management to track Menu Item Sales and Popularity Percentages?
7. Explain how a Menu Item Sales Report (with Popularity Percentages) functions, and how the information from the report is essential to preparing a Menu Item Sales Forecast.
8. Once the forecasted number of orders for each menu item for the week is determined, then a daily forecast can be calculated. How is that daily forecast stated on the Food Production Schedule?
9. List three procedures to ensure the proper dish-up.
10. A Portion Control Report is effective in controlling daily food item usage. What does the report begin with, and how are portion servings tracked?
11. Contrast the effects of under-portioning and over-portioning.
12. What are the two significant functions of the of the Food Mishap/Void Orders Report?

**Food Production
Cost Control**

Restaurant Reality

Cross-utilize a food item to eliminate waste

A 50-seat sandwich and ice cream shop was faced with the challenge of always having enough hard ripe bananas on hand for banana splits and ice cream sundae orders. The daily par amount of 36 bananas was established by the maximum amount needed based on the sales history of menu items using bananas. Produce orders were based on inventory par amounts and delivered three days per week.

The challenge for the restaurant owner was to identify an alternate use for the bananas that had become too ripe to use for banana splits and ice cream sundaes. There were some days when only 5 or 6 bananas were used, contrasted with other days when 24 to 32 were needed.

Some of the overripe bananas were used for smoothie drink orders but not enough to fully utilize all of the excess bananas. Baking banana bread was not an option because the restaurant was not set up to do any baking. The owner's wife said, "Why not peel and freeze them?" She suggested inserting a 5-inch wooden skewer about 2 inches into one end of each peeled banana and freeze it; then dip the frozen bananas in chocolate syrup, roll in them chopped walnuts, individually cover them with plastic wrap, and refreeze them. This was a great idea, especially since the restaurant was already using chocolate syrup and chopped walnuts. The only additional item needed would be the 5-inch wooden skewers.

The menu would now offer a frozen chocolate banana on a stick sprinkled with chopped walnuts. But it just didn't sound right to the owner. It needed a short, catchy name that would create curiosity and spike customer interest. One of the restaurant's young servers held the frozen chocolate banana up in an inverted position and said, "It kind of looks like a monkey's tail." That's it, thought the owner; we will name the new menu item, "Frozen Monkey Tail."

Frozen Monkey Tails soon became a popular and profitable menu item for the restaurant, requiring the banana order par amount to be increased and additional production time to be scheduled to prepare the Monkey Tails—thus cross-utilizing a perishable food item, eliminating possible waste, and in the process creating an additional restaurant menu signature item. A challenge turned into an opportunity.

7

Menu Sales Analysis and Seat Turnover

Introduction

The menu selection should be one that is "marketable" to the customer, "producible" by the staff, and "profitable" for the foodservice operation. Selecting the right menu items is the result of research, analysis and hard work. Then it becomes an ongoing process to monitor and review each menu item's sales popularity and profitability. The seat turnover rate allows management to determine the average customer dining time.

Learning Objectives

Upon succuessfully completing this chapter, readers will be able to:

1. Discuss Menu Profitability.
2. Explain the four categories that menu items may reflect in the Menu Sales Mix.
3. Know the purpose of Menu Engineering.
4. Understand how a Menu Sales Mix Report functions.
5. Demonstrate how to calculate Seat Turnover.
6. Recognize the efficiencies when using Tabletop Tablets.

Chapter Outline

Menu Profitability   Seat Turnover
Menu Sales Mix   Tabletop Tablets
Menu Engineering   Summary
Menu Sales Mix Report   Discussion Questions

Key Terms and Definitions

Begin by first reading the key terms and their definitions. An advance understanding of the terms will be helpful prior to reading the chapter.

Menu Engineering	Provides menu analysis data to review in determining menu profitability.
Menu Sales Mix	A mix of menu items that reflects varying degrees of popularity and profitability.
Menu Sales Mix Report	A version of Menu Engineering that can be prepared for the day week, or month.
Seat Turnover	The number of times a seat was "turned" (used by customers) during the course of a meal period.
Tabletop Tablets	Allows guest to quickly browse through the menu, which provides graphic descriptions and photos.

When diners use tabletop tablets or screens such as the one in the photo above to order their meals, the data is immediately recorded in the POS system. Foodservice operators can use the accurate data to easily calculate menu item sales and popularity percentages—and ultimately control food production and cost. Courtesy of Ziosk, LLC. (Photograph by Andy Post.)

Menu Profitability

The success of the foodservice operation depends to a large extent on management's ability to:

► Consistently provide the products that the customers want at the quality and price they expect

► Satisfy customers' needs and desires for new products

To accomplish the above goals, management must constantly review menu sales information, which is the data collected from customer guest checks as each item from the menu is totaled according to the amount sold and recorded on a Menu Item Sales Report (with Popularity Percentages), Figure 6.3 on p. 123. Then management needs to identify items that are strong sellers along with items that do not sell as well.

Popular items should be among the more profitable for the foodservice operation. Less popular items may need to be kept on the menu if they remain profitable and generate some loyal patronage from a select group of customers, or they need to be replaced with new items.

> **LEARNING OBJECTIVE 1**
> Discuss Menu Profitability.

Menu Sales Mix

The menu sales mix is a mix of menu items that reflects varying degrees of popularity and profitability. The menu items fall into one of four categories:

1. Popular and profitable
2. Popular and unprofitable
3. Unpopular and profitable
4. Unpopular and unprofitable

One of the easiest ways to analyze a menu sales mix is by looking at the menu item sales and popularity percentages (see Figure 6.3 on p. 123), which records the number of each item sold. It is by looking at the menu sales mix—the four categories above—that it becomes obvious which items are profitable and should be kept on the menu: The foodservice manager might use the menu sales mix to take one or more of the following actions:

► Develop a menu selection of items that are popular with customers and profitable for the foodservice operation.

► Add popular appetizers, small-plate offerings, sides, add-ons to salads, dessert options, specialty coffees and teas, and so on, to increase customer guest check averages.

► Eliminate unpopular and unprofitable items.

► Replace unpopular and unprofitable with those that are more popular and profitable.

> **LEARNING OBJECTIVE 2**
> Explain the four categories that menu items may reflect in the Menu Sales Mix.

This procedure is basic and effective, but was further enhanced by two professors from Michigan State University in 1982 when they introduced an accounting spreadsheet analysis called Menu Engineering. Since then many software programs have been developed that offer different versions of menu engineering, all with the same singular objective—to provide the necessary analysis data for management to review in determining menu profitability.

> **LEARNING OBJECTIVE 3**
> Know the purpose of Menu Engineering.

Menu Sales Mix Report

LEARNING OBJECTIVE 4
Understand how a Menu Sales Mix Report functions.

The Menu Sales Mix Report, Figure 7.1 is an example version of menu engineering. A Menu Sales Mix Report can be prepared daily, weekly or monthly as determined by the restaurant's management; it also establishes a *Target Food Cost Percentage* goal. This represents the overall food cost percentage goal that management wants to achieve when all of the menu items sold for the day, week, or month average at or below that target goal, recognizing that certain menu items may have to be sold above the target food cost percentage goal.

The Menu Sales Mix Report in Figure 7.1 is for the week with a Target Food Cost Percentage of 32%, and functions as follows: Menu Items are listed by categories taken directly from the restaurant's menu. The abbreviated example in Figure 7.1 shows Appetizers/Small Plates, Soups, Salads, Entrées, and Desserts. The cost of each of these menu items is taken directly from the item's Plate Cost Card and listed in Column B.

The Menu Price (Column C) is taken directly from the restaurant menu's selling prices. The **Food Cost Percentage** (Column D) is calculated by dividing each menu items Plate Cost by its Menu Price (Column B ÷ C = D).

Menu Sales Mix Report

Target Food Cost Percentage: 32.00%   **Week of:** January 11, 20xx

Calculations			B ÷ C = D		B x E = F	C x E = G
A	B	C	D	E	F	G
Menu Item	**Plate Cost**	**Menu Price**	**Food Cost Percentage**	**Amount Sold**	**Total Food Cost**	**Total Food Sales**
Appetizers/Small Plates						
Antipasti	$3.21	$11.00	29.18%	125	$401.25	$1,375.00
Bruschetta	$2.79	$9.00	31.00%	173	$482.67	$1,557.00
Soups						
Pasta e Fagioli	$1.19	$4.50	26.44%	118	$140.42	$531.00
Minestrone	$1.28	$5.00	25.60%	116	$148.48	$580.00
Salads						
Insalata Cesare	$1.63	$6.00	27.17%	112	$182.56	$672.00
Insalata Mista	$1.47	$5.50	26.73%	107	$157.29	$588.50
Entrées						
Farfalle Arrabbiata	$6.09	$19.00	32.05%	358	$2,180.22	$6,802.00
Salmone alla Griglia	$8.14	$26.00	31.31%	213	$1,733.82	$5,538.00
Bistecca (NY Sirloin Steak)	$9.81	$28.00	35.04%	169	$1,657.89	$4,732.00
Desserts						
Tiramisu	$2.28	$9.00	25.33%	75	$173.28	$684.00
Gelato	$1.96	$8.00	24.50%	48	$94.08	$384.00
Chocolate Torte	$2.05	$8.00	25.63%	81	$166.05	$648.00
TOTAL SUMS					**$7,518.01**	**$24,091.50**

	Sum of Total Food Costs	÷	Sum of Total Food Sales	=	Food Cost Percentage	
	$7,518.01	÷	$24,091.50	=	31.21%	

Figure 7.1   Menu Sales Mix Report.

▶ **Example:** Antipasti

Plate Cost ÷ Menu Price = **Food Cost Percentage**

$3.21 ÷ $11.00 = 0.2918 **(29.18%)**

The **Amount Sold** (Column E) is taken directly from POS customer sales reporting.

The **Total Food Cost** (column F) is calculated by multiplying Column B × E = F.

▶ **Example:** Antipasti

Plate Cost × Amount Sold = **Total Food Cost**

$3.21 ÷ 125 = **$401.25**

The **Total Food Sales** (Column G) is calculated by multiplying Column C × E = G.

▶ **Example:** Antipasti

Menu Price × Amount Sold = **Total Food Sales**

$11.00 ÷ 125 = **$1,375.00**

The **Food Cost Percentage** for the week is calculated as follows:

Sum of ÷ Sum of = **Food Cost**

Total Food Costs ÷ Total Food Sales = **Percentage**

$7,518.01 ÷ $24,091.50 = 0.31206 **(31.21%)**

The **Food Cost Percentage** of 31.21% is just below the Target Percentage of 32.00%.

When reviewing the Food Cost Percentage (Column D) for the menu items listed, all of the category items are below the 32% target goal with the exception in the Entrées. Farfalle Arrabbiata is 32.05%, Salmone alla Griglia is 31.31% and Bistecca (NY Sirloin Steak) is 35.04%. To further analyze the Entrées popularity percentages the calculations are as follows:

	Amount Sold				**Popularity %**
Farfalle Arrabbiata	358	÷	740	=	48.4%
Salmone alla Griglia	213	÷	740	=	28.8%
Bistecca (NY Sirloin Steak)	169	÷	740	=	22.8%
Total Entrées Sold	740				100%

	Total Food Cost	**Total Food Sales**
Farfalle Arrabbiata	$2,180.22	$6,802.00
Salmone alla Griglia	$1,733.82	$5,538.00
Bistecca (NY Sirloin Steak)	$1,657.89	$4,732.00
Totals	$5,571.93	$17,072.00

$5,571.93 ÷ $17,072.00 = 0.32637 **(32.64%) Food Cost Percentage for Entrées**

Farfalle Arrabbiata   popular 48.4%   profitable 32.05% Food Cost

Salmone alla Griglia   popular 28.8%   profitable 31.31% Food Cost

Bistecca (NY Sirloin Steak) popular 22.8% unprofitable **35.04% Food Cost**[*]

Overall, this is a good Menu Sales Mix Report, and keeps the focus on any possible changes in menu item popularity and profitability.

---

[*] **NOTE:** The Food Cost Percentage (35.04%) is above the Target Goal of 32.00% for this Entrée.

Possible Reasons: 1. To remain competitive with other restaurants for the same item.

2. Possible cost increase from supplier (meat prices up).

Seat Turnover

LEARNING OBJECTIVE 5
Demonstrate how to calculate Seat Turnover.

Turnover represents the number of times a seat was "turned" (used by customers) during the course of a meal period and enables management to determine the average dining time during that meal period. Furthermore, if customer counts are recorded by the hour of each meal period, a seat turnover rate can be identified for each hour during that meal period.

▶ If the average dining time is decreased while the average guest check is maintained, the number of "turns" can be increased. This can be accomplished when the service speed is improved by scheduling an adequate number of servers and kitchen staff during peak times, resulting in minimum wait times for customers.

LEARNING OBJECTIVE 6
Recognize the efficiencies when using Tabletop Tablets.

▶ Tabletop tablets that allow customers to send their food and beverage orders directly to the kitchen speed up service for fast casual and casual-dining table service restaurants, along with allowing customers to swipe their credit card for payment. An example of the various features of a tabletop tablet can be viewed at www.ziosk.com.

▶ By increasing the number of seat turns the restaurant operation is able to maximize its capacity to serve customers, which increases sales revenue for the business.

▶ Figure 7.2 shows an example of the daily and weekly seat turnover for a lunch period, using the weekly customer counts, in a restaurant with 125 available seats.

▶ Figure 7.3 on the following page shows an example of the daily and weekly seat turnover for a dinner period, using the weekly customer counts, in a restaurant with 125 available seats.

The seat turnover rate for a day (Monday) lunch period is calculated as follows:

Customers Served in Meal Period	÷	Number of Seats Available	=	**Daily Turnover Rate**
(Monday) 184	÷	125	=	1.472 rounded to **1.47**

The seat turnover rate for the weekly lunch period is calculated as follows:

125 seats × 7 = 875 Total Number of Seats Available (for the week)

Total Number of Customers Served	÷	Total Number of Seats Available	=	**Weekly Turnover Rate**
1,539 seats	÷	875	=	1.758 rounded to **1.76**

Daily and Weekly Seat Turnover

Meal Period: Lunch | | | | | | | **Week of:** January 11, 20xx

	Mon	Tues	Wed	Thurs	Fri	Sat	Sun	Total
Lunch: 11 A.M. –2 P.M.	184	189	196	204	262	246	258	1,539
Turnover Rate	1.47	1.51	1.57	1.63	2.10	1.97	2.06	1.76

Figure 7.2 Daily and Weekly Seat Turnover—Meal Period: Lunch

Daily and Weekly Seat Turnover								
Meal Period: Dinner						**Week of:** January 11, 20xx		
	Mon	**Tues**	**Wed**	**Thurs**	**Fri**	**Sat**	**Sun**	**Total**
Dinner: 5 P.M. –10 P.M.	296	311	322	341	415	438	462	2,585
Turnover Rate	2.37	2.49	2.58	2.73	3.32	3.50	3.70	2.95

Figure 7.3   Daily and Weekly Seat Turnover—Meal Period: Dinner

The seat turnover rate for a day (Monday) dinner period is calculated as follows:

Customer Served in Meal Period	÷	Number of Seats Available	=	**Daily Turnover Rate**
(Monday) 296	÷	125	=	2.368 rounded to **2.37**

The seat turnover rate for the weekly dinner period, Figure 7.3, is calculated as follows:

125 seats × 7 = 875 Total Number of Seats Available (for the week)

Total Number of Customers Served	÷	Total Number of Seats Available	=	**Weekly Turnover Rate**
2,585	÷	875	=	2.954 rounded to **2.95**

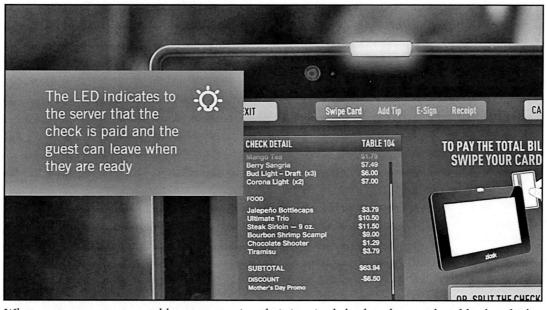

When customers can use a tablet screen to view their itemized check and pay at the table, they don't have to wait for the server to bring their check. This system facilitates increased productivity and high seat turnover rates. Courtesy of Ziosk, LLC.

Credit card processing at a POS terminal or from a hand-held tablet. Courtesy of Action Systems, Inc.

An iPad POS system is flexible and handy, allowing for orders to be placed efficiently and accurately. Courtesy of Action Systems, Inc.

Assignment 11

Calculate the **Daily and Weekly Seat Turnover Rate** for the following:

Daily and Weekly Seat Turnover

Meal Period: Breakfast (7 A.M. – 11 A.M.)   **Number of Seats:** 90   **Week of:** October 9, 20xx

	Mon	Tues	Wed	Thurs	Fri	Sat	Sun	Total
Number Served	221	219	236	215	263	259	272	_____
Turnover Rate	_____	_____	_____	_____	_____	_____	_____	_____

Daily and Weekly Seat Turnover

Meal Period: Lunch (11:30 A.M. – 3:30 P.M.)   **Number of Seats:** 180   **Week of:** December 4, 20xx

	Mon	Tues	Wed	Thurs	Fri	Sat	Sun	Total
Number Served	345	372	397	188	407	412	429	_____
Turnover Rate	_____	_____	_____	_____	_____	_____	_____	_____

Daily and Weekly Seat Turnover

Meal Period: Dinner (5:00 P.M. – 10:00 P.M.)   **Number of Seats:** 140   **Week of:** September 18, 20xx

	Mon	Tues	Wed	Thurs	Fri	Sat	Sun	Total
Number Served	315	357	382	391	495	569	548	_____
Turnover Rate	_____	_____	_____	_____	_____	_____	_____	_____

Summary

The successful foodservice operator constantly reviews menu item sales information, which is collected from customer guest checks. Each of the menu items that were sold are totaled and recorded so that management can evaluate popularity and profitability.

A Menu Sales Mix is a mix of menu items that reflect varying degrees of popularity and profitability, which typically fall into the following categories: popular and profitable, popular and unprofitable, unpopular and profitable, and unpopular and unprofitable.

The Menu Engineering procedure can provide the necessary analysis data for management to review in determining menu profitability. This is illustrated in the Menu Sales Mix Report with a Target Food Cost Percentage goal. The report represents the overall average food cost percentage for the menu items that were sold, recognizing that each menu item will have a different food cost percentage.

Seat Turnover represents the number of times a seat was "turned" during the course of a meal period. This enables management to determine the average dining times during that meal period. Tabletop Tablets, when in use, allow customers to send their food and beverage orders directly to the kitchen along with being able to swipe their credit cards for payment which speeds up service and "seat turns."

Discussion Questions

1. Explain the ongoing process required to maintain a profitable menu.
2. List the four categories that menu items may reflect in the Menu Sales Mix.
3. What is the objective of Menu Engineering?
4. How often should a Menu Sales Mix Report be prepared?
5. Explain the information that a Menu Sales Mix Report contains, and how that information can be used by the foodservice manager.
6. What is the effect for the restaurant when seat turns are increased?
7. How is Seat Turnover calculated?
8. What is the advantage of Tabletop Tablets?

Labor Cost Control

8 Controlling Payroll Costs

9 Measuring Performance and Productivity

Labor cost control results from management selecting and using the correct equipment, choosing the most productive methods and procedures, efficiently utilizing space and work flow, and effectively controlling payroll costs. But among the most challenging tasks is to hire, motivate, and retain a quality workforce.

POS software that processes labor and payroll management reports can provide the necessary daily decision-making information by the hour—all functions essential for effective labor cost control. For example, a POS system can be used to prepare work schedules, payroll budget estimates, and employee productivity reports. Further, it can monitor employee activities—employees use it when logging in the time they arrive to work and logging out when they leave; servers can use it for tip reporting.

Courtesy of Action Systems, Inc.

8

Controlling Payroll Costs

Introduction

Payroll costs have a dominating influence on the development of methods, systems, and the products used throughout the foodservice industry. The method or system, under which the lowest combined food and labor costs can be achieved without lowering quality, is the driving force that allows foodservice operators to remain competitive and profitable.

Learning Objectives

Upon successfully completing this chapter, readers will be able to:

1. Understand the essential factors that contribute to performance and operating efficiency, which leads to controlling payroll costs.
2. Analyze a Work Schedule with an adequate number of employees to meet the needs of a foodservice operation.
3. Explain how a Payroll Budget Estimate can ensure that the payroll costs for scheduled employees remain within the payroll cost percentage goal set by management.
4. Track the actual hours worked by employees with daily time card reporting.
5. Compare actual payroll costs to budgeted costs with the objective of being able to remain within the payroll cost percentage goal.
6. Determine the cost of employee turnover by calculating the direct and indirect costs associated with turnover.
7. Identify the payroll costs-saving value associated with a low employee turnover rate.

Chapter Outline

Factors That Affect Payroll Costs
Analyzing a Work Schedule
Payroll Budget Estimate
Payroll Cost Percentages
Measuring Employee
   Turnover Rate and Cost

Calculating the Turnover Rate
Calculating Employee Turnover Cost
Summary
Discussion Questions

Key Terms and Definitions

Begin by first reading the key terms and their definitions. An advance understanding of the terms will be helpful prior to reading the chapter.

Employee Meals	A form of compensation and therefore part of the payroll costs.
Employee Turnover Rate	A ratio comparison of the number of employees a business must replace compared to the average number of total employees in a specific accounting period.
Employee Turnover: Direct Costs	Position opening advertisements—websites/ newspapers—employment agency fees (if used), and management time for applicant interviews.
Employee Turnover: Indirect Costs	Loss of productivity, accounting and payroll processing expenses, and business loss.
Overtime	Occurs when an employee works more than 40 hours per week.
Payroll Budget Estimate	A planned cost estimate of payroll expenses expressed in dollar amounts and as a percentage of anticipated sales.
Payroll Cost Factors	Labor-saving kitchen equipment, well-arranged floor plans that save time and steps, ongoing training for all employees, the use of prepared foods, and a reliable workforce.
Payroll Cost Percentage	The payroll costs reported as a percentage.
Payroll Cycle	Begins when the manager prepares a Work Schedule accompanied by a payroll budget and tracked by time cards reporting actual hours worked, and is complete when the manager calculates the annual employee turnover rate and cost.
Prepared Foods	Foods that may be cheaper to buy compared to making from scratch.
Sales History	Can serve as a tremendous aid in making scheduling decisions, especially for peak sales days.
Salaries	Compensation paid weekly, bi-weekly, or monthly.
Time Cards	Recorded hours worked each day and totaled for the week.
Wages	Compensation paid for hours worked.
Work Schedule	Developed to ensure that the proper number of employees are working in order to meet the needs of customers.

Factors That Affect Payroll Costs

The primary factors that affect payroll costs are directly related to performance and operating efficiency. Those factors are essential in order to attain an optimal productive work environment, and are as follows:

1. **Labor-saving kitchen equipment.** The menu will dictate the type of equipment that a kitchen should have in place. For example, if recipes require fresh food items to be diced or grated, then a food processor would be used to save time.

2. **Well-arranged floor plans that save time and steps.** The work flow throughout the kitchen and into the customer serving areas should move with ease. This is essential for any type of foodservice operation.

3. **Ongoing training for all employees.** Advancements in preparation methods and service should be introduced to employees through an effective training program. A program that also reinforces safe food handling and safe working conditions should be set up and periodically reviewed. Also cross training, when opportunities exist for employees to be trained in more than one function, is important.

4. **The use of prepared convenience foods.** There are many choices available with prepared food items that will add efficiency and labor savings without compromising quality. Items such as, prepared vegetables and salads, refrigerated and frozen soups, and fine desserts may be cheaper to buy compared to making them from scratch—and satisfy customer expectations.

In addition to the factors above, an optimal productive work environment needs to be monitored and analyzed, beginning with managing the payroll cycle. The payroll cycle begins when the manager prepares a **Work Schedule** accompanied by a **Payroll Budget Estimate** and is tracked by time cards reporting actual hours worked. The cycle is complete when the manager calculates the annual employee turnover rate and cost.

Analyzing a Work Schedule

A Work Schedule is developed to ensure that the number of employees is adequate in order to meet the needs of customers. The Work Schedule should represent the best effort of the manager to schedule employees in anticipation of sales.

Separate Work Schedules may be prepared for the back-of-the-house (kitchen) functions, for the front-of-the-house (dining room) functions, and for managers.

Managers should follow several rules when creating Work Schedules, which are as follows:

1. **Review sales history records before making scheduling decisions.**
   A well-kept sales history can serve as a tremendous aid in making scheduling decisions, especially for peak sales days. When anticipated sales are high, a decision to schedule additional employees would be consistent with meeting the operational requirements of that day, week, or period of sales.

Holidays such as Mother's Day, Father's Day, Valentine's Day, and St. Patrick's Day are among the busiest dining-out days of the year. The previous year's sales for those days can serve as an indication of expected sales during those days for the current year.

Community events such as a local college fall homecoming weekend, a summer outdoor theater that draws large weekend crowds, a tourist season, or a large group that meets the same week annually for a convention can all bring an influx of dining-out customers that the restaurant needs to be prepared to serve.

Other conditions that may have affected sales, such as extreme weather (snow storm, hurricane), a power outage, or equipment breakdown, can provide additional insight to current scheduling when reviewing a previous year's low sales day or week. The factors that contributed to low sales may have been unusual circumstances that would not occur during the current year.

2. **Prepare schedules weekly.** A Work Schedule should be prepared weekly and planned to accommodate employee annual vacations.

3. **Post schedules at least one week in advance.** Schedules prepared one week in advance and posted the same day each week allow employees, who do not have regular schedules, to check on that day so they will know their schedule for the coming week.

   Schedules may be posted on the restaurant's POS system or website for employees to access through an employee PIN (Personal Identification Number) or access code. If a time clock is in use then the schedule may be posted nearby in the most convenient place for all employees to read.

4. **Minimize scheduling changes to avoid frustrating employees.** Although scheduling should meet the needs of business, it is also important to remember to maintain some degree of consistency. Radical or frequent changes in the schedule can frustrate and upset employees and can result in the loss of good employees, as well as result in an "employee no show" on a shift, as some employees may not check the schedule in time to be aware of the change.

5. **Schedule employee meal breaks.** Meal breaks should be scheduled for each day. The meal break schedule must be flexible enough to accommodate business. If the foodservice operation is too busy, a break should be postponed until a more convenient time.

   If breaks are postponed frequently, additional scheduling adjustments need to be made. Perhaps a portion of the kitchen preparation work may be done at a different time or an additional labor hour may need to be added.

> A well-planned Work Schedule will not eliminate job stress, but it can certainly reduce job frustration.

Reoccurring reasons that employees give for quitting a good job are frequent Work Schedule changes and not being able to take scheduled meal breaks.

The **Work Schedules—Hourly Staff**, Figures 8.1a and b on pp. 152 and 153, and the **Managers' Schedule**, Figure 8.2 on p. 154, have been created as examples for a restaurant operation to meet the needs of a 125-seat casual-dining table service restaurant that does $4.2 million in annual sales with an average customer guest check of $15 for lunch and $28 for dinner—and had served 205,000 customers during the past year. The restaurant is open daily from 11:00 A.M. to 10:00 P.M.:

Lunch—11:00 A.M. to 2:00 P.M., a 3-hour period, and

Dinner—5:00 P.M. to 10:00 P.M., a 5-hour period.

The Work Schedule is prepared for hourly staff, kitchen and dining room employees, as shown in Figure 8.1a and b, for the week of January 11, 20xx.

▶ The **Kitchen Positions** scheduled are executive chef, sous chef, chefs, cooks, and dishwashers.

▶ The **Dining Room Positions** scheduled are host, servers, and servers' assistants.

Review Figure 8.1a and b to identify positions, days worked, and hours scheduled. A brief description of each position follows:

▶ **Schedule for: Kitchen**

▷ **Executive Chef** Joe is scheduled for a 10-hour shift four days a week: Monday from 9:00 A.M. to 7:00 P.M. and Friday, Saturday, and Sunday from 10:00 A.M. to 8:00 P.M. Many of the menu items are made using fresh-from-scratch recipes according to par amounts on a daily Food Production Schedule. The executive chef meets with the manager on Monday to discuss the production needs for the week and to review any problems or concerns that may have occurred or are anticipated for the week. The executive chef is also responsible for developing new menu items and managing the kitchen staff.

▷ **Sous Chef** Jan is scheduled for a 10-hour shift four days a week: fom 10:00 A.M. to 8:00 P.M. on Thursday and from 11:00 A.M. to 9:00 P.M. Friday, Saturday, and Sunday. The sous chef assists the executive chef in managing the kitchen.

▷ **Chefs** Mike and Jose are also scheduled for 10-hour shifts four days a week; their schedules allow for coverage on Tuesdays and Wednesdays, when the other chefs are not there.

NOTE: Management may choose to offer a four-day, 10-hour-a-day, 40-hour work week for certain positions that occasionally require overtime hours or working on a scheduled day off due to unplanned circumstances. Employers have recognized the increasing emphasis on a work/life balance for high-stress, physically demanding jobs. Therefore, three consecutive days off can be an added benefit in attracting and keeping good employees.

▷ **Cooks** Ann, Evan, and Tony are scheduled for a four-day, less than a 40-hour, work week. Their schedules are staggered so one of them covers lunch and dinner every day. On Wednesday, an additional cook's schedule overlaps with the other two schedules—because Cook Ann is working as a chef (Chef Jose's schedule) on Wednesday.

NOTE: Some people prefer to work less than a 40-hour week and may be available to work additional hours if needed. There are people who choose to work beyond retirement age and enjoy working part-time as a way of staying active and supplementing their retirement income. Furthermore, a cook position can be a good learning opportunity for a responsible culinary student or recent culinary school graduate eager to work with professional chefs in a fast-paced learning environment.

▷ **Dishwashers** Don, Lester, and George are scheduled to accommodate the increased business on the busy days. Lester and George are scheduled to work less than a 40-hour week, and when needed could be scheduled for additional hours without having to pay overtime rates.

NOTE: Opportunities exist to hire people with personal challenges that may limit their ability to work demanding jobs. They often become long-term dependable employees who are able to fill positions that typically have a high turnover rate. Good employers seek to hire people with physical or learning disabilities who appreciate being treated well and respected for the important work that they perform.

▶ **Schedule for: Dining Room**

▷ **Servers** are scheduled for the week to cover the peak lunch and dinner times with additional Servers scheduled for Friday, Saturday, and Sunday. The servers and servers' assistants (bussers) are all scheduled

Work Schedule
Kitchen Staff
Week of: January 11, 20xx

Name	Position	11 Mon	12 Tues	13 Wed	14 Thurs	15 Fri	16 Sat	17 Sun
Joe	Executive Chef	9:00 AM–7:00 PM	OFF	OFF	OFF	10:00 AM–8:00 PM	10:00 AM–8:00 PM	10:00 AM–8:00 PM
Jan	Sous Chef	OFF	OFF	OFF	10:00 AM–8:00 PM	11:00 AM–9:00 PM	11:00 AM–9:00 PM	11:00 AM–9:00 PM
Mike	Chef	OFF	10:00 AM–8:00 PM	10:00 AM–8:00 PM	11:00 AM–9:00 PM	12:00 PM–10:00 PM	OFF	OFF
Jose	Chef	11:00 AM–9:00 PM	11:00 AM–9:00 PM	OFF	OFF	OFF	12:00 PM–10:00 PM	12:00 PM–10:00 PM
Ann	Cook	7:00 AM–2:00 PM	7:00 AM–2:00 PM	11:00 AM–9:00 PM	OFF	OFF	4:00 PM–10:00 PM	4:00 PM–10:00 PM
Evan	Cook	OFF	OFF	7:00 AM–2:00 PM	7:00 AM–2:00 PM	7:00 AM–2:00 PM	7:00 AM–2:00 PM	7:00 AM–2:00 PM
Tony	Cook	4:00 PM–10:00 PM	4:00 PM–10:00 PM	4:00 PM–10:00 PM	4:00 PM–10:00 PM	4:00 PM–10:00 PM	OFF	OFF
Don	Dishwasher	12:00 PM–8:00 PM	12:00 PM–8:00 PM	OFF	OFF	12:00 PM–8:00 PM	12:00 PM–8:00 PM	12:00 PM–8:00 PM
Lester	Dishwasher	OFF	OFF	5:00 PM–11:00 PM	5:00 PM–11:00 PM	3:00 PM–11:00 PM	3:00 PM–11:00 PM	3:00 PM–11:00 PM
George	Dishwasher	5:00 PM–11:00 PM	5:00 PM–11:00 PM	12:00 PM–8:00 PM	12:00 PM–8:00 PM	OFF	OFF	OFF

Figure 8.1a   Work Schedule for Hourly Employees—Kitchen Staff

for less than 40 hours per week. When additional server hours are needed for peak business periods, hours are added without having to pay overtime.

▷ Host Ricky is scheduled during the dinner hours from Wednesday through Sunday and is responsible for seating customers and managing the dining room. Mitch, the assistant manager, handles those responsibilities during his scheduled hours on Monday and Tuesday.

NOTE: Servers are often people who prefer to work part-time. A person may need to work only 15 to 20 hours a week to supplement a family income. Students may need work that fits around class schedules. Culinary and hospitality management students often seek part-time work while preparing for full-time careers. Managers employ people with a mix of different work time needs that can be accommodated with the restaurant Work Schedule.

Work Schedule
Dining Room Staff

Week of: January 11, 20xx

Name	Position	11 Mon	12 Tues	13 Wed	14 Thurs	15 Fri	16 Sat	17 Sun
Ricky	Host	OFF	OFF	4:30 PM– 10:30 PM	4:30 PM– 10:30 PM	4:30 PM– 10:30 PM	4:30 PM– 10:30 PM	4:30 PM– 10:30 PM
Lucy	Server	10:30 AM– 2:30 PM	OFF	OFF	10:30 AM– 2:30 PM	10:30 AM– 2:30 PM	10:30 AM– 2:30 PM	10:30 AM– 4:30 PM
Mary	Server	10:30 AM– 2:30 PM	10:30 AM– 2:30 PM	OFF	OFF	10:30 AM– 2:30 PM	10:30 AM– 2:30 PM	10:30 AM– 4:30 PM
Jack	Server	OFF	OFF	10:30 AM– 2:30 PM	10:30 AM– 2:30 PM	10:30 AM– 2:30 PM	10:30 AM– 2:30 PM	10:30 AM– 4:30 PM
Judy	Server	OFF	OFF	4:30 PM– 10:00 PM	4:30 PM– 10:00 PM	4:30 PM– 10:30 PM	4:30 PM– 10:30 PM	4:30 PM– 10:30 PM
Nick	Server	OFF	OFF	4:30 PM– 10:00 PM	4:30 PM– 10:00 PM	4:30 PM– 10:30 PM	4:30 PM– 10:30 PM	4:30 PM– 10:30 PM
Pam	Server	4:30 PM– 10:00 PM	4:30 PM– 10:00 PM	OFF	OFF	4:30 PM– 10:30 PM	4:30 PM– 10:30 PM	4:30 PM– 10:30 PM
Joan	Server	4:30 PM– 10:00 PM	4:30 PM– 10:00 PM	OFF	OFF	4:30 PM– 10:30 PM	4:30 PM– 10:30 PM	4:30 PM– 10:30 PM
Duane	Server	4:30 PM– 10:00 PM	10:30 AM– 2:30 PM	10:30 AM– 2:30 PM	10:30 AM– 2:30 PM	OFF	OFF	OFF
Alex	Server	OFF	4:30 PM– 10:00 PM	4:30 PM– 10:00 PM	4:30 PM– 10:00 PM	OFF	OFF	OFF
Tom	Servers' Asst.	10:30 AM– 2:30 PM	10:30 AM– 2:30 PM	10:30 AM– 2:30 PM	OFF	OFF	OFF	OFF
Rene	Servers' Asst.	OFF	OFF	4:30 PM– 10:30 PM	4:30 PM– 10:30 PM	4:30 PM– 10:30 PM	4:30 PM– 10:30 PM	4:30 PM– 10:30 PM

Figure 8.1b   Work Schedule for Hourly Employees—Dining Room Staff

		11 Mon	12 Tues	13 Wed	14 Thurs	15 Fri	16 Sat	17 Sun
Name	**Position**							
David	Manager	7:00 AM– 3:00 PM	7:00 AM– 3:00 PM	3:00 PM– 11:00 PM	3:00 PM– 11:00 PM	**OFF**	**OFF**	11:00 AM– 7:00 PM
Lynn	Assistant Manager	**OFF**	**OFF**	7:00 AM– 3:00 PM	7:00 AM– 3:00 PM	7:00 AM– 3:00 PM	7:00 AM– 3:00 PM	7:00 AM– 3:00 PM
Mitch	Assistant Manager	3:00 PM– 11:00 PM	3:00 PM– 11:00 PM	**OFF**	**OFF**	3:00 PM– 11:00 PM	3:00 PM– 11:00 PM	3:00 PM– 11:00 PM

Work Schedule
Managerial Staff   **Week of:** January 11, 20xx

Figure 8.2   Managers' Schedule

The Managers' Schedule is prepared for the manager and assistant managers for the week of January 11, 20xx, as shown in Figure 8.2 above. The manager and assistant managers are scheduled for 8-hour shifts, five days a week. The manager and assistant managers have the responsibility of opening the restaurant at 7:00 A.M. for the kitchen to begin food production—and to be available to receive scheduled deliveries as well as be involved in other beginning-of-the-day business activities. They are also responsible for making sure that kitchen and dining room closing procedures have been followed and the restaurant is cleaned and can be safely closed and secured by 11:00 P.M.

▶ **Managers' Schedule**

▷ The manager position requires a greater involvement with the operational and financial management of the restaurant operation.

▷ The assistant manager position often includes hands-on participation in the kitchen, service bar, and dining room. It would not be uncommon for an assistant manager (or when needed, the manager) to promptly help in the kitchen by dishing up food during peak periods or filling in during kitchen employee meal breaks, also by preparing drinks at the service bar, working as a host and cashier in the dining room, and assisting servers during the peak periods.

NOTE: Successful managers understand the back-of-the-house (kitchen) functions, alcohol beverage service, and the requirements for professional front-of-the-house (dining room) service.

Payroll Budget Estimate

LEARNING OBJECTIVE 3
Explain how a Payroll Budget Estimate can ensure that the payroll costs for scheduled employees remain within the payroll cost percentage goal set by management.

A Payroll Budget Estimate is a planned cost estimate of payroll expenses expressed in dollar amounts and as a percentage of anticipated sales. Payroll budgets are established based on anticipated sales—and are typically prepared at the same time the Work Schedule is determined.

To control payroll costs it is necessary to establish a Payroll Budget Estimate, as shown in Figure 8.3 on p. 158. Large properties with more than one foodservice location often require the manager of each location to prepare a Work Schedule and Payroll Budget Estimate.

A Payroll Budget Estimate includes several features necessary for effective management:

▶ **The manager can control payroll expenses.** The manager must spend the correct amount of money on payroll in relationship to the sales generated by the paid employees. The ability of the manager to control payroll costs is a significant factor in determining the level of success the restaurant may achieve. One way to control payroll costs is to calculate a payroll cost percentage.

▶ **A manager may refer to the payroll cost percentage as "labor cost."** It would be common to hear a manager say, "We run a 34% labor cost," referring to the payroll cost percentage.

▶ **As a general rule, the payroll cost percentage tends to become lower as the sales volume becomes higher.** This is the case as long as the increase in sales volume can be handled by the same number of employees while still maintaining standard levels of service.

The payroll cost percentage is calculated as follows:

Payroll Cost ÷ Sales = **Payroll Cost Percentage**

▶ **Payroll cost percentages vary according to the type of foodservice category and sales volume of the business.** The box below shows typical payroll cost percentages for the various foodservice categories as reported by industry professional associations. Each category has a payroll cost percentage range (low, medium, high) that is normal for that particular type of foodservice operation.

Typical Payroll Cost Percentages*

Foodservice Category	Low %	Medium %	High %
Fine Dining Table Service	32	36	40
Casual-Dining Table Service	30	34	38
Fast Casual	25	28	32
Quick Service (Fast Food)	20	24	28
Mobile (Food Truck/Trailer)	24	30	34
Catering Full Service	25	34	36
Cafeteria	26	30	34
Buffet	24	28	32

* Percentages include employee hourly wages and management salaries.

The Payroll Budget Estimate shown in Figure 8.3 on p. 158 identifies the following:

▶ **Hourly Staff** and **Managers** by Name, Position, Hourly Rate of Pay, Scheduled Hours, Scheduled Overtime, and Total Earned calculated in gross wages. Scheduling **overtime** may apply during the following situations:

▷ An unanticipated increase in business requires an employee to work additional hours to meet the demands of the business.

▷ An employee calls in sick resulting in another employee having to work additional hours.

▷ A family emergency requires an employee to take one or more days off resulting in other employees having to work additional hours.

▷ When an increase in business may not justify hiring an additional employee, resulting in a current employee working extra hours.

> **NOTE:** Overtime occurs when an employee works more than 40 hours per week. The minimum overtime rate is 1.5 times an employee's normal hourly rate of pay.

▶ **Estimated 12.5% of total gross wages is the allowance for payroll taxes.** Employers are required to pay federal & state unemployment taxes, FICA taxes for Social Security & Medicare (FICA—Federal Insurance Contribution Act), and workers' compensation insurance.

▷ **Hourly Staff** ($12,827.00 × 0.125 = 1,603.375 rounded up to $1,603.38)

▷ **Managers** ($4,200.00 × 0.125 = $525.00)

▶ **Estimated 30% of total gross wages is the allowance for health insurance, vacations, and sick days.**

▷ **Hourly Staff** ($12,827.00 × 0.30 = $3,848.10)

▷ **Managers** ($4,200.00 × 0.30 = $1,260.00)

> **NOTE:** The rate for health insurance can vary according to the extent of an employer's group health plan coverage. For this example—an allowance of 20% for health insurance combined with 10% for vacations and sick days brings the estimate to 30%.

▶ **Employee meals are charged at $5.00 for each employee working a shift over 4 hours.** Employee meal allowances will vary according to the amount management establishes.

▶ **Employee meals are a form of compensation and are therefore part of the payroll costs.** The total number of meals for hourly staff (100) and for managers (15) is determined by reviewing the Work Schedule and counting the number of shifts over 4 hours. A system software function will do this automatically.

▷ **Hourly Staff** (100 meals × $5.00 = $500.00)

▷ **Managers** (15 meals × $5.00 = $75.00)

> **NOTE:** The cost of employee meals is added to the payroll cost and subtracted from the food cost when calculating the food cost percentage.

Employee meals may be provided as follows:

▷ Predetermined menu items offered in an employees' cafeteria. This would occur in a large foodservice operation, hotel, resort, or casino.

The rate for unemployment taxes will vary according to the number of past employees who have filed to collect unemployment insurance. The rate for workers' compensation insurance will vary according to the accident history of the business.

▷ Selected menu items prepared each day for employees. This may occur in a large restaurant or in a healthcare or school foodservice operation.

▷ Employees allowed to select certain food and beverage items from the restaurant menu. This is what typically occurs in many restaurant operations.

NOTE: The amount charged for the employee meal is the cost of the meal not the menu selling price. For example, a $5.00 amount would represent an average cost of designated menu items (selected for employee meals) that may have a menu price range up to $18.00 on the menu or a combination of items totaling that amount.

▶ **Forecasted sales for the week ($73,540.00)** is based on the sales history—that is, sales the restaurant experienced the previous year, along with any additional factors that may have affected sales, such as holidays, community events, weather conditions, or any other related circumstances. Management reviews the information and determines an estimated amount, which becomes the forecasted sales for the week.

▶ **Estimated payroll cost percentage for hourly staff (25.54%)** is determined by dividing the estimated Hourly Staff Subtotal (gross wages plus allowance for payroll taxes, health insurance, vacations and sick days, and employee meals) by the forecasted sales for the week.

Hourly Staff Subtotal	÷	Forecasted Sales for the Week	=	**Estimated Payroll Cost Percentage for Hourly Employees**
$18,778.48	÷	$73,540.00	=	.25535 rounded to **.2554 = 25.54%**

▶ **Estimated payroll cost percentage for hourly staff & managers (33.78%)** is determined by dividing the estimated Grand Total (Hourly Staff Subtotal + Managers Subtotal) by the sales forecast for the week.

Grand Total	÷	Forecasted Sales for the Week	=	**Estimated Payroll Cost Percentage for Hourly Staff and Managers**
$24,838.48	÷	$73,540.00	=	.33775 rounded to **.3378 = 33.78%**

A Payroll Cost Percentage Goal of 34.00% would be set by management in order to achieve the desired level of profitability in conjunction with all of the other operational costs of the business. Therefore the estimated payroll cost percentage for hourly staff & managers of 33.78% would be in line with the target goal.

NOTE: The medium payroll cost percentage average for a casual-dining table service restaurant is 34%, as shown in the box on p. 155.

Complete Assignment 12 on p. 164.

Payroll Budget Estimate

Name	Position	Hourly Rate	Scheduled Hours	Scheduled Overtime	Total Earned
Joe	Executive Chef	$37.00	40		$1,480.00
Jan	Sous Chef	$30.00	40		$1,200.00
Mike	Chef	$26.00	40		$1,040.00
Jose	Chef	$24.00	40		$960.00
Ann	Cook	$22.00	36		$792.00
Evan	Cook	$22.00	35		$770.00
Tony	Cook	$22.00	30		$660.00
Don	Dishwasher	$15.00	40		$600.00
Lester	Dishwasher	$15.00	36		$540.00
George	Dishwasher	$15.00	28		$420.00
Ricky	Host	$16.50	30		$495.00
Lucy	Server	$15.00	22		$330.00
Mary	Server	$15.00	22		$330.00
Jack	Server	$15.00	22		$330.00
Judy	Server	$15.00	29		$435.00
Nick	Server	$15.00	29		$435.00
Pam	Server	$15.00	29		$435.00
Joan	Server	$15.00	29		$435.00
Duane	Server	$15.00	17.5		$262.50
Alex	Server	$15.00	16.5		$247.50
Thomas	Servers' Asst.	$15.00	12		$180.00
Rene	Servers' Asst.	$15.00	30		$450.00
TOTAL			**653**		**$12,827.00**

Allowance for payroll taxes—estimate is 0.125 of total gross wages	$1,603.38
Allowance for health insurance, vacations, & sick days—estimate is 30% of total wages	$3,848.10
Allowance for employee meals—applicable to shifts over 4 hours (100 meals × $5 each)	$500.00
Hourly Staff Subtotal	**$18,778.48**

Name	Position	Hourly Rate	Scheduled Hours	Scheduled Overtime	Total Earned
David	Manager	$45.00	40		$1,800.00
Lynn	Assistant Manager	$30.00	40		$1,200.00
Mitch	Assistant Manager	$30.00	40		$1,200.00
TOTAL			**120**		**$4,200.00**

Allowance for payroll taxes—estimate is 0.125 of total gross wages	$525.00
Allowance for health insurance, vacations, & sick days—estimate is 30% of total wages	$1,260.00
Allowance for employee meals—applicable to shifts over 4 hours (15 meals × $5 each)	$75.00
Managers Subtotal	**$6,060.00**

Week of: January 11, 20xx	**GRAND TOTAL**	**$24,838.48**

Forecasted sales for the week: **$73,540.00**	Payroll Cost Percentage Goal	34.00%
Estimated payroll cost percentage for hourly staff		25.54%
Estimated payroll cost percentage for hourly staff & managers		33.78%

Figure 8.3 Payroll Budget Estimate

Actual Hours Worked

LEARNING OBJECTIVE 4
Track the actual hours worked by employees with daily time card reporting.

The actual hours worked by each employee are recorded on an **employee time card.** Time cards are printed at the end of the week and accompany employee paychecks. A time card will include the following:

- ▶ Start and finish times for each day worked
- ▶ Start and finish times for each meal break
- ▶ Total hours worked each day, and total hours for the week
- ▶ A line for the employee to sign after having verified the hours worked as being correct

The traditional time card system with a punch-in and punch-out time clock may be used by some businesses, but this system has essentially been replaced by a computed time card that is commonly accessed through a POS terminal. The advantages of a POS system include the following:

- ▶ Each employee is able to access his or her time card by entering a PIN (personal identification number) at the POS terminal or by swiping an employee identification card.
  - ▷ The system allows employees to log in and out only at their scheduled programmed work hours, which should correspond to the Work Schedule.
  - ▷ The system also allows employees to log in and out for their meal breaks.
- ▶ When employees are requested to work longer than they were scheduled, the manager enters a code that authorizes the approval and may also enter a brief note or description code number that states the reason for the employee working longer.
- ▶ The time worked for each employee is computed and totaled for each day.

The manager can compare the hours worked with the hours that were scheduled for each day. This allows the manager to be able to keep the hours in line with the hours that were scheduled for the Payroll Budget Estimate.

LEARNING OBJECTIVE 5
Compare actual payroll costs to budgeted costs with the objective of being able to remain within the payroll cost percentage goal.

- ▶ Schedule adjustments can be made during the week in response to the actual sales compared to the sales forecast for the week.
  - ▷ If the actual sales are less than the forecasted sales, the manager can adjust the Work Schedule by reducing the number of hours that were initially scheduled, keeping the payroll costs in line with the actual sales.
  - ▷ If actual sales greatly exceeded forecasted sales, additional work hours would be needed.
- ▶ Scheduled work hours can be decreased or increased for hourly employees receiving wages: compensation paid for hours worked.
- ▶ Scheduled work hours will remain the same for managers receiving salaries: compensation paid weekly, bi-weekly, or monthly.
- ▶ A payroll report produced by the POS system (similar to the Payroll Budget Estimate) is printed at the end of the week. The report will list the total number of hours worked along with the total payroll costs.

▷ The payroll report makes it easy for the manager to compare the actual payroll cost with the Payroll Budget Estimate.

▷ If the Payroll Budget Estimate is 33.78% and the actual payroll amount is 36%, the manager would need to explain the reason for the difference.

> **LEARNING OBJECTIVE 6**
> Determine the cost of employee turnover by calculating the direct and indirect costs associated with turnover.

Measuring Employee Turnover Rate and Cost

Employee turnover rate is a ratio comparison of the number of employees a business must replace compared to the average number of total employees in a specific accounting period. A typical accounting period to measure the employee turnover rate and cost is one year.

High employee turnover can be a sign of ineffective management and/or a poor working environment, in addition to the following reasons:

▶ A large number of minimum wage positions

▶ A lack of employee benefits

▶ Limited opportunities for career advancement

Direct costs of employee turnover include:

▶ **Recruiting Costs:** Position opening advertisements—websites/newspapers—employment agency fees (if used), and management time for applicant interviews.

▶ **Training Costs:** New employees require an adequate amount of time to be properly oriented to a new work environment, and an adequate amount of training for specific functions to be performed.

Indirect costs of employee turnover are often overlooked because it is difficult to assign them a set value. Indirect costs include:

▶ **Loss of Productivity:** The new employee productivity level will be below normal until the necessary skills and speed are developed to perform the tasks for the specific position. This may require another employee to work additional hours to assist in training the new employee and to assist with some of the work.

▶ **Accounting and Payroll Processing Expenses:** The new and departing employees will need to have human resource and tax forms prepared and completed.

▶ **Loss of Business:** Possible customer loss as a result of mistakes or poor service by a new employee.

Foodservice managers should be aware of the actual cost of employee turnover and track these costs as much as possible. At the end of the year, the total dollar amount should be calculated and the information used to assess the quality of management and quality of the working environment.

Direct and indirect costs of employee turnover typically range from $500 to $5,000 per employee which has been documented by industry studies and reports. The cost per employee will vary according to the type of foodservice operation and the requirements of each position.

Calculating the Employee Turnover Rate

There are three steps to calculating the employee turnover rate. The steps below address the hourly employee turnover rate (e.g., executive chef, sous chef, chef, cook, dishwasher, or servers' assistant):

1. **Determine the average number of hourly employees.** This is done by adding the number of employees at the beginning of the year to the number of employees at the end of the year and dividing by 2. The Payroll Budget Estimate, Figure 8.3 on p. 158, lists 22 hourly employees. For this example, the number of employees at the beginning and end of the year is the same at 22—although the number of employees at any given time during the year may have been greater or less than 22.

   Number of Employees
     (beginning of the year)   22
   Number of Employees
     (end of the year)   + 22
                    Total   44 ÷ 2 = **22 Average Number of Employees**

2. **Determine the number of past hourly employees.** This is done by subtracting the number of current employees from the total number of W-2 tax forms issued at the end of the year for the hourly employees. The accountant prepared 30 W-2 year-end payroll tax forms to be sent out to current and past hourly employees. There are 22 current employees, therefore 8 past employees.

Number of W-2 Tax Forms	−	Number of Current Employees	=	**Number of Past Employees**
30	−	22	=	**8**

3. **Calculate the hourly employee turnover rate.** This is done by dividing the number of past employees by the average number of employees, as follows:

Number of Past Employees	÷	Average Number of Employees	=	**Employee Turnover Rate**
8	÷	22	=	.3636 rounded to .36 = **36%**

Calculating Hourly Employee Turnover Cost

The cost of employee turnover is calculated as follows:

Number of Past Employees	×	Cost per Employee	=	**Cost of Employee Turnover**
8	×	$500.00	=	**$4,000.00**

NOTE: $500.00 per employee was the cost amount determined for this example to replace one dishwasher, three server positions, and one servers' assistant. A chef, cook, or assistant manager position would require a different amount according to training needs of the position.

Complete Assignment 13 on p. 166.

Comparison of Hourly Employee Turnover Rates and Costs

Below is a box that shows the typical hourly employee and salaried employee turnover rates for different foodservice operations as reported by industry professional associations. We will compare the typical hourly employee turnover rate for casual-dining table service operation (108% shown in the box below) and the employee turnover rate (taken from our example in the previous section) to find out how the turnover costs in the example on the previous page compare with a typical costs.

Foodservice Category	Hourly/Employee Turnover Rate	Salaried/Employee Turnover Rate
Fine Dining Table Service	102%	15%
Casual-dining Table Service	108%	20%
Fast Casual	110%	20%
Quick Service (Fast Food)	122%	25%
Catering Full Service	105%	15%
Cafeteria	107%	15%
Buffet	107%	15%

▶ The casual-dining table service hourly/employee turnover rate of 108% is calculated as follows (the accountant prepared 52 W-2 tax forms, and there are currently 25 employees). The average number of employees (25) is derived from the industry average casual dining table service restaurant:

Number of W-2 Tax Forms	−	Number of Current Employees	=	**Number of Past Hourly Employees**
52	−	25	=	**27**

Number of Past Employes	÷	Average Number of Employees	=	**Employee Turnover Rate**
27	÷	25	=	1.08 =**108%**

▶ The Cost of Hourly Employee Turnover is calculated as follows:

Number of Past Employes	×	Cost per Employee	=	**Cost of Employee Turnover**
27	×	$500.00	=	**$13,500.00**

NOTE: The $500.00 per employee amount would need to be adjusted upward according to positions that require additional training.

▶ When comparing the 108% typical hourly/employee turnover rate average to the actual 36% turnover rate (shown in #3 on p. 161), the cost of employee turnover difference calculates as follows:

$13,500.00	(27 past hourly employees)	108% turnover
– 4,000.00	(8 past hourly employees)	36% turnover
$9,500.00	**Cost Difference**	

> **LEARNING OBJECTIVE 7**
> Identify the payroll costs-saving value associated with a low employee turnover rate.

The $9,500.00 cost difference reflects a good working environment supported by competent management. The $9,500.00 could go directly into the restaurant's profitability or a portion may be distributed to the management team as a year-end performance bonus.

An investment in training and time is made with each new employee. Therefore, every effort should be made to retain quality employees by offering the following:

1. Competitive wages for hourly employees and salaries for management

2. Health insurance with possible dental and eye care options and extended family benefits

3. Ongoing job skills training and professional development

4. Opportunities for advancement and/or additional responsibilities with increased income potential

5. A good working environment supported by competent management

Assignment 12

1. Prepare a Payroll Budget Estimate for the week of April 3, 20xx at a fine dining restaurant.
   Payroll Cost Percentage Goal: 35%
   Payroll Cost Percentage for Hourly Staff: _____%
   Payroll Cost Percentage for Hourly Staff and Managers: _____%

The following information is provided:

Forecasted sales for the week:	$66,350.00
Payroll taxes estimate:	0.125 of total gross wages
Health insurance, vacations, and sick days estimate:	30% of total wages
Employee meals (hourly staff):	$620.00
Employee meals (managers):	$85.00

Position	Hourly Rate	Scheduled Hours	Total Earned
Executive Chef	$42.00	40	$_____
Sous Chef	$31.50	40	_____
Chef	$25.50	40	_____
Pastry Chef	$23.00	30	_____
Line Cook	$19.00	40	$_____
Line Cook	$17.75	40	_____
Prep Cook	$17.00	40	_____
Dishwasher #1	$15.50	40	$_____
Dishwasher #2	$15.00	36	_____
Dishwasher #3	$15.00	30	_____
Maitre d'	$20.00	36	$_____
Server #1	$15.00	30	$_____
Server #2	$15.00	28	_____
Server #3	$15.00	25	_____
Server #4	$15.00	22	_____
Server #5	$15.00	20	_____
Server #6	$15.00	18	_____
Server #7	$15.00	16.5	_____
Server #8	$15.00	16.5	_____
Servers' Asst. #1	$15.00	30	_____
Servers' Asst. #2	$15.00	25	_____
		TOTAL	$_____
		Payroll Taxes:	_____
	Health Insurance, Vacations, Sick Days:		_____
		Employee Meals:	_____
		Hourly Staff Subtotal:	$_____
Manager	$44.00	40	_____
Asst. Manager	$32.00	40	_____
		TOTAL	$_____
		Payroll Taxes:	_____
	Health Insurance, Vacations, Sick Days:		_____
		Employee Meals:	_____
		Managers Subtotal:	$_____
		GRAND TOTAL	$_____

2. Prepare a Payroll Budget Estimate for the week of November 20, 20xx at a hotel catering department.

Payroll Cost Percentage Goal: 29%

Payroll Cost Percentage for Hourly Staff:	_____ %
Payroll Cost Percentage for Hourly Staff and Managers:	_____ %

The following information is provided:

Forecasted sales for the week:	$81,475.00
Payroll taxes estimate:	0.125 of total gross wages
Health insurance, vacations, and sick days estimate:	30% of total wages
Employee meals (hourly staff):	$490.00
Employee meals (managers):	$70.00

Overtime hours are 1.5 times the ourly rate.

Position	Hourly Rate	Scheduled Hours	Scheduled Overtime	Total Earned
Executive Chef	$38.00	40	5	$_____
Sous Chef	$30.50	40		_____
Chef	$26.50	40		_____
Pastry Chef	$25.00	36		_____
Prep Cook	$21.00	40	2	$_____
Prep Cook	$19.25	40	2	_____
Salad Prep	$18.00	40		_____
Sommelier	$22.50	40		_____
Dishwasher #1	$15.00	36		$_____
Dishwasher #2	$15.00	36		_____
Dishwasher #3	$15.00	24		_____
Server #1	$15.00	25		$_____
Server #2	$15.00	20		_____
Server #3	$15.00	22		_____
Server #4	$15.00	22		_____
Server #5	$15.00	20		_____
Server #6	$15.00	18		_____
Server #7	$15.00	14		_____
Server #8	$15.00	12		_____
Server #9	$15.00	12		_____
Servers' Asst. #1	$15.00	30		_____
Servers' Asst. #2	$15.00	25		_____
Servers' Asst. #3	$15.00	16		_____
			TOTAL	$_____
			Payroll Taxes:	_____
			Health Insurance, Vacations, Sick Days:	_____
			Employee Meals:	_____
			Hourly Staff Subtotal:	$_____
Manager	$42.00	40		_____
Asst. Manager	$31.50	40		_____
			TOTAL	$_____
			Payroll Taxes:	_____
			Health Insurance, Vacations, Sick Days:	_____
			Employee Meals:	_____
			Managers Subtotal:	$_____
			GRAND TOTAL	$_____

Assignment 13

Calculate the Employee Turnover Rate and the Cost of Employee Turnover for the following restaurants:

1. Casual-Dining Table Service Restaurant:

Number of employees at the beginning of the year:	42
Number of employees at the end of the year:	48
Number of W-2 tax forms issued at the end of the year:	77
Number of current employees:	48

Determine the average number of employees: _____

Determine the number of past employees: _____

Calculate the Employee Turnover Rate: _____

Calculate the Cost of Employee Turnover for the following hourly
  staff positions: dishwashers, servers, and servers' assistants
  at a $500.00 cost per employee.

Cost of Employee Turnover: $_____

2. Fast Casual Restaurant with high sales volume.

Number of employees at the beginning of the year:	28
Number of employees at the end of the year:	30
Number of W-2 tax forms issued at the end of the year:	51
Number of current employees:	27

Determine the average number of employees: _____

Determine the number of past employees: _____

Calculate the Employee Turnover Rate: _____

Calculate the Cost of Employee Turnover for the following hourly
  staff positions: cooks, salad and sandwich line, and cashiers
  at a $550.00 cost per employee.

Cost of Employee Turnover: $_____

3. Buffet Restaurant serving lunch and dinner.

Number of employees at the beginning of the year:	57
Number of employees at the end of the year:	61
Number of W-2 tax forms issued at the end of the year:	98
Number of current employees:	58

Determine the average number of employees: _____

Determine the number of past employees: _____

Calculate the Employee Turnover Rate: _____

Calculate the Cost of Employee Turnover for the following hourly
  staff positions: cooks, salad prep, buffet line servers, and dishwashers
  at a $525.00 cost per employee.

Cost of Employee Turnover: $_____

Summary

The primary factors that affect payroll costs are directly linked to performance and operating efficiency, and are as follows: labor saving kitchen equipment, well-arranged floor plans that save time and steps, ongoing training for all employees, and the use of prepared (convenience) foods.

The Work Schedule should represent the best effort of the manager to schedule employees in anticipation of sales. The basic rules for creating Work Schedules are as follows: review sales history records before making scheduling decisions, prepare schedules weekly, post schedules at least one-week in advance, minimize scheduling changes to avoid frustrating employees, and schedule employee meal breaks.

A Payroll Budget Estimate is usually prepared at the same time that the Work Schedule is determined, and is a planned estimate of payroll expenses stated in dollar amounts and as a percentage of anticipated sales.

The actual hours worked by each employee are recorded on an employee time card which is typically in a POS system and printed at the end of the week. The time card includes start and finish times for each day worked, start and finish times for each meal break, total hours worked each day, and total hours for the week.

High employee turnover can be a sign of ineffective management and/or a poor working environment. The Direct Costs are recruiting and training, and the Indirect Costs that are often overlooked because it is difficult to assign a set value are as follows: loss of productivity, accounting and payroll processing expenses, and loss of business.

Calculating the Employee Turnover Rate is a three-step procedure that begins with determining the average number of hourly employees, determining the number of past hourly employees, and then dividing the number of past employees by the average number of employees to arrive at the employee turnover rate. The Employee Turnover Rate cost is directly related to the type of job positions being replaced.

Discussion Questions

1. What are the primary factors affecting payroll costs that are directly related to performance and operating efficiency? List three of those factors.
2. There are several basic rules that managers should follow when creating Work Schedules. Describe five of those rules.
3. What is the purpose of a Payroll Budget Estimate?
4. How is the Payroll Cost Percentage calculated, specifically, what is the formula?
5. What are two examples of when a manager might have to schedule overtime?
6. Explain how the rate for unemployment taxes can be vary.
7. If workers' compensation insurance rates increase, what is occurring?
8. What information should be printed on an employee time card?
9. When a manager is tracking employee hours, schedule adjustments may need to be made during the week. Why?
10. Explain the Direct and Indirect Costs associated with Employee Turnover.
11. How is the Employee Turnover Rate calculated? Describe the three steps.
12. Discuss the financial savings associated with a low Employee Turnover Rate, along with how quality employees can be retained.

Restaurant Reality

When seven coffee shop line cooks were doing the work of five

A 150-seat airport terminal coffee shop with a high-volume breakfast and lunch business from 6 A.M. to 2 P.M. was experiencing customer complaints about cold toast and sloppy plate presentations. There were seven cooks scheduled to work at hourly wages. The pay rate for each cook was based on job description responsibilities and length of employment. A sense of carelessness supported by an attitude of "we're doing the best we can" seemed to prevail. The challenge for the manager was to correct the situation.

The manager observed that during the busy breakfast hours one cook was only preparing toast by placing slices of bread into a rotary toaster; another cook was only doing plate setups, which consisted of slicing and cutting fresh oranges to place on each plate. Five other cooks were busy preparing orders at the grill and pantry/sandwich station along with plating and dishing up the prepared food to be served. The obvious lack of a coordinated production flow was resulting in a cumbersome work environment.

Based on the manager's experience, he knew the situation could be corrected by reducing the number of cooks in order to free up a congested work line and consolidate food-order preparation. A cook was reassigned (with the same scheduled work hours and rate of pay) to a quick-serve foodservice location within the airport terminal, replacing another cook who was ready for new responsibilities in the dining room kitchen. A few days later a second cook left to work for another company. At that point the manager met with the remaining five cooks to present a viable option to hiring new people to fill the two positions.

The manager asked if they could function as a team of five with a wage increase to the next pay-grade level. A unanimous decision was made to accept that option. By eliminating two cook positions the hourly wage increase was more than justified. Plate presentations met company standards, which pleased the manager and customers, the line cooks were rewarded for their good work, and productivity increased. A fast-paced work flow accompanied by a coordinated effort turned a cumbersome work environment into a positive situation. So now five line cooks were doing the work of five.

9

Measuring Performance and Productivity

Introduction

Performance and productivity measurements indicate the amount of work produced in a given period of time. Management is interested in knowing if value is being obtained from employees in terms of the following: performing duties the entire time at work and according to established standards in a self-directed manner. Foodservice managers strive to maintain a desired level of kitchen staff and server performance and productivity.

Learning Objectives

Upon successfully completing this chapter, readers will be able to:

1. Understand the key factors in creating and maintaining high productivity in any type of foodservice operation.

2. Recognize the value and applied use of a job description for every position.

3. Explain the effects of ongoing training and cross training for employees.

4. Define the factors that are considered to be part of a performance and productivity standard.

5. Understand that a Kitchen Productivity Report tracks averages and can establish standards.

6. Know how to measure server performance and productivity by using a Server Productivity Report.

7. Describe the process for tip reporting as income received by servers.

8. Understand that tip income can be applied to meet the minimum wage hourly rate when employers are paying less than minimum wage to servers (tipped employees).

9. Recognize the speed, accuracy, and efficiency that is achieved with Tabletop Tablets.

Chapter Outline

Key Terms and Definitions

Begin by first reading the key terms and their definitions. An advance understanding of the terms will be helpful prior to reading the chapter.

Average Customer Sale	Computed by dividing the total sales by the total number of customers for each server.
Cross Training	Takes place when opportunities exist for employees to be trained to perform more than one function.
Customers per Employee Hour	Measures quantity of work completed by dividing the number of customers per hour served for a specific hour by the number of employee hours for that same specific hour of service.
High Productivity	When employees are meeting or exceeding performance and established productivity standards.
Job Description	Lists the qualifications, responsibilities, and functions for the work to be performed.
Kitchen Productivity Report	Tracks daily productivity of kitchen employees, which can be compared to previous days, weeks, months, and annual averages.
Low Productivity	When employees are not performing at established performance and productivity standards.
Mishaps	Measures quality of work completed by monitoring the ability of the kitchen staff to prepare food with little or no errors, as well as the food to be served with no errors.
Productivity	A term used to describe how well hourly employees perform their work.
Sales per Employee Hour	Measures efficiency of work completed by dividing the amount of sales generated for the specific hour (sales) by the number of employee hours for that same specific hour of sales.
Server Productivity Report	Allows management to analyze the performance of every server.
Tip Credit	Allows the minimum wage rate to be reduced with the remainder being supported by tip income applied to meet the minimum wage hourly rate.

Achieving High Productivity

LEARNING OBJECTIVE 1
Understand the key factors in creating and maintaining high productivity in any type of foodservice operation.

The key factors in creating and maintaining high productivity in any type of foodservice operation are the following:

1. Hire qualified people.
2. Maintain ongoing training.
3. Monitor performance and productivity standards.

Hire Qualified People

Hire people with the necessary competencies and prerequisites for each position; people who have a strong work ethic are reliable and serious about doing good work.

LEARNING OBJECTIVE 2
Recognize the value and applied use of a job description for every position.

▸ **Job Description:** A well-defined job description should be prepared for each position within the foodservice operation, and include the following:

1. **Qualifications:** Required education, experience, knowledge, skills, and abilities to effectively do the job

2. **Responsibilities:** A concise list of specific duties, tasks, and performance and productivity standards

3. **Functions:** A complete explanation of the work to be performed and the schedule of days and work hours

▸ **Hire to the Job Description:** Management can evaluate each applicant's qualifications and attributes based on a clear job description. Without the job description, the hiring process is less focused, and hiring the most qualified person becomes more difficult.

Maintain Ongoing Training

New employees are trained to perform the tasks listed in the job description. Management determines how the training takes place.

LEARNING OBJECTIVE 3
Explain the effects of ongoing training and cross training for employees.

▸ **Training** must occur on a regular basis in order to retain performance and productivity standards. Ongoing training reinforces the standards established by management and introduces new methods and procedures.

▸ **Cross training** takes place when opportunities exist for employees to be trained in more than one function. An employee may work as a dishwasher 3 days a week and be trained as a servers' assistant (busser) or cook for 1 or 2 days a week. When a servers' assistant, server, or cook position becomes available, the cross trained employee would be ready to quickly move into that position. In addition, should help be needed with washing dishes during a busy period, the cross trained employee could temporarily return to being a dishwasher.

▷ Successful managers understand the value of cross training. For employees new to the foodservice industry it provides an opportunity to be engaged in learning additional skills and earning more money; for career employees it provides an opportunity to advance.

Employee turnover and overtime hours can be reduced when the foodservice operation runs smoothly with competent employees.

Monitor Performance and Productivity Standards

Review and evaluate the performance and productivity of every employee on a regular basis.

> ▶ **Kitchen staff performance and productivity** can be compared and analyzed to focus on trends and to establish productivity standards as shown in the Kitchen Productivity Report, Figure 9.1 on p. 174.

> ▶ **Server performance and productivity** can be measured and analyzed individually and collectively by day and meal period (breakfast, lunch, dinner) in order to establish productivity standards, as shown in the Server Productivity Report, Figure 9.2 on p. 177.

> ▶ **Employee Reviews**

> > ▷ **New Employees:** Management should monitor and evaluate the performance and productivity progress of each new employee on a daily basis, and management should discuss the progress with the employee at the end of a 30-, 60-, or 90-day period.

> > ▷ **Existing Employees:** Management should review and evaluate the performance and productivity with every employee annually or as often as may be needed.

Successful managers maintain a positive work environment that promotes job satisfaction by recognizing and rewarding people for quality work performed.

The factors that are considered integral to performance and productivity standards are as follows:

LEARNING OBJECTIVE 4
Define the factors that are considered to be part of a performance and productivity standard.

1. **Efficiency** of work completed in relation to sales generated for a specific period of time.

> ▷ The sales per employee hour measures efficiency.

2. **Quantity** of work performed in relation to the number of customers served for a specific period of time.

> ▷ The customers served per employee hour measures quantity.

3. **Quality** of work in terms of mishaps (mistakes) avoided.

> ▷ Mishaps avoided is a measure of quality.

4. **Responsibility** for performing the work as demonstrated by the amount of management supervision required for the work.

> ▷ Employee responsibility measures performance.

Productivity is a term used to describe how well hourly employees perform their work.

> ▶ **High Productivity:** Employees are meeting or exceeding performance and productivity standards established by management.

> ▶ **Low Productivity:** Employees are not performing at established performance and productivity standards.

Production methods and procedures that can improve on existing employee performance and productivity are continually being developed. New and improved food products that are completely or partially prepared and advanced systems that simplify cooking procedures are introduced to the market annually.

Measuring Kitchen Staff Performance and Productivity

Kitchen staff performance and productivity can be examined daily, weekly, monthly, and annually. The days, weeks, months, and years can be compared and analyzed to focus on trends and establish averages.

The Kitchen Productivity Report, Figure 9.1 on the following page, identifies the following:

LEARNING OBJECTIVE 5
Understand that a Kitchen Productivity Report tracks averages and can establish standards.

► **Hours of Operation** (Column A) is the time kitchen employees start and finish work recorded by the hour. The report shows the Hours of Operation from 7:00 A.M. to 11:00 P.M. in one-hour increments.

   Example: 7:00 A.M.–8:00 A.M. The Kitchen Productivity Report is updated by the hour from 7:00 A.M. to 11:00 P.M. within a POS system.

► **Amount of Sales** (Column B) records the amount of sales per hour for the hours that the restaurant is serving customers (11:00 A.M. to 2:00 P.M. and 5:00 P.M. to 10:00 P.M.). The sales numbers are totaled by the hour in the POS system and transmitted to the Kitchen Productivity Report beginning with $1,035.25 for the hour from 11:00 A.M. to 12:00 P.M., followed by the sales numbers for each remaining hour that customers were served.

► **Number of Customers** (Column C) is totaled by the hour in the POS system and transmitted along with the Sales to the Kitchen Productivity Report, beginning with 69 customers from 11:00 A.M. to 12:00 P.M.

► **Number of Employee Hours** (Column D) is totaled by the hour on the POS Time Card and transmitted to the Kitchen Productivity Report. If more than one hour occurs in any given hour time frame, then additional people were working during that hour of time.

   Example: From 11:00 a.m. to 12:00 p.m., 3 employee hours were recorded, which indicates that 3 people were working during that hour of time.

► **Sales per Employee Hour** (Column E) is computed by the POS system.

   Example: The hour from 11:00 A.M. to 12:00 P.M. is computed as follows:

$$\underset{\text{(Column B)}}{\text{Sales}} \div \underset{\text{(Column D)}}{\text{Number of Employee Hours}} = \underset{\textbf{Employee Hour}}{\textbf{Sales per}}$$

$$\$1,035.25 \div 3 = \$345.80$$

Sales per Employee Hour measures *efficiency* of work completed by dividing the Amount of Sales generated for the specific hour by the Number of Employee Hours for that same specific hour of sales. The Number of Employee Hours produce a certain Amount of Sales per Hour.

The higher the sales with the same number of employee hours, the higher the productivity.

► **Customers per Employee Hour** (Column F) is also computed by the POS system.

Kitchen Productivity Report

Kitchen Hours: 7:00 A.M.–11:00 P.M.   **Day:** Friday   **Date:** Janaury 15, 20xx

Calculations				B ÷ D = E	C ÷ D = F		G ÷ C × 100 = H
A	B	C	D	E	F	G	H
Hours of Operation	Sales	Number of Customers	Number of Employee Hours	Sales per Employee Hour	Customers per Employee Hour	Mishaps	MIshap Percentage
7:00 A.M. – 8:00 A.M.			1				
8:00 A.M. – 9:00 A.M.			1				
9:00 A.M. – 10:00 A.M.			1				
10:00 A.M. – 11:00 A.M.			2				
11:00 A.M. – 12:00 P.M.	$1,035.25	49	3	$345.08	16.3		
12:00 P.M. – 1:00 P.M.	1,635.60	97	5	327.12	19.4		
1:00 P.M. – 2:00 P.M.	1,260.15	84	5	252.03	16.8		
2:00 P.M. – 3:00 P.M.			5				
3:00 P.M. – 4:00 P.M.			5				
4:00 P.M. – 5:00 P.M.			6				
5:00 P.M. – 6:00 P.M.	1,104.10	38	6	184.02	6.3		
6:00 P.M. – 7:00 P.M.	2,116.50	91	6	352.75	15.2		
7:00 P.M. – 8:00 P.M.	2,714.30	98	6	452.38	16.3	2	2.04%
8:00 P.M. – 9:00 P.M.	2,369.15	63	4	592.29	15.8		
9:00 P.M. – 10:00 P.M.	1,242.10	24	3	414.03	8.0		
10:00 P.M. – 11:00 P.M.			1				
Totals	**$13,488.15**	**544**	**60**			**2**	
Averages				**$224.62**	**9.07**		**0.368%**

Figure 9.1   Kitchen Productivity Report

Example: The hour from 11:00 A.M. to 12:00 P.M. is computed as follows:

$$\text{Number of Customers (Column C)} \div \text{Number of Employee Hours (Column D)} = \textbf{Customers per Employee Hour}$$

$$49 \div 3 = \textbf{16.3}$$

The greater the number of customers with the same number of employee hours, the greater the productivity.

Customers per Employee Hour measures *quantity* of work completed by dividing the Number of Customers served for a specific hour by the Number of Employee Hours for that same specific hour of service.

▶ **Mishaps** (Column G) are recorded in the POS system by the hour each time a mishap (mistake) occurs and the item has to be reordered and again prepared. This may include food items that were overcooked, undercooked, or dropped on the floor, or food returned to the kitchen because of a server error in placing the order. When the item is reordered, the POS system allows a reorder code or a symbol with a word to be entered in explanation for reordering.

Mishaps track *quality* of work completed for a specific hour. The purpose of tracking mishaps (mistakes) per hour is to monitor the ability of the kitchen staff to prepare food with little or no errors, and/or the server to deliver the food without any errors.

▶ **Mishap Percentage** (Column H) is the ratio of mishaps compared to the number of customers for a specific hour and is computed by the POS system.

Example: The hour from 7:00 P.M. to 8:00 P.M. is computed as follows::

$$\underset{\text{(Column G)}}{\text{Mishaps}} \div \underset{\text{(Column C)}}{\text{Number of Customers}} = \underset{\text{Percentage}}{\textbf{Mishap}}$$

$$2 \quad \div \quad 98 \quad = 0.0204 = \textbf{2.04\%}$$

The **Mishap Percentage** also measures quality of work completed for a specific hour.

▶ **Totals and Averages** are recorded on the bottom lines of the Kitchen Productivity Report and are computed by the POS software as follows:

▷ **Totals:** The Sales Total, $13,477.15, is determined by adding the Sales per Hour for each hour. The process is repeated for Number of Customers (544), Number of Employee Hours (60), and Mishaps (2) to determine the totals for each of those categories.

▷ **Average Sales per Employee Hour:** $224.62 is determined by dividing the Total Sales by the Total Number of Employee Hours.

▷ **Average for Customers per Employee Hour:** 9.07 is determined by dividing the Total Number of Customers by the Total Number of Employee Hours.

▷ **Average Mishap Percentage:** 0.368% is determined by dividing the Total Mishaps by the Total Number of Customers (and multiplying the answer by 100).

NOTE: A foodservice operation should not experience a mishap percentage rate of higher than 1%. That is, if 100 customers were served, no more than 1 food order should be wasted due to a mishap.

The Kitchen Productivity Report tracks daily productivity, which can be compared to previous days, weeks, months, and annual totals and averages. The productivity level should be consistent, but if productivity drops below the established standard totals and averages, management can quickly take corrective action. Management may also use the information that the report provides to identify where productivity could be improved.

Measuring Server Performance and Productivity

The servers are the people who take the orders from customers and enter the orders along with their server identification number at the POS terminal or on a hand-held tablet—which immediately transmits the orders to the kitchen to

LEARNING OBJECTIVE 6
Know how to measure server performance and productivity by using a Server Productivity Report.

begin preparation. The server then promptly serves the prepared food and beverages to the customers.

Server performance and productivity can be measured and analyzed individually and collectively by day and meal period (breakfast, lunch, dinner) using a Server Productivity Report.

The Server Productivity Report, Figure 9.2 on the following page, identifies the following:

> The Server Productivity Report is updated for each meal period (breakfast, lunch, dinner)within the POS system.

- ▶ **Server Name** (Column A) lists each server by name and meal period (lunch or dinner).

- ▶ **Station Number** (Column B) indicates an assigned work area. Serving areas in a dining room are identified by numbers and within each numbered area is a designated amount of tables and customer seating. Each server is assigned to a specific station to work.

  Certain stations may be more active than others, such as a station that includes counter service or attractive window views.

- ▶ **Number of Hours Worked** (Column C) lists the total number of hours that each server works serving customers. Meal break times are not included. The POS time card computes the hours worked for each server, which is transmitted to the Server Productivity Report.

- ▶ **Total Sales** (Column D) lists the total sales for the meal period (breakfast, lunch, dinner) for each server. The sales by server and meal period are totaled within the POS system and transmitted to the Server Productivity Report.

- ▶ **Sales per Server per Hour** (Column E) is computed by dividing the Total Sales by the Number of Hours Worked for each server. For Lucy, the calculation is as follows:

$$\frac{\text{Total}}{\text{Sales}} \div \frac{\text{Number of}}{\text{Hours Worked}} = \frac{\textbf{Sales per Server}}{\textbf{per Hour}}$$

$$\$1,329.35 \div 3 = \textbf{\$443.12}$$

- ▶ **Total Number of Customers** (Column F) is recorded each time servers enter customer orders into the POS terminal. The POS system transmits the Total Number of Customers along with the Number of Hours Worked and Total Sales to the Server Productivity Report.

> The Average Customer Sale is often referred to as the "Average Check."

- ▶ **Average Customer Sale** (Column G) is computed by dividing the Total Sales by the Total Number of Customers for each server. For Lucy, the calculation is as follows:

$$\frac{\text{Total}}{\text{Sales}} \div \frac{\text{Total Number}}{\text{of Customers}} = \frac{\textbf{Average}}{\textbf{Customer Sale}}$$

$$\$1,329.35 \div 79 = \textbf{\$16.83}$$

- ▶ **Sales Percent** (Column H) focuses on the sales of items that management wants to track. For the lunch period the focus is on Salads, Soups, and Espresso Drinks, and for the dinner period it is on Appetizers, Desserts, and Wines by the glass and bottle.

  Below each item listed is a percentage number.

  Example: Lunch—salads 10%, soups 25%, and espresso drinks 25%.

Server Productivity Report

Dining Room Hours: 11:00 A.M.–2:00 P.M.   **Day:** Friday   **Date:** January 15, 20xx
                    5:00 P.M.–10:00 P.M.

Calculations				D ÷ C = E		D ÷ F = G				
A	B	C	D	E	F	G		H		
								[Sales Percentages]		
Server Name	Station Number	Number of Hours Worked	Total Sales	Sales per Hour	Total Number of Customers	Average Customer Sale	Salads 10%	Soups 25%	Espresso Drinks 25%
Lunch: 11:00 A.M.–2:00 P.M.										
Lucy	1	3	$1,329.35	$443.12	79	$16.83	[8] 11	[20] 24	[20] 20
Mary	2	3	1,380.10	460.03	77	17.92	[8] 9	[19] 22	[19] 26
Jack	3	3	1,221.55	407.18	74	16.51	[7] 7	[19] 23	[19] 22
							[Sales Percentages]		
							Appetizers 25%	Desserts 50%	Wines 25%
Dinner: 5:00 P.M.–10:00 P.M.										
Jack	1	5	$2,530.15	$506.03	82	$30.86	[21] 28	[41] 52	[21] 31
Nick	2	5	2,571.20	514.24	80	32.14	[20] 26	[40] 51	[20] 29
Pam	3	5	2,190.45	438.09	77	28.45	[19] 25	[39] 49	[19] 28
Joan	4	5	2,254.35	450.87	75	30.06	[19] 24	[38] 53	[19] 21

Figure 9.2   Server Productivity Report

The percentages are sales goals that management establishes for servers based on the total number of customers for each server.

For Lucy, the percentage is calculated as follows:

$$\text{Total Number of Customers} \times \text{Percentage Goal (Item)} = \textbf{Number to Be Sold}$$

$$79 \times 0.10 \text{ (Salads)} = 7.9 \text{ rounded to } \textbf{8}$$

Lucy actually sold 11 salads—3 more than the projected goal number of 8. The process is repeated for each server and for every item with a percentage sales goal.

The POS system records the selected items sold by each server and transmits that information to the Server Productivity Report. The percentages are entered into the Server Productivity Report and the system software computes the numbers.

Management may select any number of food and beverage items to track with increased sales, including *add-ons* (items ordered in addition to the standard item), such as shrimp or crabmeat added to a salad. All items that management believes would increase sales and result in increased customer satisfaction can be tracked.

Specific comments regarding the quality of service by individual servers are often solicited on a restaurant's website as well as via social networks.

The Server Productivity Report allows management to analyze the performance of every server, recognizing that the servers are the sales force for the restaurant.

Complete Assignment 14 on p. 181.

Server Tips

Reporting Server Tips

All tips received by servers are required by law to be reported to the federal government as income received.

> ► **Reporting tip income so that the restaurant complies with the Tax Equity and Fiscal Responsibility Act (TEFRA) is the responsibility of management.** Correct tax reporting fulfills the foodservice operation's legal responsibility to the government and to its employees, and enables management to take advantage of the most beneficial tax rules.

> ► **The amount of tips that are placed on customer credit cards is totaled for each server by the POS system at the end of each day.** At the end of each shift servers should enter the total amount of their cash tips prior to entering the time that they will end their shift.

Tip Credit

Many states have mandated the legal authority to apply what is known as a tip credit.

> Section 3(m) of the FLSA [Federal Labor Standards Act] permits an employer to take a tip credit toward its minimum wage obligation for tipped employees equal to the difference between the required cash wage (which must be at least $2.13) and the federal minimum wage. Thus, the maximum tip credit that an employer can currently claim under the FLSA is $5.12 per hour (the minimum wage of $7.25 minus the minimum required cash wage of $2.13). (http://www.dol.gov/whd/regs/compliance/whdfs15.pdf)

New Jersey is an example of a state where the minimum required cash wage is $2.13 per hour.

> ► **The allowable federal minimum wage for employees who receive tips is $2.13 per hour in direct wages.** As stated above, the Fair Labor Standards Act requires payment of at least the federal minimum wage to covered, nonexempt employees.

> NOTE: If $2.13 plus tips received equals at least the federal minimum wage, the employee retains all the tips. If an employee's tips combined with the employer's direct wage of $2.13 an hour do not equal the federal minimum hourly wage, the employer must make up the difference.

Federal ($7.25) 2020 Minimum Wage for Tipped Employees

Basic combined cash and tip minimum wage per hour	Maximum tip credit against minimum wage per hour	Minimum cash wage per hour
$7.25	$5.12	$2.13

▶ **The formulas for applying a tip credit vary from state to state.** Some states do not allow a tip credit to be applied, and they may have a minimum wage that is higher than the 2020 federal minimum wage of $7.25.

Examples: California: $13.00, Oregon: $11.25, and Washington: $13.50. Twenty-nine states and Washington, DC have a minimum wage higher than the federal minimum wage.

NOTE: To see how other states do or do not apply tip credits, refer to: www.dol.gov/whd/state/tipped.htm.

Minimum Wage

All employers must comply with federal and state laws regulating the payment of minimum wage, overtime, and general working conditions. State laws supersede federal laws if they are more rigorous, noting that some states have a minimum wage that is higher than the federal minimum wage.

The foodservice industry has many jobs that fall into the minimum wage category, such as dishwashers, servers' assistants (bussers), and servers. The majority of foodservice operations pay the minimum wage to people employed in these jobs.

Many successful operators choose to pay above minimum wage rates and in so doing expect and achieve higher performance and productivity levels from employees. By having good hiring practices, ongoing training, minimizing employee turnover, and regularly monitoring performance and productivity standards, operators are able to remain competitive and profitable.

Tabletop Tablets and Apps

When current technology is brought into a restaurant operation the service speed will increase, kitchen mistakes will decrease, and guest check averages will often be higher.

> **LEARNING OBJECTIVE 9**
> Recognize the speed, accuracy, and efficiency that is achieved with Tabletop Tablets.

▶ **Tabletop tablets** allow customers to read through the menu; order food items, drinks, and desserts; and pay their guest checks—all without the help of a server. Tabletop tablets are being used in fast casual restaurants and are starting to be used in certain casual-dining table service restaurants.

▶ **Software apps** have the capability of asking different questions to customers based on the menu items the customers have ordered—further reducing the possibility of ordering errors or kitchen mistakes.

Example: When an order is transmitted to a color-coded screen in the kitchen with a red stripe over an ingredient, it means "leave it off"; a green stripe indicates an addition; and other colors will signify different options. A tabletop tablet company with various software apps is Ziosk Restaurant Tablets (www.ziosk.com).

▶ **Computerized ovens** that use conveyor belts, infrared technology, and hot air can quickly cook certain food items—which can move orders through the cooking process at a faster pace.

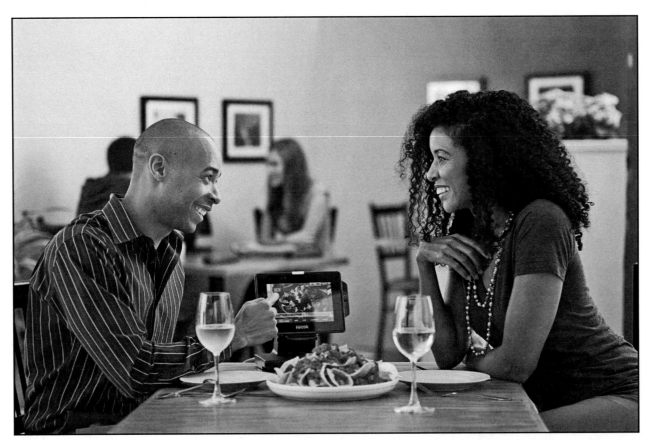

Tabletop tablets or screens allow customers to send their food and beverage orders directly to the kitchen to speed up service. Courtesy of Ziosk, LLC. (Photograph by Andy Post.)

Assignment 14

Calculate the Sales per Hour and Average Customer Sale for the following Server Productivity Report, and review and comment on the sales percentage goals in Column H.

Server Productivity Report

Dining Room Hours: 11:00 A.M.–2:00 P.M.
5:00 P.M.–10:00 P.M.

Day: Saturday

Date: January 16, 20xx

Calculations				D ÷ C = E		D ÷ F = G			
A	B	C	D	E	F	G	H		
							[Sales Percentages]		
Server Name	Station Number	Number of Hours Worked	Total Sales	Sales per Hour	Total Number of Customers	Average Customer Sale	Salads 10%	Soups 25%	Espresso Drinks 25%
Lunch: 11:00 A.M.–2:00 P.M.									
Lucy	1	3	$1,426.70	$	86	$	[9] **10**	[22] **26**	[22] **22**
Mary	2	3	1,468.50		88		[9] **8**	[22] **27**	[22] **26**
Jack	3	3	1,384.65		82		[8] **11**	[21] **21**	[21] **25**

							[Sales Percentages]		
							Appetizers 25%	Desserts 50%	Wines 25%
Dinner: 5:00 P.M.–10:00 P.M.									
Jack	1	5	$2,705.55	$	92	$	[23] **28**	[46] **60**	[23] **32**
Nick	2	5	2,690.45		90		[23] **34**	[45] **65**	[23] **37**
Pam	3	5	2,376.30		78		[20] **27**	[39] **50**	[20] **31**
Joan	4	5	2,405.85		77		[19] **26**	[39] **54**	[19] **25**

Comments on Sales Percentage Goals in Column H:

_____

_____

_____

_____

_____

_____

_____

_____

_____

_____

_____

_____

_____

Summary

The foodservice organizations that are able to create and maintain high productivity are consistent in hiring qualified people, maintaining ongoing training, and monitoring performance and productivity standards. It begins with well-defined job descriptions for each position that specifically identify the qualifications, responsibilities, and functions required for the job position.

Successful managers maintain a positive work environment that promotes job satisfaction by recognizing and rewarding people for quality work performed. This includes evaluating performance and productivity standards based on efficiency, quantity, and quality of work along with the responsibility for performing the work.

Productivity is a term used to describe how well hourly employees perform their work, which can be defined by two measures: High Productivity—meeting or exceeding performance and productivity standards established by management, or Low Productivity—not performing at established performance and productivity standards.

Measuring kitchen staff performance and productivity can be accomplished by using a Kitchen Productivity Report. Measuring server performance and productivity can be done for individual servers or for all of the servers together using a Server Productivity Report.

All tips received by servers are required by law to be reported to the federal government as income received which is the responsibility of management. Tip Credit is applicable in many states, which allows tips to be applied toward meeting the federal minimum hourly wage.

Tabletop tablets and apps can increase the service speed, increase sales, and reduce the potential for ordering and kitchen errors.

Discussion Questions

1. What are the three key factors in creating and maintaining high productivity in any type of foodservice operation?
2. A well-defined job description should be prepared for each position within the foodservice operation and specifically describe what three points?
3. What are the effects of ongoing training?
4. Discuss the value of cross-training in the typical foodservice operation.
5. Explain the four factors that are considered integral to performance and productivity standards.
6. Contrast high productivity with low productivity.
7. When reviewing a Kitchen Productivity Report, how is *efficiency* measured? How is *quantity* and *quality* tracked?
8. Why is it import for management to review the Server Productivity Report and to establish sales goal percentages for certain food and beverage items?
9. Explain the process for reporting server tip income.
10. Describe how Tip Credit is applied in the states where it is authorized.
11. Explain the function of Tabletop Tablets and Apps in achieving speed, accuracy, and efficiency for customer ordering.

Project Exercises

1. Research the formula rule for applying a tip credit (if applicable) in the state that you are currently living in along with the formula rules for two neighboring states. Write a report detailing how each state law governs tip credit and identify the state minimum wage.
Visit: www.dol.gov/whd/state/tipped.htm

2. Visit a casual dining table service restaurant that is using tabletop tablets and document your experience in a one-page written report. Attention should be given to ease of reading and searching the menu, and ordering food items that may include special requests, such as salad dressing on the side or medium rare roast beef. Also note the manner in which the server brought the food and beverage to your table and interacted with you—the follow-up for beverage refills, water, condiments needed, etc. And, if you were inclined to leave a server tip.

Beverage Cost Control

Alcohol and espresso drinks are primary beverage categories within the foodservice industry and represent a significant amount of sales for foodservice operators. To maximize the strong profit potential from the sale of these beverages, cost control procedures must be recognized, described, and effectively implemented.

A POS system with reporting features is essential for management to have the necessary decision-making information to control beverage costs. These features can record each sale when it happens; maintain a sales history with reports by beverage category for each hour, day, week, month and year to date; facilitate inventory control reporting, such as with bar-code scanners for taking inventory and reordering; and read customer credit cards and print customer receipts.

Contributing Author

KAREN GOODLAD Associate Professor, New York City College of Technology, CUNY is a Certified Specialist of Wine with the Society of Wine Educators and is an active member of Les Dames d'Escoffier International, New York Chapter. She was among hospitality educators recognized by *Total Food Service* and named in the Top Woman in Metro New York Foodservice & Hospitality 2019 and 2020. Professor Goodlad is the lead coauthor of "Place-Based Learning across Disciplines: A Living Laboratory Approach to Pedagogy," *InSight: A Journal of Scholarly Teaching*, vol. 66 no. 3 (2018), and "Comparing Faculty and Student Perception of Academic Performance, Classroom Behavior, and Social Interactions in Learning Communities," *College Teaching*, vol. 13 (2018). Her professional experience in food and beverage management is leveraged in the classroom, where she teaches beverage management courses and is the faculty advisor to students participating in the Walt Disney World College Program.

Alcohol Beverage Control

The cycle of Alcohol Beverage tracking for a food and beverage operation begins when the orders are placed with the distributors and follows a path to when the bar requisitions are fulfilled and the empty bottles returned (exchanged for full bottles).

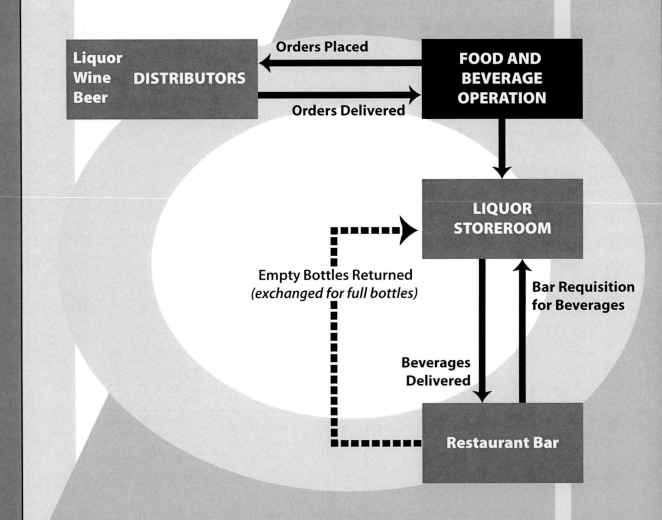

10

Alcohol Beverage Service

Introduction

Alcohol beverage management principles will be presented with a concentration on the terminology and operating procedures that are required for controlling pour (drink) costs. The task of management is to ensure that the procedures are in place and responsible beverage service is provided to customers.

Learning Objectives

Upon successfully completing this chapter, readers will be able to:

1. Discuss an Alcohol Beverage Menu.

2. Explain the different places in a foodservice operation where Alcohol Beverage Service can take place.

3. Understand the function of a Standardized Drink Recipe.

4. Describe Pour Methods that ensure drink ingredients are dispensed properly.

5. Recognize commonly serviced alcohol beverages and the methods in which they are served.

6. Explain the differences between *well liquor* and *call brands*.

7. Understand how to determine Liquor Portion Cost.

8. Calculate the cost of an alcohol beverage using a Drink Cost Card.

9. Discuss the common percentages of loss associated with alcohol beverage service.

10. Understand Liquor Sales and Liability.

11. Describe Responsible Beverage Service.

Chapter Outline

Key Terms and Definitions

Begin by first reading the key terms and their definitions. An advance understanding of the terms will be helpful prior to reading the chapter.

Alcohol Beverage Menu	Consists of the following categories: wine list, alcohol-based drinks, bottled beer, ale, draft beer, and non-alcohol drinks.
Alcohol Server Training	Everyone involved with the preparation and service of alcohol beverages should take the training program before beginning to work in a beverage operation.
Aperitifs, liqueurs, cordials	Types of liquors, served from the bottle or used in recipes of multiple alcohol beverages.
Automated Control System	A fully integrated system that allows for separate pumps to be attached to each 1.75 L bottle of liquor for dispensing.
Bottle Control System	A device used to control the amount of beverage poured from a bottle.
Call Brand	Higher quality, more expensive premium liquors that customers order by name.
Cocktails	A combination of two or more alcohol beverages, sometimes referred to as a blended drink.
Dram Shop Liability	A body of law that governs the liability of establishments that sell alcohol beverages to visibly intoxicated persons or minors.
Evaporation and Spillage	Liquors: 5%, Wine: 5%, Draft Beer: 8 to 20%.
Free Pouring	When a bartender pours the alcohol beverage straight from the bottle, estimating how much liquid has left the bottle.
Front Bar	Located in a public area of the restaurant, in full view of the dining room area.
Incident Report	Possibly the best defense, as part of a third-party liability claim, if ever sued, is to record incidents that occurred in serving or denying service to customers.
Jigger	A stainless steel measuring device in an hourglass shape, typically, one side measurese 1.5 ounces and the other 1 ounce.

Lounge	Part of the foodservice operation and is located in a separate room that is expressly designed for serving alcohol beverages.
Measured Pouring	The bartender pours the alcohol beverage into the shot glass or jigger and then pours the alcohol into the serving glass.
Minimum Menu Price	The lowest menu drink price or minimum selling price for the beverage item, determined by dividing the portion cost by the beverage portion cost %.
Mixed Drink	A combination of an alcohol beverage and water or some other non-alcohol ingredient, such as club soda, ginger ale, and so on.
Neat Drink	An alcohol beverage poured from the bottle into a glass and consumed—no ice, water, or anything added.
Overpouring	Cheats the beverage operation by pouring too much alcohol into a glass.
Pour Gun	A hand-held device used by the bartender to control pouring.
Prudent Person Rule	A prudent or responsible person would not serve alcohol to someone who is intoxicated.
Reconciling Sales	The manager compares what the POS system indicates was sold to what the inventory indicates was sold.
Rocks Drink	An alcohol beverage poured from the bottle into an ice-filled glass.
Service Bar	Often in or next to the kitchen, it is used by servers to pick up beverages to go with meals.
Shot Glass	The bartender pours to the line in the glass that represents a certain amount of liquor, and then pours the liquor from that glass into the serving glass.
Special Function Bar	A portable bar used for private parties, catered events, and group functions.
Standardized Drink Recipes	Must be established and uniformly followed to maintain a consistent beverage presentation.
Underpouring	Cheats the customer by pouring less than the standard amount of alcohol into a glass.
Well	A stainless steel shelf with a short front edge that keeps bottles aligned for immediate use, easily accessed from behind the bar at about the height of the bartender's knees. Often called "The Speed Rack."
Well Liquor	The most used liquor in any given bar may also be referred to as "house brand" or "pouring brand" liquors.

Alcohol Beverage Service Overview

▶ **An alcohol beverage menu is the first step in the cost control process.** Each operation must determine its own menu based on research and customer preferences. The menu categories consist of the following:

▷ Wine list (by the glass and bottle)

▷ Alcohol-based drinks (traditional and specialty)

▷ Bottled beer, ale, and tap (draft beer) selections

▷ Non-alcohol drinks

▶ **Standard recipes for each drink must be established and uniformly followed in the same manner in which food recipes are followed.** Once the alcohol beverage menu is developed, proper "drink" recipes must be followed to maintain a consistent beverage presentation. If the beverage operation does not have standardized recipes, bartenders will prepare drinks according to their own preferences or the way they were previously trained.

▶ **The objective of management is to promote responsible alcohol beverage service.** Increasingly, law enforcement agencies are holding alcohol beverage operations responsible for ensuring that the customer does not drink too much. The financial consequences of serving too much to a customer may be devastating to the operation, server, and customer.

▶ **Alcohol beverage service can take place in four different places (or settings) in a foodservice operation**, and are as follows:

1. **Front Bar:** located in a public area of the restaurant, in full view of the dining room area.

2. **Service Bar:** often in or next to the kitchen. It is used by servers to pick up beverages served at guest tables. It may also be accessed by the front bar.

3. **Special Function Bar:** portable and used for special events, private parties, catered events, and group functions.

4. **Lounge or Bar:** located in a separate room that is expressly designed for serving alcohol beverages. It may also serve as a service bar for a nearby dining room.

Alcohol Beverage Portion Control

▶ **Controlling the alcohol served is accomplished by consistently pouring the correct amount of alcohol into a glass.** Bartenders who believe they should be able to customize drinks according to customer taste are not consistently pouring the same amount of alcohol beverage for the same type of drink. When bartenders do this, it becomes difficult to price drinks and control use.

The primary way of controlling pour costs *(the cost of individual drink servings)* is to ensure that the bartender is using standardized recipes.

Standardized Drink Recipe

Drink Name: Bloody Mary

File Code: Cocktail - 1

Yield: 1 serving

Glassware: 10-ounce glass, highball glass

Equipment:	jigger	shaker
	ice scoop	

Ingredients	Measure
Vodka (well)	1.5 ounces
Tomato juice	3 ounces
Celery salt	1 dash
Ground black pepper	1 dash
Tabasco sauce	1 dash
Worcestershire sauce	3 dashes
Horseradish	⅛ teaspoon
Lemon juice	1 dash
Ice (small cube)	½ glass
Celery stalk (trimmed)	1 stalk
Lemon	⅛ wedge

Method of Preparation:

1. Fill half of glass with small cube ice.
2. Pour vodka and tomato juice into shaker.
3. Add celery salt, ground black pepper, Tabasco sauce, Worcestershire sauce, horseradish, and lemon juice.
4. Shake four times and pour into serving glass.

Service Instruction:

1. Put trimmed celery stalk into serving glass.
2. Lemon wedge placed on the rim of the glass and served at the 2 o'clock position relative to the customer.
3. Serve drink on a cocktail napkin.

Figure 10.1 Standardized Drink Recipe

As with food items, every drink sold should have a standardized recipe that identifies the following, as shown in Figure 10.1:

▷ Drink Name

▷ Recipe File (code that aligns with the POS system)

▷ Yield (standard portion size)

▷ Glassware

▷ Equipment

▷ Ingredients and Quantity

▷ Method of Preparation

▷ Service Instruction

LEARNING OBJECTIVE 3
Understand the function of a Standardized Drink Recipe.

▶ **Wine and tap (draft beer) products also have standard portion sizes and glassware.** A recipe for these types of drinks is still required, because it identifies the portion size necessary to determine the cost of one serving and, subsequently, the menu price. Some typical examples are the following:

▷ **Draft Beer:** served in a 12-ounce tapered cone pilsner glass with a 1-inch foam head.

▷ **Red Wine:** 5 ounces served by the glass in a 12-ounce rounded stemmed glass. (See Figure 10.3, Common Glassware Shapes and Sizes, on p. 194.)

▶ **Pour Methods:** After the recipes have been determined, one of the following six pour methods should be used to ensure drink ingredients are dispensed properly:

1. **Free Pouring:** when a bartender pours the alcohol beverage straight from the bottle, estimating how much liquid has left the bottle. A professionally experienced bartender will pour with a high degree of accuracy, on average.

A significant margin of error exists with the free pouring system as bartenders will overpour or underpour drinks, which creates a control issue.

> **LEARNING OBJECTIVE 4**
> Describe Pour Methods that ensure drink ingredients are dispensed properly.

▷ **Overpouring** cheats the beverage operation.

▷ **Underpouring** cheats the customer.

NOTE: As a general rule, **free pouring** will result in 3 to 4 drinks out of 100 being spilled by the bartender. A **wireless spout cap** can be used to measure the amount of the free pour and will transmit that information to a POS system. The wireless spout does not control the portion size.

2. **Measured Pouring:** when the bartender uses a marked measuring glass, called a **shot glass,** or a stainless steel measuring cone, called a **jigger.** The bartender pours the alcohol beverage into the shot glass or jigger and then pours the alcohol into the serving glass.

> Historically, the free pour method is preferred by both the bartender and the customer. Some customers believe they actually get more alcohol beverage when a free pour is used, as the bartender displays the personal touch of pouring and mixing the drink.

▷ The **shot glass** is marked with a line so the bartender pours to the line that represents a certain amount of liquor. Typical amounts are ⅞ ounce, 1 ounce, 1⅛ ounce, 1¼ ounce, and 1½ ounce.

▷ The **jigger** has two opposing cones in an hourglass shape. Typically, one cone measures 1 ounce and the opposite cone measures 1½ ounce, although cones are available in sizes ranging from ¾ ounce to 2 ounces.

3. **Bottle Control System:** when devices are used to control the amount of beverage poured from a bottle.

▷ A special type of **pouring cap** is placed in the bottle top. This cap releases a set measurement when poured, reducing the possibility of overpouring or underpouring. Use of the pouring cap has the feel of free pouring, although the pour is controlled.

▷ Management may choose to use a **collar ring** to control the portion size and instantly record the amount sold to a POS system. The collar ring, with a retractable cord is attached to a POS terminal, and when placed over the pourer cap releases a preset amount of liquor for pouring.

Collar Ring
Pouring Technology

An example of a collar ring is the Berg All-Bottle Brand ID ring pouring top liquor control with radio frequency microchip technology that enables tracking of the specific brand, portion size, and price for every pour.

Pourers inserted into the liquor bottles are secured with a tamper-evident security seal and placed at the bar ready for pouring.

LaserTouch Pour Gun

An example of an advanced pour gun is the Berg Laser Touch, which can dispense beverage and liquor with touch screen and cocktail ability. A total of 16 brands of liquor can be dispensed individually or up to 48 cocktail mixes with five brands of liquor dispensed at the same time.

A microchip embedded in each pourer is assigned to each liquor bottle's specific brand at the control station. The activator ring (collar ring) controls and records every pour, which will not dispense unless engaged with the activator ring. This ensures that each drink is dispensed accurately and recorded.

To pour a drink, the bartender simply brings the selected bottle up to the activator ring and pours the drink with a conventional pouring motion. The activator ring controls and records the pour. The brand is displayed on the liquor control unit's screen for quick, easy confirmation and the drink selling price is sent to the POS terminal.

Figure 10.2   Collar Ring and LaserTouch Pour Gun. Courtesy of Berg Company LLC.

▷ A **liquor clicker** may also be used, which is a pouring cap that controls the amount of each pour, as set by management, and records the number of pours on an "odometer style" counter.

4. **Pour Gun:** hand-held device used by the bartender to control pouring alcohol drinks.

   The pour gun has a series of buttons on the back handle; each button indicates the type of alcohol beverage to be dispensed.

   Example: If the bartender presses the appropriate button for gin, a prescribed amount of gin comes out. A pour gun can also be used to dispense house brand wine.

   The **non-alcohol pour gun** is typically used for club soda, seltzer, tonic, ginger ale, and cola. The bartender estimates the amount actually poured.

Shot Glass
1- to 2-ounce capacity
Lined or unlined

Old-Fashioned
6 to 9 ounces, average 8 ounces
Used for "on the rocks"

Roly Poly
5 to 15 ounces
Used for "on the rocks"
Adaptable for many drinks

Standard Highball or Tumbler
8- to 12-ounce capacity
Straight-sided shell or sham

Cooler
Tall slim glass of varied capacity for
summer beverages
14- to 16-ounce capacity is popular
Often frosted

Stemmed Cocktail Glass
3- to 4-ounce capacity
Martini, manhattan, etc.

Margarita
8- to 12-ounce capacity

Alternative Cocktail Glass
4½- to 7½-ounce capacity

Whiskey Sour
3½- to 4½-ounce capacity

Cordial
1-ounce capacity is normal
Sometimes called a Pony

Tulip Champagne
6- to 8-ounce capacity
Sometimes hollow stemmed

All-Purpose Wine
4- to 8-ounce capacity
Stemmed glass

Standard White Wine
8- to 12-ounce capacity
Stemmed glass

Standard Red Wine
8- to 22-ounce capacity
Stemmed glass

Sherry
2-ounce capacity is normal

Brandy Snifter
6- to 12-ounce capacity
Designed to enhance aroma

Tapered Cone Pilsner
8- to 12-ounce capacity

Sham Pilsner
8- to 12-ounce capacity

Stem Pilsner
8- to 12-ounce capacity
10-ounce size is most popular

Goblet
6- to 10-ounce capacity

Stein or Beer Mug
8- to 12-ounce capacity

Figure 10.3 Common Glassware Shapes and Sizes

194

5. **Automated Control System:** when a fully integrated method is used that allows for separate pumps to be attached to each 1.75 L bottle of liquor in a nearby storage area or dispensing room. The system allows drinks to be poured simultaneously and has the capability to mix drinks and make cocktails.

> NOTE: The disadvantage to the automated control system is that atmosphere and personal service, which are pleasing to customers, may be difficult to create.

> ▷ An **automated draft beer control system** measures the amount of beer poured and can function continuously—when an empty keg shuts off and a full keg is automatically connected for uninterrupted service.

> ▷ A **turbo tap** is a draft beer dispensing device that can be attached to an existing draft beer tap to increase the speed of beer flow from the tap to the glass or pitcher; it allows for faster pours with minimized waste.

6. **Specific Size Serving Glass:** The size of the serving glass is another method by which the portion size of an alcohol beverage can be controlled. Most alcohol drinks are served in specific, standard glassware. The standardized recipe specifies the type of glass used. Figure 10.3 shows examples of glassware commonly used to serve alcohol beverages.

Alcohol Beverages and Service Methods

The following is a list of alcohol drinks by type, description, and service method:

▶ Beer is available in a range of styles including ales and lagers as well as tap (draft beer). Beer is served by the bottle, and tap (draft beer) by the glass or pitcher.

▶ Wine is served by the glass, carafe, or bottle.

▶ Liquors are available in a wide range of products and quality levels. The most basic quality level would be considered a well liquor or house brand. The higher quality levels are considered a call brand and are often more expensive then the "well" brand.

Liquor can be used and served in the following ways:

▶ **Aperitifs, liqueurs,** and **cordials** are types of liquors, served from the bottle or used in recipes of multiple alcohol beverages.

▶ **Cocktails** use a combination of two or more alcohol beverages, sometimes referred to as a blended drink.

▶ **Mixed drinks** use a combination of an alcohol beverage and water or some other non-alcohol ingredient, such as club soda, ginger ale, etc.

▶ **Neat drinks** are alcohol beverages poured from the bottle into a glass and consumed—no ice, water, or anything added.

▶ **Rocks drinks** are alcohol beverages poured from the bottle into an ice-filled glass.

> **LEARNING OBJECTIVE 5**
> Recognize commonly serviced alcohol beverages and the methods in which they are served.

> **LEARNING OBJECTIVE 6**
> Explain the differences between *well liquor* and *call brands.*

Pour Cost (Drink Cost)

Each drink must have a standard portion cost. This is commonly referred to as the **pour cost.** It is the total cost of all ingredients used in a drink as served to the customer. Pour costs are calculated the same way as food costs.

To determine the Liquor Portion Cost do the following:

STEP 1   Divide the Purchasing Cost (bottle cost) by the Bottle Yield (number of ounces in the bottle) to identify the Unit Price (cost per ounce).

$$\text{Purchasing Cost} \div \text{Bottle Yield} = \textbf{Unit Price}$$

STEP 2   Multiply the Liquor Quantity Serving Size (in ounces, taken from the Drink Recipe) by the Unit Price (cost per ounce from Step 1) to determine the Liquor Portion Cost.

$$\begin{array}{c}\text{Liquor} \\ \text{Quantity} \\ \text{Serving Size}\end{array} \times \begin{array}{c}\text{Unit} \\ \text{Price}\end{array} = \begin{array}{c}\textbf{Extended Cost} \\ \textbf{(Liquor} \\ \textbf{Portion Cost)}\end{array}$$

Drink Costing Using a Drink Cost Card

A **Drink Cost Card** is used to determine the pour cost for each type of drink. Figure 10.4 on the following page shows an example of a Drink Cost Card for a Bloody Mary. The procedure for costing alcohol beverages is exactly the same as costing for food recipes. The Quantity (Column B) is multiplied by the Unit Price (Column C) to determine the Extension (Column D). In the case of beverage costing, however:

▶ Recipes are typically for one serving.

▶ The average serving will hold from ⅞ ounce to 1½ ounces of liquor.

▶ The unit price is typically measured in cost per ounce.

▶ The measurement for bottle sizes will be in the metric system, but almost every American bar and recipe book gives measurements for individual drinks in ounces.

    1.75 Liter = 59.2 ounces

    1.0 Liter = 33.8 ounces

    750 mL = 25.4 ounces

The brand of vodka (well) used in the Bloody Mary recipe (refer to Figure 10.4) is Smirnoff, purchased in 1.75 L bottles (59.2 ounces per bottle). If the cost of one bottle is $23.70 (Purchasing Cost), use the formula introduced above in Step 1:

$$\begin{array}{c}\text{Unit} \\ \text{Purchasing Cost}\end{array} \div \text{Yield} = \begin{array}{c}\textbf{Unit} \\ \textbf{Price}\end{array}$$

$$\$23.70 \div 59.2 \text{ ounces} = \textbf{\$0.40} \text{ per ounce}$$

Drink Cost Card

Drink Name: Bloody Mary   **File Code:** Cocktail - 1

Glassware: 10-ounce glass; highball glass

Minimum Menu Price: $6.05

Portion Cost: $1.21

Calculations

$B \times C = D$

A	B	C	D
Ingredients	**Quantity**	**Unit Price**	**Extension**
Vodka (well)	1.500 ounces	$0.40 per ounce	$0.60
Evaporation loss	5.00% alcohol	$0.60 per drink	$0.03
Tomato juice	3.000 ounces	$0.07 per ounce	$0.21
Celery salt	1.000 dash	$0.01 per dash	$0.01
Ground black pepper	1.000 dash	$0.01 per dash	$0.01
Tabasco sauce	1.000 dash	$0.02 per dash	$0.02
Worcestershire sauce	3.000 dashes	$0.02 per dash	$0.06
Horseradish	0.125 teaspoon	$0.08 per teaspoon	$0.01
Lemon juice	1.000 dash	$0.01 per dash	$0.01
Celery stalk (trimmed)	1.000 stalk	$0.18 per celery stalk	$0.18
Lemon	0.125 lemon wedge	$0.56 per lemon	$0.07
Ice (small cube)	1/2 glass	$0.00	$0.00

Total Portion Cost:			**$1.21**

Portion Cost ÷ Beverage Cost Percentage (20%) = Minimum Menu Price

$1.21   ÷   0.20   = $6.05

Figure 10.4   Drink Cost Card

Next, to determine the extended cost for the Liquor Portion Cost, calculate using the second step in the formula above.

$$\frac{\text{Liquor Quantity}}{\text{Serving Size}} \times \frac{\text{Unit}}{\text{Price}} = \frac{\textbf{Extended Cost}}{\textbf{(Liquor Portion Cost)}}$$

1.5 ounces   × $0.40 per ounce =   **$0.60**

NOTE: Well liquor is the **house brand liquor** used by bartenders to mix drinks whenever a customer does not specify a higher-price brand name. Management identifies certain brands for the operation's "well liquor." The bottles of liquor (750 mL or 1 Liter size) are located in an easy access "well" at about the height of the bartender's knees, which positions the bottles for immediate use. The "well" is a stainless steel shelf with a short front edge that keeps the bottles in place. The well is also often called "the speed rack." Well vodka and gin are often dispensed through a pour gun connected to 1.75 L bottles.

Higher-price brand-name liquors ordered by customers, referred to as **call brand liquors**, command a higher drink price because they are more expensive to purchase than well liquors.

Tomato juice is usually purchased in #3 tall cans at about $3.22 per can (Unit Purchasing Cost). There are approximately 46 servable ounces in one can. The cost for one ounce is determined using the same process previously illustrated for vodka:

$$\begin{array}{ccccc} \text{Unit} & & & & \textbf{Unit Price} \\ \text{Purchasing Cost} & \div & \text{Yield} & = & \textbf{(Cost per Ounce)} \\ \$3.22 & \div & 46 \text{ ounces} & = & \textbf{\$0.07} \text{ per ounce} \end{array}$$

Three ounces of tomato juice are needed for the drink, so the final extension is determined by multiplying:

$$\begin{array}{ccccc} \text{Quantity Serving Size} & \times & \text{Unit Price} & = & \textbf{Extended Cost} \\ 3 \text{ ounces} & \times & \$0.07 \text{ per ounce} & = & \textbf{\$0.21} \end{array}$$

▶ **The concepts of evaporation and spillage are unique to beverage costing.** The following are common percentages of loss for different alcohol beverages:

LEARNING OBJECTIVE 9
Discuss the common percentages of loss associated with alcohol beverage service.

  ▷ Liquors: 5%

  ▷ Wine: 5%

  ▷ Tap (draft beer) products: 8 to 20%

Since keg beer is delivered sealed, loss of the product is more often than not from overpouring and spillage, rather than from evaporation. Experience has shown that about 8 to 20% of tap (draft beer) products are lost. Each beverage operation should calculate its actual loss.

Figure 10.4 shows the evaporation loss amount as a separate line item after the cost of the vodka. The evaporation loss is calculated as follows:

$$\begin{array}{ccccc} \text{Liquor Portion Cost} & \times & \text{Evaporation Loss (5\%)} & = & \textbf{Extended Cost} \\ \$0.60 & \times & 0.05 & = & \textbf{\$0.03} \end{array}$$

▶ **To calculate the cost of the remaining ingredients the process is the same as that used for costing food recipes.** When the cost for certain ingredients is difficult to calculate—such as celery salt, ground black pepper, Tabasco sauce, Worcestershire sauce, horseradish, lemon juice and ice—an adequate cost estimate should be made to cover the amount of the ingredient.

▶ **The most common method of computing the minimum menu (selling) price is shown in Figure 10.4** (see page 197).

The minimum menu price would be the lowest menu price for the drink and the starting point from which the actual drink menu price is determined by management.

> NOTE: The **Beverage Cost Percentage** is set by management at 20%. Review Alcohol Beverage Cost and Cost Percentage, Chapter 11, p. 217.

The same guidelines are used in setting alcohol beverage menu pricing as used for food menu pricing, which include:

1. **Type of Operation:** upscale associated with fine dining, mid-level range, or theme type such as a sports bar.

2. **Location:** in a neighborhood, on a busy street, in a mall, on a highway, etc. A premium location—resort, sporting event, airport, or ocean view—can justify higher prices versus a neighborhood restaurant or tavern.

3. **Market Conditions:** the number and type of competing places that sell the same or similar drinks.

4. **Entertainment Provided:** piano player (possibly a piano bar) or a professional recording artist or small band.

Complete Assignment 15 on p. 201.

Liquor Sales and Liability

A well-managed beverage operation effectively controls the cost of liability insurance associated with serving alcohol beverages. Management will implement procedures and training that will reduce the possibility of lawsuits against the beverage operation and its employees.

A serious responsibility comes with the privilege of having a liquor license issued by a State Liquor Control agency that authorizes a business to sell alcohol beverages within strict governing laws. Therefore, it is in every operator's best interest to be vigilant in protecting that license. Stringent standard operating procedures are necessary to prevent the loss of the license and to protect against lawsuits that could financially devastate the business.

> ► **Dram Shop liability** refers to a body of law that governs the liability of bars, taverns, restaurants, and other establishments that sell alcohol beverages to minors or to visibly intoxicated persons who may cause death or injury to third parties (persons not having a relationship to the bar) as a result of alcohol–related car or other type accidents.
>
> **Dram shop** is a legal term referring to a bar or establishment where alcohol beverages are sold. The name, "dram shop" originated with reference to a shop where spirits were sold by the dram, a small unit of liquid.

> ► Legally, those who serve alcohol beverages are increasingly being held to the **prudent person rule**, which specifically asks, "What would a prudent person do in this or a similar situation?" The basic answer to the question is that a prudent or responsible person would not serve alcohol to someone who is intoxicated. Nor would a prudent person allow someone who is visibly intoxicated to drive a vehicle anywhere.

> ► **Those who serve alcohol beverages are liable for serving people who are considered legally drunk.** Therefore, the beverage operation must take every means possible to safeguard against potential Third-Party Liability lawsuits.

LEARNING OBJECTIVE 10
Understand Liquor Sales and Liability.

Responsible Beverage Service

Management proves that it is a responsible provider of alcohol beverages in several of the following ways:

1. **Set and enforce a house policy that specifically states the house (alcohol beverage operations) rules concerning visibly intoxicated persons.** Management writes the house policy indicating how employees are to behave in given situations of alcohol beverage service. The house policy would be posted in a conspicuous place in order to allow access for everyone to read the policy.

LEARNING OBJECTIVE 11
Describe Responsible Beverage Service.

Information about Responsible Beverage Service Certification can be found on the National Restaurant Association website: www.nraef.org/servsafe

Possibly the best defense, as part of a third-party liability claim, if ever sued, is to complete an Incident Report.

2. **Support an alcohol beverage server training program for beverage managers and all servers.** A certified alcohol server training program (ServSafe) is available from the National Restaurant Association Educational Foundation. Other alcohol server training programs may be available in various states. Rules governing alcohol beverage service are set forth by individual State Liquor Control agencies. Everyone involved with the preparation and service of alcohol beverages should go through an alcohol server training program before beginning to work in a beverage operation.

3. **Review reports from POS systems, which may provide information regarding the number of items sold, as well as specific quantities, dates, and times sold.** This keeps management informed of any irregularities or out-of-the-ordinary occurrences that might give cause for concern and might result in additional or renewed alcohol server training.

4. **Complete an Incident Report for any problem occurring with a customer.** This is a form used to record incidents that occurred in serving or denying service to customers.

   The Incident Report is used to record a description of any episodes that occur and is signed by the person reporting the incident, employee(s) involved, the manager, and any witnesses. The report effectively documents irresponsible behavior and helps an establishment avoid a lawsuit. Figure 10.5 below is an example of an Incident Report.

   Many liability cases that go to court end up with witnesses providing conflicting testimony. Often, the case comes down to just one person's word against another. A written record clearly documents and dates what took place and can be submitted in a court of law. An Incident Report can provide that written report.

Figure 10.5   Incident Report

Assignment 15

Complete the following Drink Cost Card.

The well gin—Gordon's brand, used in the Tom Collins—is purchased in 1.75 L bottles at a cost of $22.50 per bottle.

Drink Cost Card

Drink Name: Tom Collins	**File Code:** Cocktail - 2

Glassware: 10-ounce glass; highball glass

Minimum Menu Price:
Portion Cost:

Calculations   B × C = D

A	B	C		D
Ingredients	**Quantity**	**Unit Price**		**Extension**
Gin (well)	1.500 ounces		per ounce	
Evaporation loss	5.00% alcohol		per drink	
Lemon juice	0.750 ounces	$0.07	per ounce	
Simple syrup	0.250 ounces	$0.06	per ounce	
Club soda	2.000 ounces	$0.04	per ounce	
Lemon	0.125 lemon slice	$0.56	per lemon	
Ice (small cube)	3/4 glass	$0.00		

Total Portion Cost:

Portion Cost ÷ Beverage Cost Percentage (20%) = Minimum Menu Price

÷   0.20   =

Summary

An alcohol beverage menu is the first step in the cost control process. The menu may offer wine by the glass and bottle, traditional and specialty alcohol-based drinks, bottled beer, ale and tap (draft beer) selections, and non-alcohol drinks. Alcohol service can take place in four different places: Front Bar, Service Bar, Special Function Bar, and Lounge or Bar.

Alcohol beverage pour costs are controlled by ensuring that the bartender is following a Standardized Drink Recipe for every drink; then ensuring that drink ingredients are dispensed properly by following a specific pour method. Furthermore, the alcohol beverage categories of beer, wine, and liquors have individual serving methods in place.

Each drink must have a standard portion cost which is the total cost of all ingredients used in a drink as served to a customer. This is accomplished by using a Drink Cost Card which also accounts for the common evaporation and spillage loss percentage.

A serious responsibility comes with the privilege of having a liquor license issued by a State Liquor Control agency. Therefore, management must at all times be a responsible provider of alcohol beverages. This begins with a policy stating rules concerning visibly intoxicated persons, supporting an alcohol beverage server training program for managers and all servers, reviewing POS system reports, and completing incident reports for any problems occurring with customers.

Discussion Questions

1. What is typically listed on an Alcohol Beverage Menu?
2. List and explain the four different places in a foodservice operation where Alcohol Beverage Service can take place.
3. Explain the purpose of a Standardized Drink Recipe and discuss what it should include.
4. Contrast "Free Pouring" with "Measured Pouring".
5. How does the Automated Control System work and what can be a disadvantage when using this type of system?
6. Explain how a Bottle Control System functions.
7. What is a Neat Drink?
8. Explain the difference between a Cocktail and a Mixed Drink.
9. Describe the two-step method used to determine Liquor Portion Cost.
10. Explain how the Minimum Menu Price is determined when completing a Drink Cost Card.
11. What is the Evaporation and Spillage Loss percentage associated with liquors and wines?
12. Describe the reasons for a beer loss percentage being high, and explain how it can be controlled.
13. Explain the "prudent person rule" when serving alcohol beverages.
14. Discuss how management demonstrates Responsible Beverage Service.
15. How is an Incident Report used?

Project Exercises

Complete the following:

1. A 5-ounce glass of red wine has a menu price of $15.75. The Beverage Manager sets a beverage cost percentage of 20%. The 750 mL bottle of wine was purchased for $15.24 so determine if it is accurately priced on the menu. Check it out by preparing a Drink Cost Card.

2. Prepare a Standardized Drink Recipe for an Alcohol Beverage of your choice, and complete the Standardized Drink Recipe form that is available in Excel for this text/work book. Then prepare a Drink Cost Card for that recipe using the form provided in Excel.
   Helpful beverage sites: www.allrecipes.com/recipes/133/drinks/cocktails; www.drinksmixer.com

   NOTE: If you completed the project exercise that began in chapter 1, creating a semi á la carte menu, consider selecting an alcohol beverage that would complement that menu.

11

Purchasing and Selling Alcohol Beverages

Introduction

The application of the laws governing the sale of alcohol beverages along with the standard procedures to purchasing and cost management, sales and cost analysis, and alcohol beverage cost and cost percentages are presented with application examples.

Learning Objectives

Upon successfully completing this chapter, readers will be able to:

1. Recognize the similarities between food product and alcohol beverage purchasing.

2. Know that a state can sell alcohol beverages as a License State or a Control State.

3. Understand soft drink and bar ingredient purchasing.

4. Describe how Alcohol Beverage and Supply Requisitions and Transfers track beverage costs along with being processed through a POS system.

5. Describe how a POS system can reconcile sales by comparing them to guest check receipts.

6. Analyze sales using an Alcohol Beverage Sales Report.

7. Calculate alcohol cost percentages using an Alcohol Beverage Category Sales and Cost Report.

8. Discuss the reasons for higher-than-normal alcohol beverage cost percentages.

9. Explain why beverage cost percentages may differ from one beverage operation to the next.

Chapter Outline

Alcohol Beverage Purchasing
Alcohol Beverage Governance
Alcohol Beverage Distributors
Soft Drink and Ingredient
   Purchasing
Beverage Requisitions
   and Transfers

Reconciling Sales
Alcohol Beverage Sales and Cost Analysis
Alcohol Category Sales and Cost Report
Alcohol Beverage Cost and Cost Percentage
Summary
Discussion Questions
Project Exercises

Key Terms and Definitions

Begin by first reading the key terms and their definitions. An advance understanding of the terms will be helpful prior to reading the chapter.

Alcohol Beverage Category Sales and Cost Report	Tracks bar sales and cost percentages by categorizing alcohol beverages according to liquor, wine, and beer.
Alcohol Beverage Sales Report	Tracks bar sales by identifying trends and fluctuations by date, day, shift, and daily sales for a one-week period.
Alcohol Beverage Requisition	Empty liquor, wine, and beer bottles are counted and subtracted from par amounts to determine the order amount, which is entered on this form.
Beverage Cost	The total "cost of goods sold" for a specific accounting period (day, week, month).
Beverage Cost Percentage	The beverage cost reported as a percentage of the "cost of goods sold" for a specific accounting period.
Bottle Exchange	Empty bottles are exchanged for full bottles.
Control State	Beverage operations buy directly from state-controlled stores or distribution centers.
License State	Beverage operations buy directly from alcohol (liquor, wine, beer) distributors licensed by the state.
Par Amount	A standard amount established on the basis of usage and in anticipation of sales.
Post-mix System	Delivers the mixer flavor in a bag-in-a-box (BIB); the syrup is then mixed in a carbonator with water to produce a carbonated beverage.
Pour Cost	The cost of preparing a single drink.
Pre-mix System	Delivers a ready-to-drink soda (same as sold in cans and bottles) in a 5-gallon stainless steel tank.
Supply Requisition	Inventoried non-alcohol items are subtracted from established par amounts to determine the amount needed for this form.
Transfer	Used to track the movement of alcohol beverages from the bar to the kitchen or from a special function bar to the bar or between bars in a multi-outlet operation.

Alcohol Beverage Purchasing

The standard functions of purchasing, receiving, storing, and inventory control are applied when purchasing alcohol beverages.

Due to the high cost involved and the responsibility required, the beverage manager, general manager, or owner typically receives most of the alcohol beverages on behalf of the operation.

> **Purchase orders are compared with invoices and checked for accuracy at the time of delivery.** The items received are immediately inventoried and placed in locked storage.

> **The purchasing objective for alcohol beverages—like that for food products—is to purchase the best quality product at the lowest price for its specific use.** The purchase of alcohol beverages should be based on criteria developed by management, called specifications, for liquor, wine, beer, and all other ingredients in alcohol beverages.

> ▷ All alcohol beverages are purchased primarily by brand name, unit size (bottle/keg), and price. Because of this, specifications are written within these parameters.

> ▷ Management identifies certain brands to act as the operation's "well liquor"— the most used liquor in any given bar, also referred to as house brand or pouring brand.

> ▷ Because of considerable quality variations, management may choose specific brands for its well liquor or may identify several acceptable brands within common liquor categories—bourbon, vodka, gin, Canadian (whisky*), Scotch, blended American whiskey, tequila, rum, and so on.

> *Whiskey is spelled without the letter "e" in Canada.

> ▷ Call brand liquors are higher-quality premium liquors that customers order by name. Call brands command a higher drink price because they are more expensive to purchase than well liquors. Sales records, customer requests, and beverage trends help determine the variety and quality of call brands stocked.

LEARNING OBJECTIVE 1
Recognize the similarities between food product and alcohol beverage purchasing.

It is the buyer's function to compare supplier price lists and purchase the appropriate brands with the lowest prices.

Alcohol Beverage Governance

A three-tier system for alcohol beverage distribution in the United States was established following the repeal of alcohol prohibition on December 5, 1933 and is still in force. The three-tier system is as follows:

> **Tier 1.** Producer / Winery / Distillery / Brewery

> **Tier 2.** Wine and Liquor Distributor / Beer Distributor / Control Board (state controlled)

> **Tier 3.** Retailer / Restaurant / Bar / Supermarket

The three-tier system was established with the intent that only the third tier would sell alcohol beverages to the consumer.

Alcohol Beverage Distributors

The purchase of alcohol beverages within the United States is subject to the laws of each state or municipality. A state is designated as either a License State or a Control State.

> ▶ **License State:** Beverage operations buy directly from alcohol distributors (liquor, wine, beer) licensed by the state. Competitive product pricing among distributors is common when offering the same brand products, although some distributors may carry only certain brands and some imports may restrict distribution to one distributor within a state and set the selling price.

> ▶ **Control State:** Beverage operations buy directly from state-controlled stores or distribution centers. The state determines the prices for all of the available alcohol products. Some states may deliver to beverage operations based on a set minimum quantity ordered to qualify for delivery. Other states require beverage operations to arrange for transportation from a distribution center or store. A Control State may regulate the sale of all alcohol products (liquor, wine, beer) or may sell only liquor and wine, while beer can be sold through licensed distributors.

In many states, the method of payment made by the beverage operation to the supplier is governed by state law. Typically, the payment must be made within a specified period of time. In some states, regulations require that all deliveries be on a COD (cash-on-delivery) basis with a certified bank check or a bank-funds transfer the day of the delivery.

Example: New York law requires beverage operators to pay wine, liquor and beer distributors within 30 days (based on credit terms set forth by each distributor) for beverage products, which are delivered directly to the beverage operation. Pennsylvania law requires beverage operators to pay cash (COD) for beverage products, which they must pick up from a central distribution center controlled by the Pennsylvania Liquor Control Board.

Soft Drink and Ingredient Purchasing

> ▶ **Soda Drinks:** Management identifies the brand of soda drinks preferred by customers, such as Coke or Pepsi, and purchases those brands from a local soft drink distributor. The price that the beverage operation will pay for these drinks is often determined by the volume of products purchased. A higher volume results in a lower price.

Dispensing soda to mix drinks may be in any one or more of the following ways:

> ▷ Cans
>
> ▷ Bottles
>
> ▷ Pre-mix soda beverage system
>
>> ◆ Delivers a ready-to-drink soda (same as sold in cans and bottles) in a 5-gallon stainless steel tank.

▷ Post-mix soda beverage system

- ◆ Delivers the mixer flavor as a syrup in a bag-in-a-box (BIB). The syrup is then mixed in a carbonator with water to produce the soda beverage. The post-mix system is the most economical and provides the soda at the lowest cost. It is often used in high-volume operations.

- ◆ To assure a consistent quality flavor, the soft drink distributor, on request, may visit the bar operation to test the soda by measuring the sweetener (Brix) content ratio. The Brix reading is conducted with a small testing device known as a refractometer that can quickly identify blending ratios to determine if correct ratios are in place.

- ◆ Management may choose to sample the soda—take a Brix reading—on a regular or random basis with its own refractometer.

▶ **Bar Juices:** Fruit juices used in mixed drinks, such as cranberry, grapefruit, orange, pineapple, and tomato, may be purchased in Liters, #3 (46-ounce) cans, or 5-ounce individual serving cans.

▶ **Mixers:** Examples of mixers used to prepare or flavor alcohol beverages include collins mix, mai tai mix, margarita mix, sweet and sour mix, and so on, and are purchased from broadline distributors or wholesale suppliers.

▶ **Bar Items:** These may include seasonings, spices, flavored syrups, juice concentrates (lemon, lime), cherries, cocktail onions, olives, peanuts, coffees, cream, half-and-half, milk, fresh fruits (oranges, lemons, limes), and so on, and are available from broadline distributors or wholesale suppliers.

Requisitions and Transfers

Alcohol Beverage and Supply Requisitions

The bar manager or bartender prepares an Alcohol Beverage Requisition to restock alcohol beverages from the alcohol beverage storeroom and a Supply Requisition to restock items, such as bar juices, mixers, beverage napkins, stir sticks, straws, etc., from the foodservice storeroom. Requisitions (see Figures 11.1 and 11.2 on the following page) are typically done prior to or at the start of the first shift of the day or at the close of the last shift in anticipation of a morning delivery of the items requisitioned.

▶ **To prepare Alcohol Beverage and Supply Requisitions,** an inventory is taken of the products on hand. The inventoried amounts are subtracted from the established par amounts to determine the amount needed to restore the par amount for each item.

▶ **Par amounts (standard starting amounts)** for bottles of alcohol, juices, mixers, bar items, and supplies are established on the basis of usage and in anticipation of sales. Par amounts are periodically adjusted to meet an increase or decrease in sales for individual items.

When a post-mix system is in use, the taste of the soda is affected by the quality of the local water supply and properly working carbonator. A special filtration system may be needed to avoid undesirable flavors in highly chlorinated or hard water.

LEARNING OBJECTIVE 4
Describe how Alcohol Beverage and Supply Requisitions and Transfers track beverage costs along with being processed through a POS system.

The objective in establishing par amounts is to maintain an adequate supply of items to meet the needs of the bar while at the same time not having more than is needed.

Alcohol Beverage Requisition

From: Bar
To: Alcohol Beverage Storeroom
Date: 01/16/20xx
Time: 8:10 A.M.

Item Description	Unit Size	Par	On Hand	Order
Bourbon				
Early Times	750 mL	5	2	3
Jack Daniels	750 mL	5	4	1
Wine				
Robert Mondavi - Pinot Noir	750 mL	4	2	2
Beer				
Heineken	12 oz.	36	12	24

Figure 11.1 Alcohol Beverage Requisition

Supply Requisition

From: Bar
To: Foodservice Storeroom
Date: 01/16/20xx
Time: 8:20 A.M.

Item Description	Unit Size	Par	On Hand	Order
Juices				
Orange Juice	1.75 L	2	1	1
Tomato Juice	#3 can	3	1	2
Mixers				
Collins	1 L	2	1	1
Mai Tai	1 L	3	1	2
Bar Items				
Lemons	each	18	3	15
Limes	each	18	2	16
Cherries	quart jar	2	1	1
Olives	quart jar	2	1	1
Napkins	case	1	1/4	1

Figure 11.2 Supply Requisition

▶ **POS software programs with inventory reordering capability can generate an Alcohol Beverage Requisition and a Supply Requisition.** The bar manager or bartender takes an inventory of the empty liquor bottles using a hand-scanner to scan the bottle bar codes. The bottle par stock amounts remain a constant in the program and may be adjusted as needed. The inventoried empty bottle amounts are automatically subtracted from the par amounts to prepare the Alcohol Beverage Requisition—refer to Figure 11.1.

An inventory would also be taken of actively used bar supply items and entered in the POS system, which would automatically subtract the inventory amounts from the par stock amounts to prepare the Supply Requisition—refer to Figure 11.2.

> NOTE: A complete liquor inventory can be taken daily by scanning the bottle bar codes of all full and partially used bottles. The partially used bottles would be measured in tenths of a bottle with an entry to the scanner screen that would record actual amounts in open bottles.

▶ **An empty bottle exchange for full bottles will take place.** When a bottle is emptied it is stored in a convenient location within the bar. The empty bottles will be exchanged for the requisitioned full bottles when the full bottles are delivered to the bar.

> NOTE: Each state has its own specific law regarding the disposal of empty liquor bottles. The empty bottles may be recycled (glass recycle), or a law may require that bottles be broken with a bottle crusher.

Transfers

When alcohol is used in the kitchen—wine for cooking, rum or liqueur for dessert items—the chef or kitchen manager prepares a Transfer—refer to Figure 11.3 on the following page. The Transfer is used to track the movement of the alcohol from the bar to the kitchen. The alcohol items are removed from the bar inventory and added to the kitchen inventory.

> NOTE: It may be the policy of some restaurant operations to have the kitchen prepare a Requisition directly to the alcohol beverage storeroom, avoiding the transfer of any liquor items from the bar to the kitchen.

A Transfer would also be used between bars in multi-outlet operations. During an excessively busy shift, a bar location may need an additional bottle of a specific brand of liquor due to an above-average consumption of that brand. Therefore, the manager or bartender may submit a transfer request to another bar location in order to fulfill an immediate need.

Transfer

| From: | Bar | Date: | 01/16/20xx |
| To: | Kitchen | Time: | 10:15 A.M. |

Item Description	Unit Size	Quantity
Grand Marnier	750 mL	1
Bacardi dark rum	750 mL	2
Taylor dry sherry	750 mL	1

Figure 11.3 Transfer

Special-Function Bar Requisition and Transfers

When a special-function bar is used an Alcohol Beverage Requisition is prepared based on the brands (liquor, wine, beer) requested by the host of the special-function bar. A Supply Requisition is also prepared for bar juices, mixers, and bar items needed, as well as for any canned or bottled soft drinks.

▶ The bar manager or a catering manager may assist the host in determining the brand selections and quantities needed.

▶ The special-function bar is stocked with bottles of alcohol from the alcohol beverage storeroom and supplied with all of the necessary bar juices, mixers, and bar items from the foodservice storeroom. Special-function bars are not supplied from other bars within the operation.

NOTE: If items run out during an event when the special-function bar is in use, additional bottles of alcohol and other needed items may be added with the host's approval. A second Alcohol Beverage Requisition and/or Supply Requisition would be prepared for those items.

The special-function bar is inventoried at the end of its use. The remaining full and partially used bottles of liquor along with remaining amounts of bar juices, mixers, and bar items are transferred to the bar. The bar manager or catering manager prepares a Transfer, listing all of the items that are then added to the bar inventory.

Reconciling Sales

When reconciling sales, the manager compares what the POS system indicates was sold to what inventory shows. The reconciliation method must include the following three steps:

1. The server or bartender must either write a guest check or directly enter the order into a POS terminal for every drink ordered by a customer. Thus, no drinks are prepared unless they are accounted for.

2. Every drink is issued a POS receipt, which is placed on the table or bar with the drink by the server or bartender. By issuing receipts, the manager may be able to quickly look at a table or the bar and know that a customer has paid.

3. Guest check and/or POS totals are reconciled with inventory.

   ▷ If guest checks are used, the guest check totals should be the same as the POS system totals when compared at the end of each shift. This protects against most cash shortage problems. And the POS system inventory should balance with the actual inventory sold amount.

   ▷ If drink orders are directly entered into the POS terminal, then the POS system total should balance with the total amount of cash in the POS terminal drawer. The inventory sold amount should also balance with the actual inventory sold amount, which is monitored with effective inventory controls.

LEARNING OBJECTIVE 5
Describe how a POS system can reconcile sales by comparing them to guest check receipts.

An attentive manager supervises the entire process to ensure policies are followed consistently.

Alcohol Beverage Sales and Cost Analysis

Alcohol beverage sales and costs need to be checked frequently because sales and costs are crucial in judging how well a beverage operation is performing.

▶ If a POS system is used, it may have the capability to prepare reports daily, by shift, and even hourly, depending on the program. These reports serve to inform management of operational efficiencies, and are similar to those presented in Figures 11.4 on p. 214 and 11.5 on p. 216.

When employees are aware that management maintains tight control, they tend to be motivated to perform their best.

Sales Report

An Alcohol Beverage Sales Report (refer to Figure 11.4) tracks bar sales by identifying trends and fluctuations by date, day, shift, and daily sales for a one-week period. The report can be produced weekly or for whatever period of time management determines to be effective.

LEARNING OBJECTIVE 6
Analyze sales using an Alcohol Beverage Sales Report.

▶ **Increasing beverage sales** may be the result of a **growth trend** for various reasons: for example, a greater number of tourists or conventioneers coming to the community or perhaps popular musical entertainment (a band or singer) appearing at the beverage establishment.

▶ **Decreasing sales amounts** would alert management to a potential problem that would need to be immediately identified and corrected.

▶ **Fluctuations in sales** would be reflected by a greater or less than typical sales amount for a given day, shift, or period of time when reports are compared (example: compared weekly or with prior weeks or months). The explanations for the fluctuations could be as follows:

> To reduce avoidable fluctuations, management must forecast demand accurately and schedule labor accordingly.

1. An increase in business resulting from large groups of people patronizing the bar following gatherings such as business meetings, weddings, or sporting events

2. A decrease in business because of hazardous weather conditions

3. A decrease in sales resulting from bar operating procedures not being correctly followed, such as incorrect drink prices or errors being made when drink sales were recorded at the POS terminal

4. An increase and decrease in sales occurring when a bartender's shift or scheduled days off are changed, which would draw immediate attention to the possibility of bartender theft

Alcohol Beverage Sales Report

Bar Name: Lounge

Period Beginning: 01/11/20xx
Period Ending: 01/17/20xx

Date	Day	Shift	Sales	Daily Sales Total
January 11	Sunday	Shift 1	$253.50	$736.40
		Shift 2	$482.90	
January 12	Monday	Shift 1	$271.25	$910.40
		Shift 2	$639.15	
January 13	Tuesday	Shift 1	$301.50	$1,057.80
		Shift 2	$756.30	
January 14	Wednesday	Shift 1	$328.25	$1,171.10
		Shift 2	$842.85	
January 15	Thursday	Shift 1	$329.40	$1,317.15
		Shift 2	$987.75	
January 16	Friday	Shift 1	$575.15	$2,406.80
		Shift 2	$1,831.65	
January 17	Saturday	Shift 1	$611.10	$2,536.60
		Shift 2	$1,925.50	

Totals

Shift 1: 9:00 AM–5:00 PM $2,670.15

Shift 2: 5:00 PM–1:00 AM $7,466.10

All Shifts $10,136.25

Figure 11.4 Alcohol Beverage Sales Report

▶ A POS system can automatically categorize beverage sales when the bartender enters the sale of each drink. Daily and weekly sales totals for each category—liquor, wine, beer—and shift are recorded, and weekly cost percentages are calculated for liquor, wine, and beer along with a total cost percentage.

Category Sales and Cost Report

Trends and fluctuations within the categories of liquor, wine, and beer can be tracked by date, day, and shift for a one-week period. Weekly reports can be compared to previous weeks or the same weeks in a previous year. The sales totals shown in Figure 11.4 on the previous page have been transferred to the Category Sales section of the Alcohol Beverage Category Sales and Cost Report, Figure 11.5 on the following page, which tracks the sales and cost percentages for the categories of liquor, wine, and beer.

The Cost Report section of Figure 11.5 includes the following information:

▶ **Cost of Goods Sold** (Column B) are dollar amounts by category—liquor, wine, beer—taken directly from the Alcohol Beverage Inventory and Sales Control Report (the use and function of the Alcohol Beverage Inventory and Sales Control Report is explained in Chapter 12), along with the Total Sales Value sums that are determined through inventory and price calculations. Cost of Goods Sold are calculated on the basis of the actual inventory (opening and closing amounts) and tracked with Requisitions. The difference (when calculated) is the number of units sold.

▶ **Sales: Week Total** (Column C) are the amounts generated by the POS system—the actual dollar amount (cash taken in) from the recorded sales—and indicate the total sales for each category for the week and also show the total sales of all three categories for the week.

▶ **Alcohol Beverage Cost %** (Column D) is determined by dividing the Cost of Goods Sold (Column B) by the Sales Total for the week (Column C) and multiplying that answer by 100 to get the percentage (Column D). A total of the liquor, wine, and beer percentages determines the total Alcohol Beverage Cost Percentage for the beverage operation.

▶ **Total Sales Value** (Column E)—See the following example:

Example: 8.4 bottles of Early Times at $11.75 per bottle = $98.70 cost of goods sold for that brand. From that amount, based on the standardized drink recipes (1.5 ounces) the number of drinks sold is calculated and multiplied by the price per drink for that brand to determine the total sales value.

▶ **Over or (Short)** (Column F) is determined by subtracting the Total Sales Value (Column E) from the Sales Total (Column C). Sales is the actual dollar amount (cash taken in) compared to the potential dollar amount (total sales value) that should have been collected. Management determines an acceptable over (short) variance range, which is typically between 0.005 and 0.01%.

Typically less than 0.01% short is a result of evaporation loss that was discussed in chapter 10. An over amount would raise concern that there could have been an error when the inventory was taken or mistakes were made when returning dollar amount change to customers—shortchanging the customer. During extremely busy shifts honest mistakes can occur.

LEARNING OBJECTIVE 7
Calculate alcohol cost percentages using an Alcohol Beverage Category Sales and Cost Report.

Alcohol Beverage Category Sales and Cost Report

Period Beginning: 01/11/20xx   **Period Ending:** 01/17/20xx

Category Sales

A	B Sunday 01/11/xx	C Monday 01/12/xx	D Tuesday 01/13/xx	E Wednesday 01/14/xx	F Thursday 01/15/xx	G Friday 01/16/xx	H Saturday 01/17/xx	I Week Total
Shift 1								
Liquor	$156.50	$184.40	$211.80	$238.45	$233.25	$476.70	$517.35	$2,018.45
Wine	$51.20	$43.55	$46.10	$48.20	$55.75	$50.30	$47.70	$342.80
Beer	$45.80	$43.30	$43.60	$41.60	$40.40	$48.15	$46.05	$308.90
Shift 1 Total	$253.50	$271.25	$301.50	$328.25	$329.40	$575.15	$611.10	$2,670.15
Shift 2								
Liquor	$312.85	$370.60	$425.50	$524.35	$591.90	$1,159.95	$1,052.70	$4,437.85
Wine	$76.70	$78.90	$82.50	$82.10	$85.95	$149.15	$259.25	$814.55
Beer	$93.35	$189.65	$248.30	$236.40	$309.90	$522.55	$613.55	$2,213.70
Shift 2 Total	$482.90	$639.15	$756.30	$842.85	$987.75	$1,831.65	$1,925.50	$7,466.10
Daily Total	$736.40	$910.40	$1,057.80	$1,171.10	$1,317.15	$2,406.80	$2,536.00	$10,136.25

Cost Report

Calculation Formulas   (B ÷ C) × 100 = D   C – E = F

A Category	B Cost of Goods Sold	C Sales: Week Total	D Alc. Beverage Cost %	E Total Sales Value	F Over (Short)
Liquor	$1,310.65	$6,456.30	20.30%	$6,507.00	($50.70)
Wine	$295.15	$1,157.35	25.50%	$1,159.75	($2.40)
Beer	$461.65	$2,522.60	18.30%	$2,549.40	($26.80)
Total	$2,067.45	$10,136.25	20.40%	$10,216.15	($79.90)

Figure 11.5 Alcohol Beverage Category Sales and Cost Report

If cost percentages are not in line according to planned percentages, management needs to identify the problem, which could be in one or more of the following areas:

1. Theft by employees
2. Beverage recipes not being followed
3. Inaccurate portioning is occurring
4. Suppliers have raised their prices
5. Drink selling prices are too low

LEARNING OBJECTIVE 8
Discuss the reasons for higher-than-normal alcohol beverage cost percentages.

Alcohol Beverage Cost and Cost Percentage

Alcohol beverage cost is the **cost of goods sold** in the preparation of alcohol beverages and includes the cost of the following:

1. **Alcohol ingredients** (liquor, wine, beer)
2. **Mixers** used in beverage production
3. **Condiments** used in beverage production
4. **Garnishes** and any other items used for drinks
5. **Waste and spillage**

The terms "pour cost" and "bar cost" are often used interchangeably with the term "beverage cost" by people working in food and beverage operations. So not to be confused, remember that:

► **Pour cost** is the cost of preparing a single drink: (drink cost).

► **Beverage cost** is the **total cost of goods sold** for a specific accounting period (day, week, month), **similar to food cost.**

► **A manager may refer to the beverage cost percentage as "bar cost."** It would be common to hear a manager say, "We run a 20.5% bar cost," referring to the beverage cost percentage.

► **Beverage cost percentages may differ** from one operation to the next, depending on the following:

1. Type of operation
2. Location
3. Market conditions
4. Entertainment provided

Beverage cost percentages are calculated by category, such as liquor, wine, and beer, as shown in the box below, which lists typical beverage cost percentage ranges (which is a composite of averages from beverage industry professional associations)

Beverage cost percentage is the beverage cost reported as a percentage of total beverage sales, similar to a food cost percentage, which is the food cost reported as a percentage of total food sales.

LEARNING OBJECTIVE 9
Explain why beverage cost percentages may differ from one beverage operation to the next.

	Low	Median	High
Liquor	14%	18%	26%
Wine*	25%	40%	60%
Beer**	12%	24%	36%

　* Wine is served by the glass, from a bottle, or carafe.
** Beers and ales are served by the bottle or drawn from a keg and served by the glass or pitcher.

Complete Assignment 16 on page 218.

Assignment 16

1. Calculate the **Alcohol Beverage Cost Percentages** in each category along with the Total Beverage Cost Percentage for a one-week period at a Casual-Dining Restaurant Bar:

Category	Cost of Goods Sold	Week's Sales Totals	Beverage Cost %
Liquor	$1,826.50	$9,460.85	_____%
Wine	784.35	3,378.15	_____%
Beer	938.15	4,745.50	_____%
Total	$3,549.00	$17,584.50	_____%

Calculations:

2. Calculate the **Alcohol Beverage Cost Percentages** in each category along with the Total Beverage Cost Percentage for a one-week period at a Sports Bar:

Category	Cost of Goods Sold	Week's Sales Totals	Beverage Cost %
Liquor	$3,615.75	$18,892.15	_____%
Wine	1,309.50	3,156.75	_____%
Beer	2,137.50	10,025.00	_____%
Total	$_____	$_____	_____%

Calculations:

3. Calculate the **Alcohol Beverage Cost Percentages** in each category along with the Total Beverage Cost Percentage for a one-week period at a Cocktail Lounge:

Category	Cost of Goods Sold	Week's Sales Totals	Beverage Cost %
Liquor	$1,967.25	$10,756.10	_____%
Wine	1,042.50	4,492.25	_____%
Beer	815.50	3,635.25	_____%
Total	$_____	$_____	_____%

Calculations:

Summary

When purchasing, receiving, and storing alcohol beverages the same procedures are applied that are used when purchasing food products. The purchasing objective for alcohol beverages is the same objective that is used for buying food: to purchase the best quality product at the lowest price for its specific use.

The way in which alcohol beverages are purchased in the US is determined by the state law that governs the sale of alcohol beverages. A state will either be a **License State** with authorized licensed distributors or a **Control State** requiring beverage operations (restaurants, bars, etc.) to buy directly from state-controlled stores or distribution centers. Soft drink and beverage related ingredients are typically purchased from local soft drink and foodservice distributors.

Alcohol Beverage and Supply Requisitions often include a "Par" amount along with an "On Hand" amount to accurately determine the Requisition "Order" amount that adequately identifies the product items needed for the day or shift. A POS system software can speed the requisition process for the products and for accurate tracking. Transfers will also function in the same manner but do not include "Par" and "Order" amounts.

Reconciling Sales and Alcohol Beverage Sales and Cost Analysis are essential procedures that require the constant attention of management. If cost percentages are not in line according to planned percentages, the problem needs to be identified; problems such as, employee theft, beverage recipes not being followed, inaccurate portioning, suppliers having increased prices, or drinks selling prices being too low.

Alcohol beverage cost percentages are calculated by category, such as liquor, wine, and beer. Also, beverage cost percentages may differ from one operation to the next based of the type of operation, location, market conditions, and if entertainment is provided.

Discussion Questions

1. When comparing alcohol beverage purchasing to food product purchasing, what is the common purchasing objective?
2. Describe the functional differences between a License State and a Control State.
3. Contrast the difference between a pre-mix soda beverage system and a post-mix system.
4. What are the essential bar ingredients that are purchased?
5. Explain how Alcohol Beverage and Supply Requisitions track beverage costs.
6. How are beverage and supply par amounts established?
7. A complete liquor inventory can be taken by scanning the bottle bar codes of all full and partially used bottles. What unit of measurement is used to record the amounts in partially used bottles?
8. Explain what is meant by an empty bottle–full bottle exchange when fulfilling a Beverage Requisition from the bar.
9. If the kitchen needed a bottle of dark rum from the bar (taking it from the bar inventory) to prepare a dessert item, would that be on a Requisition or Transfer?
10. Explain how a POS system can reconcile sales by comparing them to guest check receipts.
11. When analyzing sales using an Alcohol Beverage Sales Report, what would be some of the reasons for a greater- or less-than-average sales amount fluctuation?
12. The Alcohol Beverage Category Sales and Cost Report tracks the sales and cost percentages for the categories of liquor, wine, and beer. If cost percentages are not in line according to planned percentages, what could be the possible reasons? List five.
13. Identify the four reasons why beverage cost percentages may differ from one beverage operation to the next.

Project Exercises

1. Compare the laws for purchasing alcohol beverages (License State or Control State) in the state that you are currently living in with two bordering states. Begin by doing an Internet search for each state's State Liquor Control Board. Write a detailed explanation of your findings for each state.

   Directory—Alcohol Beverage Control Boards

   www.ttb.gov (go to Resources, ABC Boards)

   www.nabca.org (National Alcohol Beverage Control Association)

   If the state is a License State, identify the names and web addresses of the major liquor, wine, and beer distributors.

2. If a bartender's days off change from Sunday and Monday to Tuesday and Wednesday, and bar sales increase on Sunday and Monday by about $150 each day and decrease on Tuesday and Wednesday by about $140 each day, on the same shift that the bartender had been working, there is reason to be concerned. Why? Explain what you suspect is happening and how you would resolve the issue.

12

Alcohol Beverage Inventory and Control

Introduction

The many factors that determine the type and size of an alcohol beverage inventory are discussed, along inventory turnover rates and sales tracking. Alcohol beverage service by its very nature has tempting opportunities for theft to occur, but with the appropriate management control procedures in place it can be prevented. This will be explained and reviewed with examples.

Learning Objectives

Upon successfully completing this chapter, readers will be able to:

1. Explain the factors that determine Alcohol Beverage Inventory stock levels and the number of brands an establishment might carry.
2. Demonstrate how to calculate an Alcohol Beverage Inventory Turnover Rate.
3. Identify the factors influencing different rates of inventory turnover.
4. Utilize an Alcohol Beverage Inventory and Sales Control Report to track alcohol beverage inventory.
5. Understand the importance of monitoring the financial investment in inventory with the use of an Alcohol Beverage Storeroom Inventory Report.
6. Recognize and understand how theft can occur with managers, bookkeepers, bartenders, servers, and customers.
7. Explain how control procedures can discourage and prevent theft.

Chapter Outline

Key Terms and Definitions

Begin by first reading the key terms and their definitions. An advance understanding of the terms will be helpful prior to reading the chapter.

Alcohol Beverage Inventory and Sales Control Report	The report can be used to compare what should have happened against what did happen.
Alcohol Beverage Inventory Turnover Rate	Cost of goods sold divided by average liquor inventory.
Alcohol Beverage Storeroom Inventory Report	The report tracks the inventory to determine if it is being properly managed.
Beverage Cost Percentage	The beverage cost reported as a percentage of the "cost of goods sold" calculated by dividing cost of goods sold by the total sales value.
Beverage Inventory Size	Primarily determined by the sales volume along with several other factors.
Closing Inventory on Hand	The actual physical count of all items at the bar.
Cost of Goods Sold	The amount sold multiplied by the requisition cost per unit.
Item Purchase Price	The actual cost paid by the beverage operation for the products. The cost price is taken directly from invoices.
Number of Drinks Sold	Number determined by multiplying the amount sold by the drink portion size.
Opening Inventory on Hand	The previous accounting period's closing inventory.
Price per Drink	The price the customer pays.
Total Inventory Cost	The closing inventory on hand multiplied by the purchase price per unit.
Total Sales Value	Determined by multiplying the number of drinks sold by the price per drink.
Wine Inventory Turnover Rate	Cost of goods sold divided by average wine inventory.

Alcohol Beverage Inventory and Sales Tracking

The greatest concentration of dollars invested in food and beverage inventory is associated with alcohol beverages. The number of products offered can vary greatly in price and it is not uncommon for an upscale restaurant to have wine bottles ranging from $20 per bottle to over $500 per bottle.

Like food products, all alcohol beverages must be:

► Accounted for when used

► Inventoried

► Constantly monitored

LEARNING OBJECTIVE 1
Explain the factors that determine Alcohol Beverage Inventory stock levels and the number of brands an establishment might carry.

Alcohol Beverage Inventory

Management determines how large an inventory to stock and how large a selection of brands to carry based on the following:

1. **Sales volume:** low volume—limited offerings; high volume—a large selection of liquors, wines, and beers, plus all the major call brands
2. **Customer preferences** for specific brands
3. **Amount of inventory storage space available**—temperature controlled security locked rooms
4. **Supplier delivery schedules** and minimum order requirements
5. **Supplier price specials** and volume order discounts
6. **Availability of vintage and imported wines:** a larger inventory amount (bigger purchases) for wines in limited supply
7. **Food menus** that call for specific cooking wines, rum, or liqueurs for desserts, or additional wines may be needed to be served with certain menus
8. **Banquets or catered events** that require additional purchases to supply the needs of the function
9. **Holidays** such as St. Patrick's Day, Cinco de Mayo, July 4th, and New Year's Eve that may require additional purchases to meet the needs of increased business
10. **Size of financial investment in inventory: a budgeted dollar amount**

Depending on the sales volume, desired inventory turnover rate, and budgeted dollar amount, alcohol beverage purchasing may be weekly, every two weeks, or monthly.

► **Inventory turnover** rate is usually separated by alcohol beverage category—liquor, wine, and beer—and is calculated as follows:

LEARNING OBJECTIVE 2
Demonstrate how to calculate an Alcohol Beverage Inventory Turnover Rate.

STEP 1   To determine the Average Inventory in each category—liquor, wine, and beer—add the Opening Inventory and the Closing Inventory for each category and divide the total by 2.

$$\frac{\text{Opening Inventory} + \text{Closing Inventory}}{2} = \textbf{Average Inventory}$$

NOTE: The Alcohol Beverage Storeroom Inventory Report, Figure 12.2 on p. 228, or a similar report would have the Opening and Closing Inventory amounts.

STEP 2   **To determine the turnover rates for liquor, wine, and beer, divide the Cost of Goods Sold for each category by the Average Inventory for each category.**

Cost of Liquor Sold ÷ Average Inventory = **Liquor Turnover Rate**

Cost of Wine Sold ÷ Average Inventory = **Wine Turnover Rate**

Cost of Beer Sold ÷ Average Inventory = **Beer Turnover Rate**

NOTE: The Alcohol Beverage Inventory and Sales Control Report, Figure 12.1 on p. 226, or a similar report would have Cost of Goods Sold amounts for each category: liquor, wine, and beer.

The numbers used in the following example have been selected to demonstrate the math function when calculating a Liquor Inventory Turnover Rate.

STEP 1   **Determine the Average Liquor Inventory:**

$$\text{Opening Inventory} + \text{Closing Inventory} = \text{Total} \div 2 = \textbf{Average Inventory}$$

$$\$1,605.20 + \$1,582.50 = \$3,187.70 \div 2 = \textbf{\$1,593.85}$$

STEP 2   **Calculate the Turnover Rate:**

$$\text{Cost of Liquor Sold} \div \text{Average Inventory} = \textbf{Turnover Rate}$$

$$\$1,310.60 \div \$1,593.85 = \textbf{.82}$$

LEARNING OBJECTIVE 3
Identify the factors influencing different rates of inventory turnover.

Liquor, wine, and beer inventory turnover rates will fluctuate depending on how quickly the beverage operation uses the inventory and how often products are reordered.

Typical turnover rates for liquor, wine, and beer are represented in the box below.

	Low	Median	High
Liquor	0.50	0.75	1.50
Wine	0.10	0.25	0.75
Beer	0.75	1.25	2.00

NOTE: Wine inventory turnover rates will vary greatly depending on the type of wine and number of SKUs (Stock Keeping Unit—Product Code) on the wine list. A wine list with a larger selection (more SKUs) will have a lower turnover rate than one with a smaller selection. The range of prices will also impact turnover rates and may require subcategories within the wine inventory.

Complete Assignment 17 on p. 235.

Alcohol Beverage Inventory and Sales Control

Alcohol Beverage Inventory and Sales Control can be divided into two functions:

1. Determining if the inventory has been used properly

2. Calculating the value of the Alcohol Beverage Storeroom Inventory

When an alcohol beverage control system is in place, it is a simple matter to have complete inventory control over alcohol beverages. The control system:

1. Accounts for all alcohol beverage usage

2. Reconciles receipt of bottles into the bar against bottles used

3. Automatically reorders alcohol beverages

The Alcohol Beverage Inventory and Sales Control Report, Figure 12.1 on p. 226 and the Alcohol Beverage Storeroom Inventory Report, Figure 12.2 on p. 228, provide a complete view for helping to manage alcohol beverage inventory.

The Alcohol Beverage Inventory and Sales Control Report, Figure 12.1, is one of the best ways to manage and comprehensively track alcohol beverage inventory.

If more than one bar exists within a foodservice operation, a report should be prepared for each bar location.

> **LEARNING OBJECTIVE 4**
> Utilize an Alcohol Beverage Inventory and Sales Control Report to track alcohol beverage inventory.

The Alcohol Beverage Inventory and Sales Control Report keeps track of:

▶ Opening and closing inventories

▶ Use of product by day and by period (week)

▶ The number of drinks that should have been sold

▶ The total sales value of the drinks that should have been sold

▶ Beverage cost percentages by brand and category (liquor, wine, beer)

The report is organized by column (refer to Figure 12.1), as the following column descriptions are explained:

▶ **Item Description** (Column A) lists each type of beverage according to beverage category: liquor, wine, beer. In our example, Figure 12.1, only Bourbon is listed, which would be under the Liquor category.

▶ **Unit Size** (Column B) is the size of the purchasing unit described in Column A (such as, 750 mL, 1 L, 1.75 L).

   NOTE: If beer were listed, the purchasing unit would be 12-oz. bottle, 0.5 keg or other size container.

▶ **Opening Inventory on Hand** (Column C) is the previous accounting period's Closing Inventory on Hand. As is done with food products, at the end of each accounting period, a physical inventory hand count is taken and valued. This is called the Closing Inventory on Hand.

▶ **Requisitions by Day** (Column D) is a Requisition from the Bar to the Alcohol Beverage Storeroom, which should be prepared daily. This enables the bar to maintain a par amount stock.

Alcohol Beverage Inventory and Sales Control Report

Period Beginning: 01/11/20xx　　**Period Ending:** 01/17/20xx　　**Bar Location:** Cedar Room

Calculation Formulas

C + D = E　　E − F = G　　G × H = I　　J × K = L　　(I ÷ L) × 100 = M

A	B	C	D (11)	D (12)	D (13)	D (14)	D (15)	D (16)	D (17)	E	F	G	H	I	J	K	L	M
Item Description	Unit Size	Opening Inventory on Hand	Requisitions by Day January 20xx 11	12	13	14	15	16	17	Opening Inventory + Requisitions	Closing Inventory on Hand	Number of Units Sold	Requisition Cost per Unit	Cost of Goods Sold	Number of Drinks Sold	Price per Drink	Total Sales Value	Beverage Cost Percentage
Bourbon																		
Early Times	750 mL	4.3	1	2	1	4		2		14.3	5.9	8.4	$11.75	$98.70	134	$4.50	$603.00	16.37%
Jack Daniels	750 mL	3.2		2		1	4			10.2	4.1	6.1	$19.20	$117.12	97	$6.00	$582.00	20.12%
Jim Beam	750 mL	2.4	3		1				1	7.4	2.9	4.5	$18.00	$81.00	72	$5.75	$414.00	19.57%
Item Total														$296.82			$1,599.00	**18.56%**
Wine																		
Robert Mondavi - Pinot Noir	750 mL	3.1	1		3	1			2	10.1	2.9	7.2	$19.00	$136.80	36	$9.50	$342.00	40.00%
Kendall-Jackson - Merlot	750 mL	4.5			2	2			2	10.5	3.7	6.8	$17.00	$115.60	34	$8.50	289.00	40.00%
Item Total														$252.40			$631.00	**40.00%**
Beer																		
Budweiser	0.5 keg	1.5	1			1	1		1	5.5	1.3	4.2	$89.30	$375.06	693	$3.50	$2,425.50	15.46%
Heineken	12 oz	27	72		24		24	48		195	33	162	$1.15	$186.30	162	$5.00	$810.00	23.00%
Samuel Adams	12 oz	21	48		24		24	24		141	25	116	$1.25	$145.00	116	$5.25	$609.00	23.81%
Item Total														$706.36			$3,844.50	**18.37%**
GRAND TOTAL														$1,255.58			$6,074.50	**20.67%**

Figure 12.1 Alcohol Beverage Inventory and Sales Control Report

NOTE: As requisitions are filled and used, the information is for-
warded to the Alcohol Beverage Inventory and Sales Control
Report daily. Every item taken is accounted for. A POS system
can forward the requisition amounts to a system-generated
Alcohol Beverage Inventory and Sales Control Report.

▶ **Opening Inventory + Requisitions** (Column E) equals the Opening
Inventory plus the Requisitions by Day of the period (Column C + D =
Column E).

▶ **Closing Inventory on Hand** (Column F) is the actual physical count of
all items at the bar. This is usually done the morning after the last day of
the ending period, before the bar opens. If the last day of the accounting
period is a Saturday, the inventory would be taken Sunday morning,
before opening.

Some beverage operations take inventory daily. Full bottles are either
manually counted or bottle bar codes are scanned. Bottles that are in
use can either be weighed or scanned and are measured in tenths of a
bottle. A half-full bottle of liquor would be visually assessed, scanned, or
weighed and reported at 0.05. A partially used keg would be weighed with
a keg scale or with a keg-check attached to the side of the keg, or with a
high-tech device that sends a soundwave through the keg to determine
the level of beer in the keg.

> If a bottle of liquor is almost empty, it *should not* be poured into an-
> other bottle of the same liquor as a convenient way for taking inven-
> tory. The procedure, known as "marrying bottles," is in direct violation
> of the law and could result in having an operator's liquor license being
> revoked. Marrying bottles of liquor is viewed as altering the liquor that
> results in a misrepresentation of the product.

▶ **Number of Units Sold** (Column G) indicates the number of bottles or
parts of bottles sold by subtracting the Closing Inventory on Hand from
the Opening Inventory + Requisitions (Column E – F = Column G).

▶ **Requisition Cost per Unit** (Column H) is the actual cost (amount paid)
for products. The cost price is taken directly from invoices.

▶ **Cost of Goods Sold** (Column I) is the Number of Units Sold multiplied
by the Requisition Cost per Unit price (Column G × H = Column I).

▶ **Number of Drinks Sold** (Column J) is determined by multiplying the
Number of Units Sold by the Drink Portion Size (Column G × Drink Portion Size* = Column J).

* For Drink Portion Size, see Standardized Drink Recipe (Figure 10.1 on p. 191)
or Drink Cost Card (Figure 10.3 on p. 197).

Examples of portion sizes for liquor, wine, and beer:

▷ A **liquor** portion per drink of 1½ ounces from a 750 mL bottle (25.4
ounces) would yield **16** or **17 drinks.** Subtracting a 5% loss for evaporation and spillage—25.4 ounces × 0.05% = 1.27 ounces (25.40 – 1.27
= 24.13 ounces)—would result in **16 drinks per 750 mL bottle** (24.13
ounces ÷ 1.5 ounces = 16.09—**rounded to 16 drinks**).

Alcohol Beverage Storeroom Inventory Report

Period Beginning: 01/11/20xx **Period Ending:** 01/17/20xx **Category:** Liquor

Calculation Formulas

		C	D	C + D = E				Requisitions by Day January 20xx				Week Total G	E – G = H	I	I – H = J	K	I x K = L
A Item Description	**B** Unit Size	Opening Inventory on Hand	Purchases	Opening Inventory + Purchases	11	12	13	14	15	16	17	Total Requisitions	**H** Inventory Balance	Closing Inventory on Hand	Balance + or –	Item Purchase Price	Total Inventory Cost
Bourbon																	
Early Times	750 mL	7	12	19	1	2	1	4			2	10	9	9		$11.75	$105.75
Jack Daniels	750 mL	2	12	14		2		1		4		7	7	6	–1*	$19.20	$115.20
Jim Beam	750 mL	3	12	15	3		1			1		5	10	10		$18.00	$180.00
Old Grand-Dad	750 mL	3		3				1				1	2	2		$16.45	$32.90
Total																	**$433.85**
Canadian																	
Canadian Club	750 mL	9		9	1			1				2	7	7		$15.25	$106.75
Seagram's VO	750 mL	7		7	2		1					3	4	4		$19.25	$77.00
Seagram's CR	750 mL	5		5			1					1	4	4		$22.00	$88.00
Total																	**$271.75**
Gin																	
Beefeater	750 mL	12		12	2			1				3	9	9		$18.75	$168.75
Tanqueray	750 mL	8		8			1			1		2	6	6		$22.50	$135.00
Total																	**$303.75**
Rum																	
Bacardi's	750 mL	17		17	3			2			1	6	11	11		$28.35	$311.85
Captain Morgan	750 mL	4		4			1					1	3	3		$17.50	$52.50
Total																	**$364.35**
Vodka																	
Absolute	750 mL	1	12	13	1			1		2		4	9	9		$20.25	$182.25
Grey Goose	750 mL	6		6			1			1		2	4	4		$26.45	$105.80
Total																	**$288.05**
TOTAL																	**$1,661.75**

* **Explanation:** 1 bottle of Jack Daniels broken **Date:** 01/12/20xx **Cause:** Fell off service cart

Figure 12.2 Alcohol Beverage Storeroom Inventory Report

- ◆ Most bars will use 750 mL bottles for ease in handling when pouring. Other bars may prefer 1 L bottles or a combination of 1 L and 750 mL bottles. Pouring systems will use 1.75 L bottles.

  ▷ A **wine** portion per glass of approximately 5 ounces from a 750 mL (25.4 ounces) bottle would yield 5 drinks per bottle. Subtracting a 5% loss for evaporation and spillage—25.4 ounces × 0.05 = 1.27 ounces (25.4 – 1.27 = 24.13 ounces)—would result in 5 drinks per 750 mL bottle (24.13 ounces ÷ 5 ounces per serving = 4.83 average serving size)—**rounded to 5 glasses of wine.**

  ▷ A **beer** served in a 12-ounce glass from a 0.5 keg (1,984 ounces) typically yields 165 drinks. This accounts for an 8% loss for evaporation and spillage (about 1 ounce per 12 ounces) with approximately a 1-inch head to fill a 12-ounce glass. 1,984 ounces × 0.08% = 158.72 ounces loss (1,984.00 ounces – 158.72 = 1,825.28 ounces) yields 165 drinks per 0.5 keg (1,825.28 ÷ 11 ounces per serving = 165.94)—**rounded down to 165 drinks,** allowing the 0.94 amount for loss.

  - ◆ Bottled beer is sold by the bottle.

- ▶ **Price per Drink** (Column K) is the price the customer pays (the menu price).

  NOTE: This price should be used even if the beverage is used to make a cocktail.

- ▶ **Total Sales Value** (Column L) is determined by multiplying the Number of Drinks Sold by the Price per Drink (Column J × K = Column L).

- ▶ **Beverage Cost Percentage** (Column M) is the cost in relationship to Total Sales Value and is calculated by dividing Cost of Goods Sold by the Total Sales Value and multiplying by 100 (Column I ÷ L × 100 = Column M).

  Cost percentages are identified for each product, by product category (liquor, wine, beer), and by the total for all alcohol beverages.

The benefit of maintaining the information provided by the Alcohol Beverage Inventory and Sales Control Report is that it can be used to compare what should have happened against what did happen.

> The beverage cost percentage will fluctuate with an increase or decrease in the cost of the beverage products, as determined in the market.

Example: In Column L, if the Total Sales Value of all drinks sold is reported at $6,074.50, and the amount reported by the POS system is $6,069.00, there is a $5.50 difference.

Usually, the differences are not very large. In this example, there may have been some spillage or a partially used bottle incorrectly inventoried.

Similarly, the Beverage Cost Percentages should compare to the ones established when pricing drinks. If a cost percentage is higher than what it should be, the possible reasons for the fluctuations (differences) should be checked.

The Alcohol Beverage Storeroom Inventory Report (see Figure 12.2 on the facing page) tracks the inventory to help determine if it is being properly managed and kept track of:

> **LEARNING OBJECTIVE 5**
> Understand the importance of monitoring the financial investment in inventory with the use of an Alcohol Beverage Storeroom Inventory Report.

- ► Opening and closing inventories

- ► Liquor, wine, and beer purchases

- ► Requisitioned use of product by day and by period (week)

- ► Any plus or minus inventory item quantity differences

- ► Individual product item purchase price

- ► The quantity and value of the inventory

The report is organized by column, as the following column descriptions are explained:

- ► **Item Description** (Column A) lists each type of beverage according to its beverage category: liquor, wine, and beer.* For speed and convenience, when taking a physical inventory count, the bottles should also appear in the same order on the storeroom shelves.

  * In our example, Figure 12.2, only liquor items are listed.

- ► **Unit Size** (Column B) is the size of the purchasing unit described in Column A.

- ► **Opening Inventory on Hand** (Column C) is the previous accounting period's Closing Inventory on Hand. Like with food products, at the end of each accounting period, a physical inventory hand count is taken and valued. This is called the Closing Inventory.

- ► **Purchases** (Column D) are the quantities that have been purchased during the period (week).

  NOTE: When inventory items fall below established par amounts those items are reordered/purchased.

  Alcohol beverage items are typically purchased by the case.
  - ▷ Liquor and wine purchased by the case:

    750 mL and 1 L bottles, 12 bottles per case

    1.75 L bottles, 4 bottles per case
  - ▷ Bottled beer (Imported and Domestic) purchased by the case:

    12-ounce bottles, 24 bottles per case

- ► **Opening Inventory + Purchases** (Column E) includes the Opening Inventory + Purchases for the period (Column C + D = Column E).

- ► **Requisitions by Day** (Column F) are the bottle items that the bar needs to replace with requisitioned bottle amounts that are recorded daily.

- ► **Total Requisitions** (Column G) is the total number of each item requisitioned for the period (week).

- ► **Inventory Balance** (Column H) is determined by subtracting Total Requisitions from Opening Inventory + Purchases (Column E − G = H). Inventory Balance is the remaining inventory.

- ► **Closing Inventory on Hand** (Column I) is the actual physical count of all items in the Alcohol Beverage Storeroom. This is typically completed (inventory taken) the morning after the last day of the ending period. If the last day of the accounting period was a Saturday, the inventory could be taken Sunday morning. Some beverage operations may take inventory daily.

A POS system with the appropriate configuration can maintain a perpetual inventory and track usage and purchases by the day, week, month, etc.

▶ **Balance + or –** (Column J) is determined by comparing the Closing Inventory on Hand to the Inventory Balance to identify any differences between what was actually used and what should have been used (Column I compared with Column H to identify any differences).

> **Example:** If 8 bottles of Jack Daniels should have been used but only 7 were actually used, then there is a one-bottle difference. In this example (as shown in Figure 12.2), the bottle was broken and noted on the report. A broken bottle would normally be kept in order to confirm the actual breakage to management.

> ▷ The most common reasons for differences are:

> > ◆ Inventory Error

> > ◆ Breakage

> > ◆ Theft

▶ **Item Purchase Price** (Column K) is the actual cost paid for each item. The cost price is taken directly from invoices.

▶ **Total Inventory Cost** (Column L) is the Closing Inventory on Hand multiplied by the Item Purchase Price, which determines the Total Inventory Cost for each item along with the Total Inventory Cost for each category: liquor, wine, beer, and the Total Inventory Cost for all alcohol beverages (Column I × K = Column L).

> Management can regularly compare the actual inventory cost with the amount that has been budgeted for the inventory.

Protecting Against Theft

Management's responsibility is to create a system that promotes honesty and accuracy among managers, bookkeepers, bartenders, and servers, which begins with an awareness of the common points of theft.

Management and Bookkeepers

Always present are the improper temptations for managers and bookkeepers, such as the following:

> **LEARNING OBJECTIVE 6**
> Recognize and understand how theft can occur with managers, bookkeepers, bartenders, servers, and customers.

1. **Unauthorized Consumption by Managers:** A recommended rule is that all employees, including managers, may not drink on the job.

2. **Kickbacks and Bribes to Managers:** Suppliers may offer money to managers to promote their products, rather than offer legitimate discounts for volume purchases. This is called a **kickback**.

   A manager may also be offered a **bribe** to carry certain brand products, such as free tickets to a sporting event or a gift card for an electronics store. Although the bribe is not necessarily stealing from the operation, the practice usually leads to overpricing and other costs to cover the bribe.

3. **Bookkeeping Theft:** Bookkeepers/accounting staff may steal by not making deposits or by reporting cash shortages. If they are responsible for paying invoices, they may create fictitious invoices payable to friends or relatives.

4. **Inventory Theft:** A manager may steal bottles of alcohol from inventory and cover the loss by falsely reporting the bottles as still being in inventory or under-reporting a bottle in order to steal it later.

Bartenders and Servers

Some bartenders and servers are tempted to cheat the bar operation or customers when serving alcohol beverages. The most common methods of dishonesty are as follows:

1. **Misusing the POS Terminal:** The following are ways that a bartender or server may tamper with the sales process:

   ► The bartender does not enter the drink sale into the POS terminal and keeps the money, or enters a drink item of lesser cost and keeps the difference.

   ► The bartender voids the drink sale and keeps the money and reports the void amount as an incorrect entry that needed to be voided.

      ▷ A legitimate void may occur if a customer rejects a drink or walks out without paying—the bar manager would be immediately informed in order to verify the void. A manager's password may be needed for a POS system to process a void.

   ► The bartender serves drinks during a shift change, when the POS terminal is not in use, and keeps the money.

   ► The server reuses guest checks and POS receipts to order drinks that have not really been ordered, pocketing the money from the sales of the "second drinks." When this occurs, the server and bartender are colluding (have a secret agreement) to steal from the operation.

   NOTE: A policy that the cash drawer to the POS terminal never be left open between sales must be clearly stated and monitored by management. Also the manager should frequently observe the bartender's activities near the POS terminal.

   If a bartender is not entering a drink sale into the POS terminal or enters a lesser amount or voids a sale, he or she must have a way to keep track of those dollar amounts at the end of the shift. He or she does this by removing the unaccounted for money taken in, allowing the POS terminal recorded drink sales total to balance with the cash drawer total. A bartender who is stealing, may keep track of stolen drink sales by placing a drink stir stick into an empty glass near the POS terminal each time a drink sale is not recorded. Then prior to the end of the shift the bartender counts the number of stir sticks and multiplies that number by the cost of each drink. For example: 12 stir sticks for drinks that sold for $6.00 per drink (12 × $6 = $72.00—the amount to be removed, *stolen*).

2. **Phony Walkouts:** A server claims a phony customer walkout after the customer has paid, and keeps the money. If a bar operation allows a customer to "run up a tab" (order drinks on account), the amount taken by the server and/or bartender could be sizable.

3. **Phantom Bottle:** A bartender brings in his or her own bottle of liquor (a phantom bottle) onto the shift and pockets the money from the sale

> An attentive manager will notice any unusual occurrence near the POS terminal that may indicate a dishonest activity.

of drinks he or she makes and serves from that bottle. The phantom bottle is typically a popular brand of alcohol beverage. Several bottles of that brand are used during a shift. The bartender does not enter any of the drink sales into the POS terminal that are served from the phantom bottle. This often occurs during a busy period when the POS cash drawer could remain partially open for change to be made without a drink order being entered. Before the end of the shift, the bartender removes the money collected from the phantom bottle drink sales so that the cash drawer dollar amount will balance with the POS terminal recorded drink sales amount. The empty phantom bottle mysteriously disappears in the same manner in which it appeared.

> A way to guard against phantom bottles is to have a policy that prohibits employees from bringing in any large purses, jackets, or bags to the bar.

4. **The Short Pour:** In a short pour situation, drinks are prepared with less than the recipe amount of alcohol beverage. The difference between the amount that should have been sold and the amount that was sold is kept by the bartender. This method can also be used when a bartender and server collude in selling the amount of the difference and equally pocketing the money.

5. **Overcharging Customers:** The customer is deliberately charged more than the menu price. The difference between the menu price and the amount collected is kept by the bartender or server or both. Another way this is done is when a customer signs a credit card voucher in advance and then is overcharged for drinks or charged for drinks not served.

6. **Diluting Bottles:** When a bartender dilutes bottles, he or she substitutes water for liquor, then uses the "diluted liquor" for making cocktails or mixed drinks. The liquor poured off before the bottle was diluted is also sold, and the bartender steals the money from those drinks.

7. **Outright Theft:** Sometimes, employees decide to practice outright theft, wherein they physically take bottles of liquor, wine, or beer from the bar or storage areas.

Control Procedures

> **LEARNING OBJECTIVE 7**
> Explain how control procedures can discourage and prevent theft.

A sound beverage management system will help to prevent theft from the operation and from the customer. Discouraging and preventing theft can be accomplished by:

1. **Maintaining tight controls over inventory.**

2. **Controlling pouring techniques.** By using a bottle control system, pour guns, or an automated control system, pouring can be controlled. Although automated control systems represent a significant investment, they typically pay for themselves in a short period of time when used in a high-sales-volume beverage operation.

3. **Creating an order system that documents drink orders.** A variety of systems are available to help track drink orders and their preparation. The basic principle behind these systems is to separate the ordering and preparation of the drinks so that a double-check system is in place. All orders should be submitted on guest checks or entered into a POS terminal that conveys the drink order to the bartender for preparation. This creates evidence of an order and helps management to track problems that may occur.

> Drinks ordered by customers at the bar directly from the bartender are the most difficult to track.

Management may determine that a "cash drop" should randomly occur as a security check against employee theft.

4. **Conducting random "cash drop" checks.** As a security measure, a POS terminal cash drawer may be removed when the cash amount becomes too high. The drawer would be immediately replaced with a second drawer so as not to interrupt the operation of the POS terminal. The second drawer—as with the first drawer—would contain a beginning bank, which typically consists of $250 to $350 in coins and small-denomination (less than $20) dollar bills. The excessive amount of cash from the first drawer would be deposited into a safe.

If at any time the cash amount in the POS drawer does not balance with the recorded POS sales amount, the employee would be held accountable.

Example: During a random "cash drop" management finds $80 more in cash than what is reported in the POS system sales total. This would immediately create the suspicion of theft, unless a legitimate reason for the difference could be found.

NOTE: If theft is occurring, the random "cash drop" check does not allow the employee time to remove the excess amount of stolen money. The employee would normally remove the stolen money near or at the end of the employee's shift, thereby allowing the cash drawer amount to balance with the recorded POS transaction totals.

Assignment 17

1. Calculate the **Alcohol Beverage Inventory Turnover Rate** for liquor, wine, and beer categories for a one-week period at a Casual-Dining Restaurant Bar:

Category	Cost of Goods Sold	Beginning Inventory	Ending Inventory	Average Inventory	Inventory Turnover Rate
Liquor	$1,854	$1,554	$1,285	$_____	$_____
Wine	2,234	1,995	2,100	$_____	$_____
Beer	3,525	2,985	3,622	$_____	$_____

Calculations:

2. Calculate the **Alcohol Beverage Inventory Turnover Rate** for liquor, wine, and beer categories for a one-week period at a Sports Bar.

Category	Cost of Goods Sold	Beginning Inventory	Ending Inventory	Average Inventory	Inventory Turnover Rate
Liquor	$3,615.75	$2,739.50	$2,698.50	$_____	$_____
Wine	1,309.50	974.50	1,051.50	$_____	$_____
Beer	2,137.50	1,593.00	1,605.25	$_____	$_____

Calculations:

3. Calculate the **Alcohol Beverage Inventory Turnover Rate** for liquor, wine, and beer categories for a one-week period at a Cocktail Lounge within a Fine Dining Restaurant.

Category	Cost of Goods Sold	Beginning Inventory	Ending Inventory	Average Inventory	Inventory Turnover Rate
Liquor	$1,967.25	$1,794.50	$1,744.50	$_____	$_____
Wine	1,042.50	862.25	905.25	$_____	$_____
Beer	815.50	685.00	710.50	$_____	$_____

Calculations:

Summary

Management will determine how large of an alcohol beverage inventory to stock and how large a selection of brands to carry based on the following: sales volume, customer preferences, amount of inventory storage space available, supplier delivery schedules, supplier price specials, availability of vintage and imported wines, food menus, banquet or catered events, holidays, and a budgeted financial investment.

The alcohol beverage inventory turnover rate for each beverage category—liquor, wine, and beer—is calculated by dividing the cost of goods sold for each category by the average inventory for each category. The turnover rates can fluctuate depending on how quickly the beverage operation uses the inventory and how often products are ordered.

The objective of an alcohol beverage control system is to have complete control over alcohol beverages. This begins with accounting for all alcohol beverage usage, reconciling receipts of bottles into the bar against bottles used, and automatically reordering as needed. This can be accomplished when using an Alcohol Beverage Inventory and Sales Control Report and an Alcohol Beverage Storeroom Inventory Report.

Protecting against theft from managers, bookkeepers, bartenders, servers, and customers requires a comprehensive beverage management system. There are numerous ways in which cheating can occur, therefore maintaining tight controls over inventory, controlling pouring techniques, creating an order system that documents drink orders, and conducting random "cash drop"checks are all effective means.

Discussion Questions

1. When determining how large of an alcohol beverage inventory to stock along with how large a selection of brands to carry, what must management consider? List five critical points.

2. The Alcohol Beverage Inventory Turnover Rate is usually calculated by category—liquor, wine, and beer. Explain the two-step procedure for each category.

3. What can cause fluctuating inventory turnover rates?

4. Describe how an alcohol beverage inventory and sales control system functions.

5. Explain the purpose of the Alcohol Beverage Storeroom Inventory Report.

6. Discuss two possible methods of theft by managers and bookkeepers.

7. Describe the methods that bartenders and servers may use to cheat. List five.

8. An effective beverage management system can discourage and prevent theft. What should that system include?

9. During a very busy shift, management conducts a random "cash drop" and finds $120 more in cash than what is reported in the POS system sales total. What could be a possible explanation?

**Beverage
Cost Control**

Restaurant Reality

Workers collude in theft

A large restaurant and banquet facility located in a major city was experiencing a food cost percentage increase every week. The volume of business had been consistent, there were no significant price increases from suppliers or distributors, the dining room and banquet managers and chefs had been long-term employees, tight management controls were in place, and nothing seemed out-of-the-ordinary except for the increasing food cost percentage. A central kitchen serviced the restaurant dining room and banquet facility. Something mysterious was happening.

The general manager reviewed the inventory par amounts, requisitions, POS guest checks, banquet sales, and purchases for the dining room and banquet departments. The meat and seafood purchases had been increasing, specifically 6-ounce filet mignon steaks, 10-ounce NY steaks, and lobster tails. Those were the items that did not balance: customer orders, requisitions to the central kitchen from the storeroom, and purchases. Upon further analysis, the requisitions and purchases were accounted for, but something was happening in the kitchen. The product items requested and delivered to the kitchen did not all get sold to dining room or banquet customers. A significant amount of those items was missing. Theft was occurring.

The dining room and banquet managers along with the chefs were furious and determined to find whomever was responsible. But the immediate issue was to identify how the items were being taken out of the kitchen refrigerators. There were no surveillance cameras in the kitchen, so the general manager began walking through the kitchen, the refrigeration area, all the way to the loading and receiving area at the rear of the building. He was looking for something, anything that would solve this mystery. As he was standing in that area, he noticed 12 cases of empty imported beer bottles that would be exchanged for full cases with the beer delivery scheduled for later that day. Two of the boxes were marked with a small black X, which raised his curiosity. He pulled those boxes out and found randomly placed steaks and lobster tails packed among the empty beer bottles. Part of this mystery was solved.

The chefs began watching the dishwasher, who was also responsible for cleaning and wiping down the refrigerators during his shift; an older, slightly mentally impaired man who would not do something like this on his own. When caught in the act of putting steaks and lobster tails in an empty trash bag and taking it to the loading and receiving area, he said that the liquor storeroom attendant would then do the rest. He further said that the liquor storeroom attendant told him that they weren't being paid enough for their work and this was a way to earn some extra money. The beer truck driver was selling the steaks and lobster tails for cash that he would split with the liquor storeroom attendant and the dishwasher.

The mystery was solved. Although alcohol beverages were not stolen, the people entrusted with the security of those items were responsible for the theft of expensive food items, which resulted in losing their jobs and having criminal records.

13

Espresso Drink Control

Introduction

This chapter provides an introduction to how espresso drinks are prepared and priced to market conditions, and how ingredient costs are identified and controlled.

Learning Objectives

Upon successfully completing this chapter, readers will be able to:

1. Understand how espresso drinks are prepared.
2. Explain the difference between latte, cappuccino, and mocha drinks.
3. Calculate espresso drink cost percentages.
4. Understand how syrups are used to flavor espresso drinks.
5. Know how alcohol spirits and liqueurs can be added to espresso and coffee.

Chapter Outline

Espresso Process and Equipment

Espresso Drinks

Espresso Drink Cost Analysis

Disposable Paper Items

Spirited Espresso and Coffee Drinks

Summary

Discussion Questions

Project Exercises

Key Terms and Definitions

Begin by first reading the key terms and their definitions. An advance understanding of the terms will be helpful prior to reading the chapter.

Barista	The person who prepares espresso drinks.
Cappuccino	An approximate mixture of 10% espresso, 45% steamed milk, and 45% milk foam.
Cost Percentage	Will fluctuate with an increase or decrease in the cost of ingredients, as determined by market conditions.
Crema	Thin layer of foam that floats on top of espresso.
Demitasse	2- to 3-ounce cup used to serve espresso.
Espresso Coffee	Specialty blended and roasted coffee, finely ground, brewed rapidly—20 to 25 seconds—under pressure, through a fine mesh screen filter.
Espresso Shot	Typically made from 7 grams of fine ground coffee.
Latte	An approximate mixture of 10% espresso, 80% steamed milk, and 10% milk foam.
Mocha	An approximate mixture of 10% espresso, 8% chocolate syrup, and 82% steamed milk.
Syrups	Used to enhance the taste of lattes and cappuccinos.

Espresso Process and Equipment

Espresso is the method of brewing not the bean. There is a large variety of beans and blends of beans used.

Espresso is an Italian style of coffee produced through a process in which a specialty blended and roasted coffee, finely ground, is brewed rapidly—20 to 25 seconds—under pressure, through a fine mesh screen filter.

LEARNING OBJECTIVE 1
Understand how espresso drinks are prepared.

▶ A **barista** is the person who prepares espresso drinks.

▶ **Espresso is traditionally served in a demitasse**—2- to 3-ounce—cup with a thin layer of foam—called crema—floating on top of the drink.

▶ **An espresso machine** consists of a pump to create pressure, a steam boiler tank with an element to produce hot water/steam, and a continuous flow cycle through heat exchange to produce freshly extracted espresso coffee. The machine also includes a hot water valve and a steam valve with a steaming wand to steam milk.

▶ **Automatic espresso machines** allow the press of a single button to start the entire process, which begins with grinding the coffee beans. A keypad allows for several different one-touch drink buttons (that is latte, cappuccino, etc.) for quick, precise drinks. Espresso and milk quantities are set for each drink according to predetermined drink sizes.

Automatic machines are usually the most used because they save time and ensure quality and consistency.

Espresso Drinks

Among the most popular espresso drinks are lattes, cappuccinos, and mochas. They are made with different amounts of the same ingredients, with one exception as follows:

Latte

An approximate mixture of   10% espresso
80% steamed milk
10% milk foam

LEARNING OBJECTIVE 2
Explain the difference between latte, cappuccino, and mocha drinks.

Cappuccino*

An approximate mixture of   10% espresso
45% steamed milk
45% milk foam

* When made with half-and-half instead of milk it is called "Café Breva."

Mocha

An approximate mixture of   10% espresso
8% chocolate syrup
82% steamed milk

NOTE: The above percentages will vary according to the size of the drink and according to the various drink combinations created by baristas. For example, by adding an additional shot of espresso and/or syrups, a variety of flavored drinks can be created, changing the percentages shown above.

Each customized espresso drink can result in a different selling price based on the customer's choice of ingredient combinations.

The selling price for espresso drinks is often determined by the following:

1. **Type of Operation:** Fine dining, theme restaurant, or coffee house
2. **Location:** Fast-paced, high traffic, or neighborhood community
3. **Market Conditions:** The number and type of competing coffee houses that may sell similar drinks and food items

Espresso Drink Cost Analysis, Figure 13.1 on p. 244, is an example of a standard that is set forth by management in establishing drink sizes and identifying ingredient costs, selling prices, and cost percentages in relationship to selling prices. Refer to Figure 13.1 as the calculations in the next section are explained.

Espresso Ingredient Calculations

Espresso

> **LEARNING OBJECTIVE 3**
> Calculate espresso drink cost percentages.

▶ **One shot of espresso** is typically made from 7 grams of fine ground coffee as per espresso machine setting and will produce an average of 1.5 ounces of espresso.

One pound of espresso coffee with an average waste factor of 0.07% **will yield approximately 60 shots of espresso**, calculated as follows:

$$1 \text{ pound} = 453.6 \text{ grams}$$

Multiply the total number of grams by the average waste factor to determine the number of grams lost due to waste.

$$453.6 \text{ grams} \times 0.07\% = \textbf{31.75 grams lost due to waste}$$

From the total number of grams subtract the number of grams lost due to waste to identify the **yield.**

$$453.6 \text{ grams} - 31.75 \text{ grams} = \textbf{421.9 grams}$$

Divide the yield by the number of grams per shot (7) to identify the number of shots per pound.

421.9 grams ÷ 7 grams per shot = 60.27 rounded to **60 shots per pound**

▶ **Espresso coffee on average may cost about $7.50 per pound.** A unit price (cost per shot) is therefore calculated as follows:

Unit Cost (per-pound cost)	÷	Yield (shots per pound)	=	**Unit Price (cost per shot)**
$7.50	÷	60	=	**$0.125 per shot**

NOTE: Premium brands of espresso coffee will be priced several dollars per pound higher.

▶ **The typical drink serving sizes are:** small—12 ounces; medium—16 ounces; and large—20 ounces.

▷ 12-ounce drinks usually contain a single shot of espresso.

▷ 16- or 20-ounce drinks usually contain double shots of espresso.

◆ 20-ounce drinks may contain a triple shot of espresso.

◆ Customers may order additional shots, which would be charged as "added shots," ranging in price from 40 to 60 cents per shot.

Milk

▶ Milk is poured into a stainless steel pitcher and placed under the steam wand nozzle to be heated and steamed—unless an automatic machine is used.

▷ When steamed, milk will foam up and expand. The expansion will typically range from 20 to 50 percent, depending on the intended use (latte, cappuccino, or mocha).

▷ There is an average waste factor of about 10% for the amount of milk that remains unused in the pitcher, which would have to be calculated into the portion cost for each serving size of milk. The waste factor is eliminated with an automatic espresso machine.

▶ To determine the milk portion cost:

Milk is often purchased in half-gallon sizes at about $1.92 per half-gallon (unit cost). There are approximately 64 servable ounces in a half-gallon. The cost for 1 ounce is calculated as follows:

				Unit Price
Unit Cost	÷	Yield	=	**(Cost per Ounce)**
$1.92	÷	64 ounces	=	**$0.030 per ounce**

For the 12-ounce Latte—10 ounces of steamed milk is required, which is calculated as follows:

Steamed Milk		Unit Price		**Extended Price**
per Serving	×	per Ounce	=	**(Milk Portion Cost)**
10 ounces	×	$0.030	=	**$0.30**

NOTE: The same procedure is followed to determine the Milk Portion Cost for all of the drinks in Figure 13.1.

▷ Customers may request non-fat milk (skim milk), 2%, half-and-half, soy, or almond milk. Some operators will charge extra for half-and-half, soy, and almond milk, but most operators will not.

▷ **Half-and-Half** is often purchased in half-gallon sizes at about $5.10 per half-gallon.

				Unit Price
Unit Cost	×	Yield	=	**(Cost per Ounce)**
$5.10	×	64 ounces	=	**$0.079 per ounce**

▷ **Soy Milk and Almond Milk** are often purchased in half-gallon sizes at about $3.80 per half-gallon.

				Unit Price
Unit Cost	÷	Yield	=	**(Cost per Ounce)**
$3.80	÷	64 ounces	=	**$0.059 per ounce**

Espresso Drink Cost Analysis

Drink Type	Small 12 ounces		Medium 16 ounces		Large 20 ounces	

Latte

Ingredient	Amount	Cost	Amount	Cost	Amount	Cost
Espresso	1 shot	$0.125	2 shots	$0.250	3 shots	$0.375
Steamed Milk	10.0 oz	$0.300	12.0 oz	$0.360	15.0 oz	$0.450
Foam (no cost)						

	Small	Medium	Large
Total Cost of Goods Sold:	$0.425	$0.610	$0.825
Selling Price:	$3.50	$4.00	$4.50
Cost Percentage:	**12.1%**	**15.3%**	**18.3%**
[Total Cost ÷ Selling Price]	[$0.425 ÷ $3.50 = 0.121]	[$0.610 ÷ $4.00 = $0.153]	[$0.825 ÷ $4.50 = $0.183]

Cappuccino

Ingredient	Amount	Cost	Amount	Cost	Amount	Cost
Espresso	1 shot	$0.125	2 shots	$0.250	3 shots	$0.375
Steamed Milk	7.5 oz	$0.225	9.5 oz	$0.285	11.5 oz	$0.345
Foam (no cost)						

	Small	Medium	Large
Total Cost of Goods Sold:	$0.350	$0.535	$0.720
Selling Price:	$3.50	$4.00	$4.50
Cost Percentage:	**10.0%**	**13.4%**	**16.0%**
[Total Cost ÷ Selling Price]	[$0.350 ÷ $3.50 = 0.100]	[$0.535 ÷ $4.00 = $0.134]	[$0.720 ÷ $4.50 = $0.160]

Mocha

Ingredient	Amount	Cost	Amount	Cost	Amount	Cost
Espresso	1 shot	$0.125	2 shots	$0.250	3 shots	$0.375
Chocolate Syrup	1.0 oz	$0.150	1.5 oz	$0.225	2.0 oz	$0.300
Steamed Milk	8.5 oz	$0.255	10.5 oz	$0.315	13.0 oz	$0.390

	Small	Medium	Large
Total Cost of Goods Sold:	$0.530	$0.790	$1.065
Selling Price:	$3.85	$4.35	$4.85
Cost Percentage:	**13.8%**	**18.2%**	**22.0%**
[Total Cost ÷ Selling Price]	[$0.530 ÷ $3.85 = 0.138]	[$0.790 ÷ $4.35 = $0.182]	[$1.065 ÷ $4.85 = $0.220]

Cost Per Unit

Espresso	$0.125	per shot
Milk	$0.030	per ounce
Chocolate Syrup	$0.150	per ounce
Syrup	$0.207	per ounce
Half & Half	$0.079	per ounce
Soy Milk	$0.059	per ounce
Almond Milk	$0.059	per ounce
Whipped Cream	$0.100	per ounce

Selling Price

Additional Shot	$0.50
Syrup	$0.40
Half & Half	$0.45
Soy Milk	$0.40
Almond Milk	$0.40
Whipped Cream	$0.40

Figure 13.1   Espresso Drink Cost Analysis

Chocolate Syrup

▶ Chocolate syrup is often purchased in half-gallon sizes at about $9.60 per half-gallon.

▶ To determine the chocolate syrup cost:

				Unit Price
Unit Cost	÷	Yield	=	**(Cost per Ounce)**
$9.60	÷	64 ounces	=	**$0.15 per ounce**

For the 12-ounce Mocha—1 ounce of chocolate syrup is required which is calculated as follows:

Syrup				**Extended Price**
Serving Size	×	Unit Price	=	**(Chocolate Syrup Portion Cost)**
1 ounce	×	$0.15 per ounce	=	**$0.15 per portion**

> NOTE: The same procedure is followed to determine the Chocolate Syrup Portion Cost for all of the Mocha drinks.

The typical serving size is 1 ounce of chocolate syrup for a 12-ounce mocha, 1.5 ounces for a 16-ounce mocha, and 2 ounces for a 20-ounce mocha. A hand push-down pump is placed in every new bottle of syrup and automatically set to dispense 1 ounce of syrup when fully pressed down. A 0.05-ounce serving is dispensed when pressed half-way down.

Syrups

▶ **Lattes and cappuccinos** can be enhanced with a number of different syrups that are available in a variety of flavors, such as caramel, vanilla, raspberry, almond, hazelnut, Irish cream, and butter rum.

▶ To determine the syrup cost:

Syrups are typically purchased in 750 mL bottles at about $5.25 per bottle. There are approximately 25.4 servable ounces in a 750 mL bottle. The cost for 1 ounce is calculated as follows:

				Unit Price
Unit Cost	÷	Yield	=	**Unit Price**
$5.25	÷	25.4 ounces	=	**$0.207 per ounce**

A 1-ounce serving of syrup is calculated as follows:

Syrup		Unit		**Extended Price**
Serving Size	×	Price	=	**(Syrup Portion Cost)**
1 ounce	×	$0.207 per ounce	=	**$0.207 per portion**

The typical serving size for a 12-ounce latte or cappuccino is 1 ounce of syrup. For 16- and 20-ounce drinks, a double or triple serving of syrup flavor is needed. The average charge for syrup flavoring is between 30 and 60 cents per flavor.

> **LEARNING OBJECTIVE 4**
> Understand how syrups are used to flavor espresso drinks.

> Syrup brands will have different costs and flavor intensities. Therefore, management determines the syrup brand that best matches customers' preferences.

Toppings

▶ **Whipped cream topping** is a favorite choice for many customers and may be offered for an additional charge when requested. The average cost for a serving of whipped cream is 10 cents. Most operators will include the whipped cream topping with the price of the drink at no additional charge.

▶ **The whipped cream may be topped off** with a swizzle of chocolate or caramel syrup, chocolate sprinkles, cinnamon, nutmeg, vanilla powder, ground sweet chocolate, hazelnut, or a variety of other garnishes at no additional charge.

> NOTE: When syrup or garnishes are used the additional ingredient cost must be determined and added to the total cost of the drink. The cost of the ingredients would be divided by the estimated number of applications. A per drink cost would be identified and added to the total cost of each drink, which may range from $0.005 to $0.01 per drink.

Iced Espresso Drinks

▶ **When espresso drinks are served with ice** an additional selling price may range from 20 to 40 cents per drink.

Drink Cost Percentage

▶ A Drink Cost Percentage is calculated for each drink as shown in Figure 13.1.

In the first example—12-ounce Latte—the cost of the espresso is $0.125, which is added to the cost of the steamed milk of $0.300 to determine the total ingredient cost of $0.425 (Cost of Goods Sold). The Selling Price for the drink is $3.50.

Cost of Goods Sold	÷	Selling Price	=	**Drink Cost Percentage**
$0.425	÷	$3.50	=	.121 = **12.1%**

▶ The Drink Cost Percentage will fluctuate with an increase or decrease in the cost of ingredients, as determined by market conditions.

Complete Assignment 18 on p. 249.

Disposable Paper Items

The majority of espresso drinks that are sold in coffee houses, from espresso carts, and in drive-thrus are prepared in disposable cups. The cost of the cups, lids, stir sticks, straws, coffee cup sleeves, and napkins must be identified.

The cost of these items will vary according to quantities purchased. The greater the volume amount purchased the lower the price. An average price range is as follows:

Cups	$0.05–0.10 per cup (depending on size of cup)
Lids	$0.02–0.04 per lid (depending on size of lid)
Stir Sticks	$0.001–0.002 per stick
Straws	$0.003–0.005 per straw
Sleeves	$ 0.03–0.05 per coffee cup sleeve
Napkins	$0.002–0.004 per napkin

Other Popular Drinks

▶ **Café au Lait**—half coffee, half steamed milk, and a bit of milk foam.

▶ **Americano**—a single shot of espresso with hot water served in a 6- or 8-ounce cup.

▶ **Macchiato**—a shot of espresso topped off with a small amount of foamed milk served in a demitasse cup.

▶ **Espresso Con Panna**—the same as Macchiato except using a dab of whipped cream instead of foamed milk.

Spirited Espresso and Coffee Drinks

Alcohol spirits and liqueurs can be added to espresso and coffee drinks, typically served with a dollop of whipped cream. The popularity of these drinks is increasing; they are often offered in fine-dining restaurants as an after-dinner beverage.

> **LEARNING OBJECTIVE 5**
> Know how alcohol spirits and liqueurs can be added to espresso and coffee.

▶ The espresso and coffee drinks may be served in a traditional 6- or 8-ounce coffee cup or clear glass coffee cup or mug.

▶ The selling prices for spirited espresso and coffee drinks may range from $7.50 to $12.50 per drink depending on the type of restaurant and market conditions.

NOTE: Each spirited espresso and coffee drink would have a Standardized Drink Recipe (see Figure 10.1 on p. 191) and a Drink Cost Card (see Figure 10.3 on p. 197).

Popular Spirited Espresso Drinks

Café Amaretto	Café Bueno	Café Don Juan
¾ cup Espresso	¾ cup Espresso	¾ cup Espresso
1 ounce Amaretto	1½ ounce Brandy	1 ounce Dark Rum
1 ounce Kahlúa	1½ ounce Kahlúa	1 ounce Kahlúa
Whipped Cream	Whipped Cream	Whipped Cream

Popular Spirited Coffee Drinks

Bailey's Irish Cream Coffee*	**Irish Coffee**	**Café Royale**
10 ounces Coffee	¾ cup Coffee	1 cup Coffee
1½ oz Bailey's Irish Cream	1½ oz Irish Whiskey	4 tsps Brandy
Whipped Cream	1 tbl Brown Sugar	1 cube Sugar
	Whipped Cream	Whipped Cream

Others may include the following:

Café Brulot	Café Diablo	Kioki Coffee	Spanish Coffee
Café Corretto	Frangelico Coffee	Mexican Coffee	Venetian Coffee

*Served in a 12-oz. Wine Glass

Popular Non-Caffeinated Drinks

Hot Chocolate

A single shot of chocolate syrup, vanilla, hot milk, and a dab of whipped cream.

Steamers or Creamers

Made with steamed milk and flavored with syrups such as vanilla, hazelnut, cinnamon, almond, etc., and topped with whipped cream.

Assignment 18

Calculate the cost percentage of a 16-ounce latte with the following information:

Espresso Coffee: $10.50 per pound, 60 shots per pound

12 ounces of steamed milk: $0.36

Selling Price: $4.50

Cost Percentage Calculations:

Summary

Espresso is an Italian style of coffee that is traditionally served in a 2- to-3-ounce demitasse cup with a thin layer of foam—called crema—floating on the top of the drink. The barista is the person who prepares the espresso drinks.

Among the most popular espresso drinks are lattes, cappuccino, and mochas. The selling price for espresso drinks is often determined by the type of operation (fine dining, theme restaurant, or coffee house), the location, and the market conditions.

A shot of espresso is typically 1.5 ounces and a pound of espresso ground coffee will yield approximately 60 shots of espresso. The cost of the ground coffee and ingredients can fluctuate with an increase or decrease depending on market conditions.

There is a variety of popular espresso drinks including Café au Lait, Americano, Macchiato, and Espresso Con Panna. Also, there are spirited espresso drinks such as Café Amaretto, Café Bueno, and Café Don Juan, and the popular spirited coffee drinks—Bailey's Irish Cream Coffee, Irish Coffee, and Café Royale.

Discussion Questions

1. Describe the process in preparing an espresso drink.
2. Explain the difference between a latte, cappuccino, and mocha.
3. What are the three factors that determine the selling price for espresso drinks?
4. List the typical espresso drink serving sizes.
5. How are syrups dispensed into espresso drinks?
6. Discuss why espresso drink cost percentages will fluctuate.
7. When adding alcohol spirits or liqueurs to espresso or coffee drinks, why would it be important to have a Standardized Drink Recipe for each drink?

Project Exercises

1. Visit two different coffee houses (e.g., Starbucks, Dunkin', or independently owned) in your community and compare the menu selling prices for three of their most popular espresso drinks. Review the information on the factors that determine the selling prices that was presented in the chapter. Write a one-page report comparing and contrasting the similarities and differences between the two establishments, and if you prefer one over the other, discuss the reasons why.

2. Prepare a Standardized Drink Recipe for a Spirited Espresso or Coffee Drink of your choice and complete the Standardized Drink Recipe form that is available in Excel for this text/workbook. Helpful beverage sites:
   www.allrecipes.com/recipes/134/drinks/coffee
   www.allrecipes.com/making-espresso-drinks/

   — Then prepare a Drink Cost Card for that recipe using the form provided in Excel.

   NOTE: If you completed the project exercise that began in chapter 1, creating a semi á la carte menu, consider selecting a spirited espresso or coffee drink that would complement that menu.

Financial and Operational Reporting

14 Income Statements
and Budgets—Cash
and Card Reporting

The financial position of a foodservice operation has to be monitored in order to identify areas of concern that could possibly jeopardize the profitability and continued success of the business. The sales, often referred to as revenue, along with all of the expenses and profit, has to be documented and analyzed during a scheduled reporting period.

To understand how the foodservice operation is performing, an income statement is prepared, which can quickly provide that information. The manager needs to be able to interpret the information provided and measure the actual results against the planned results, and then establish a plan of action for the next reporting period.

When handling cash and processing credit and debit cards, there must be strict procedures in place.

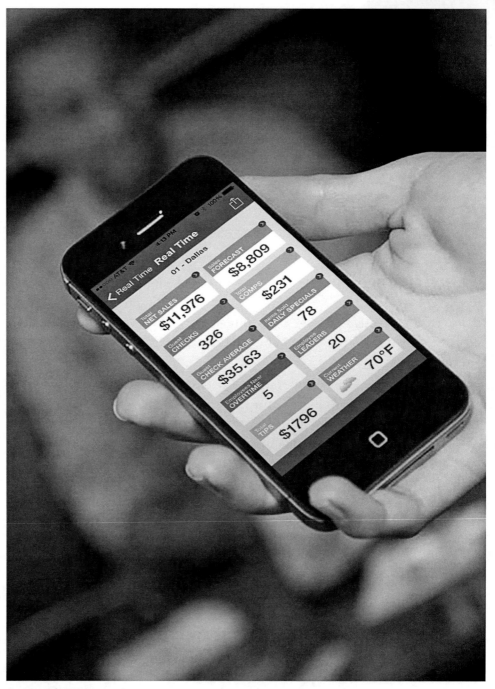

Courtesy of NCR Corporation.

14

Income Statements and Budgets—Cash and Card Reporting

Introduction

The Income Statement is a report of all income, expenses, and profit (or loss) for a specific accounting period. An Income Statement is also referred to as a Profit and Loss Statement commonly known as the P & L.

Restaurant owners and managers use the Income Statement to report the financial performance of the business in order to keep the operation focused and performing according to budgeted goals.

Cash and Card Reporting must be secured with control procedures for handling cash and processing credit and debit cards.

Learning Objectives

Upon successfully completing this chapter, readers will be able to:

1. Describe how an Income Statement is used in foodservice operations.
2. Assess the performance of Income Statement categories: sales, cost of goods sold, controllable expenses, occupational costs, and profit or loss.
3. Understand expense detail line items.
4. Recognize favorable and unfavorable variances from forecasted amounts and budget goals.
5. Identify possible reasons for unacceptable variances.
6. Recognize when corrective action needs to be implemented in order to improve results.
7. Explain how cash and card transactions are tightly controlled and documented.

Chapter Outline

Understanding the Income Statement
Expense Detail
Analyzing the Costs by Category
Reviewing Performance

Cash and Card Reporting
Summary
Discussion Questions

Key Terms and Definitions

Begin by first reading the key terms and their definitions. An advance understanding of the terms will be helpful prior to reading the chapter.

Cash Turn-In Report	Identifies the currency (notes and coins), quantity and amount of each, beginning with opening bank amount and final amount at the end of the cashier's shift.
Cash & Card Sales Report	Checks the accuracy of the cashier, reports credit and debit card transactions, and gift card redeemed amounts. Tracks food and beverage sales, amount of sales tax collected, and amount of staff tips collected.
Controllable Costs	The costs that can be managed—that is, costs within the manager's control.
Controllable Expenses	All operating costs directly related to generating sales revenue.
Cost of Goods Sold	All of the product costs incurred by each revenue center: food and beverage.
Direct Operating Expenses	Cleaning supplies, paper goods, china, glassware, flatware, uniforms, table linens, kitchen smallwares, contract services such as trash removal and pest control.
Expense Detail	Identifies costs in the major purchasing categories.
Fixed Costs	The costs that stay the same for a period of time.
Income Statement	Profit performance presented in an accounting report.
Mixed Costs	The costs that are made up of both variable and fixed costs.
Occupation Costs	The noncontrollable fixed costs, which remain the same.
Operating Cost	An expense incurred to generate sales revenue.
Prime Costs	The categories of food, beverage, and labor, which are typically reported daily and weekly through a POS system.
Profit	The amount of income left when all of the expenses are paid from income.
Sales Mix	The ratio of income earned from each source of total sales.
Variable Cost	The amount of money allocated to an item will fluctuate or change with an increase or decrease in sales.
Variance	The difference between a budget goal percentage and an actual percentage, which can be favorable or unfavorable.

Understanding the Income Statement

Profit performance is presented in an accounting report known as the Income Statement. An Income Statement is simply subtracting expenses from income and is typically prepared for the month, quarter (every three months), and annually. It can also be prepared weekly by averaging the monthly fixed costs into weekly amounts.

The Income Statement, as shown in Figure 14.1 on p. 257, for the month period ending 01/31/20xx, has the following components:

> ▸ **Sales** reports income earned from sales to customers, commonly referred to as the sales revenue. The sales revenue was generated from two revenue centers: Food and Beverage.

> ▸ **Cost of Goods Sold** reports all of the product costs incurred by each revenue center: Food and Beverage.

> ▸ **Controllable Expenses** are all other operating costs directly related to generating sales revenue.

> ▸ **Occupation Costs** are fixed costs—the costs that have to be paid whether the business is open or closed, busy or slow.

> ▸ **Profit or Loss** reports income left when all of the expenses are paid from income—the profit or loss is what is reported for the accounting period.

LEARNING OBJECTIVE 1
Describe how an Income Statement is used in foodservice operations.

Sales

The Sales in Figure 14.1 represent income earned from two sources: Food and Beverage. The **sales mix percentage** of each source category is its ratio to the Total Sales and is calculated using the following formula:

Food Sales	÷	Total Sales	=	**Sales Mix %**
$220,679	÷	$275,849	=	0.7999 rounded up to **80%**

Beverage Sales	÷	Total Sales	=	**Sales Mix %**
$55,170	÷	$275,849	=	0.2000 or **20%**

Therefore, 80 percent of the restaurant sales is derived from food sales and 20 percent from beverage sales. The sales mix ratio of food and beverage sales is frequently monitored—any shift in the sales pattern can affect overall profit because beverage sales are more profitable than food sales.

Other Components of the Income Statement

Cost of Goods Sold	
Food Cost	The cost of all food and non-alcohol beverages.
Beverage Cost	The cost of liquor, wine, beer and serving ingredients.

Controllable Expenses	
Payroll Cost	The cost of wages and salaries, payroll taxes, workers' comprehensive insurance, health insurance, vacation and sick days, and employee meals.
Direct Operating Expenses	Cleaning supplies, paper goods, china, glassware, flatware, uniforms, table linens, kitchen smallwares, and contract services such as trash removal and pest control.
Advertising & Marketing	Advertising in newspapers, direct mail, TV, and Internet, and all costs for promotion and marketing programs.
Music & Entertainment	Music license fees, entertainment such as a pianist for live piano entertainment in the dining room or lounge.
Utilities	Gas, electric, oil (for heating), water, telephone, Internet, and cable television.
Maintenance & Repairs	Maintenance and repairs of kitchen equipment, dining room and bar equipment, fixtures and furnishing, fire safety systems, POS systems, the parking lot, landscaping, snow removal, etc.
Administration and general	Office supplies, accounting, human resource and training costs, banking fees, etc.

The terms of a commercial triple net lease require a business to pay for the building maintenance and repair, property tax, and property insurance.

Occupation Costs	
Rent	Rent for a building or business space within a building or mall property; a lease contract may be for a fixed monthly rent or may be for a monthly base rent amount plus a percentage of the monthly sales.
Property Tax	A lease may require the business to pay the property tax for the building or portion of the tax for the space leased within the building.
Other Taxes	Some state and municipalities impose a property tax on the value of the equipment owned and used by the business and may also impose a city transit tax applied to all businesses.
Property Insurance	A lease may require the business to pay for insurance of the building against any loss resulting from fire, hurricane, flood, etc.
Interest Expense	The interest paid on loans for the purchase of equipment or property for the business.
Depreciation	A building or space within a building (if it has been purchased), furnishings, fixtures and equipment, along with leasehold improvements of a rental building—a portion of the original cost of those investments is charged for using them during the accounting period.

Using an Income Statement to Evaluate Profit Performance

The Income Statement is a record of what had occurred during an accounting period and is used to answer the following questions:

1. Did the sales revenue meet the forecasted goals for the period?
2. Why did sales revenue increase or decrease?
3. Which expenses increased more or less than the budget amounts?

> **LEARNING OBJECTIVE 2**
> Assess the performance of Income Statement categories: sales, cost of goods sold, controllable expenses, occupational costs, and profit or loss.

Income Statement

Period Ending: 01/31/20xx

Sales		
Food	$220,679	80.00%
Beverage	55,170	20.00%
Total Sales:	**$275,849**	**100.00%**
Cost of Goods Sold		
Food Cost	$70,196	31.81%
Beverage Cost	12,255	22.21%
Total Cost of Goods Sold:	**$82,451**	**29.89%**
Gross Profit:	$193,398	70.11%
Controllable Expenses		
Payroll Cost	$93,132	33.76%
Direct Operating Expenses	12,715	4.61%
Advertising & Marketing	8,280	3.00%
Music & Entertainment	1,875	0.68%
Utilities	13,989	5.07%
Maintenance & Repairs	7,674	2.78%
Administration & General	3,250	1.18%
Total Controllable Expenses:	**$140,915**	**51.08%**
Income before Occupation Costs:	$52,483	19.03%
Occupation Costs		
Rent	$16,050	5.82%
Property Tax	4,115	1.49%
Other Taxes	1,769	0.64%
Property Insurance	2,956	1.07%
Interest Expense	2,437	0.88%
Depreciation	5,765	2.09%
Total Occupation Costs:	**$33,092**	**12.00%**
Restaurant Profit before Taxes:	**$19,391**	**7.03%**

Figure 14.1 Income Statement

Expense Detail

The expense detail identifies costs in the major purchasing categories, which allows management to analyze the expense details in each of those categories. Therefore, the expense amounts for each category contain the details that identify all the individual expenses that make up a specific line item, such as food cost $70,196 or beverage cost $12,255 under cost of goods sold.

The Expense Detail for Food Cost would be as follows:

Meats	$16,560	7.50%
Poultry	9,392	4.26
Seafood	13,110	5.94
Dairy	4,324	1.96
Bakery	3,719	1.69
Grocery	17,149	7.77
Produce	5,942	2.69
Total Food Cost	**$70,196**	**31.81%**

The Expense Detail for Beverage Cost would be as follows:

Liquor	$6,306	11.43%
Wine	2,610	4.73
Beer	3,339	6.05
Total Beverage Cost	**$12,255**	**21.21%**

The sum of the Total Food Cost and Total Beverage Cost ($82,451) comprises the Total Cost of Goods Sold. The Cost of Goods Sold percentage is calculated as follows:

$$\frac{\text{Cost of}}{\text{Goods Sold}} \div \text{Total Sales} = \frac{\textbf{Cost of}}{\textbf{Goods Sold \%}}$$

$$\$82,451 \div \$275,849 = 0.2989 = \textbf{29.89\%}$$

If a manager wants to know the cost percentage of a particular item (e.g., meats or liquor), he/she would use the following calculations:

$$\frac{\text{Total Cost}}{\text{of Meats}} \div \frac{\text{Total}}{\text{Food Sales}} = \textbf{Meats Cost \%}$$

$$\$16,560 \div \$220,679 = 0.075 = \textbf{7.5\%}$$

$$\frac{\text{Total Cost}}{\text{of Liquor}} \div \frac{\text{Total}}{\text{Beverage Sales}} = \textbf{Liquor Cost \%}$$

$$\$6,306 \div \$55,170 = 0.1143 = \textbf{11.43\%}$$

The same calculating procedure is followed for each category item, as well as for each line item expense listed under controllable expenses and occupational costs.

Analyzing the Costs by Category

To analyze the Income Statement and to assess how the business is performing, you have to know what to look for and have to understand cost characteristics and behaviors when sales revenue changes and how each category has an effect on profit.

▶ **What is an operating cost, and why is it controllable and variable?** An **operating cost** is an expense incurred to generate sales revenue. As such, it is considered variable in relationship to sales because as sales increase or decrease, more or fewer dollars have to be spent to generate the new level of sales.

Spending more or fewer dollars to generate that increase or decrease in sales is acceptable, which is the controllable aspect of the cost.

▶ **Controllable costs** are costs that can be managed—that is, costs within the manager's control. These are the operating costs that are incurred as part of the day-to-day business operation. Standard operating procedures are in place to control each cost: food and beverage—listed under cost of goods sold—and payroll—listed under controllable expenses. The **prime cost** categories of food, beverage, and labor are typically reported daily and weekly through a POS system software program, and when unacceptable variances occur they can be promptly corrected.

▶ **Variable costs** are variable because the amount of money allocated to that line item has to fluctuate or change with sales. For example: food cost is a variable cost—it is the amount of money spent to purchase food needed to generate food sales.

> The most important point to understand about variable costs is that even though the dollars might be changing because of sales increases or decreases, the percent-to-sales ratio must not change.

▷ The amount to purchase is determined by the par amounts on the order sheets, which were computed by standardized HACCP Recipes, standardized portion sizes, and customer count forecasts. Therefore, the amount of food purchased for a forecast amount of 3,500 customers will not be the amount of food needed if sales are actually running closer to 4,000 customers—more food will have to be purchased. So the dollar value of the food cost on the Income Statement will be more (or less if sales were to decline to 3,000 customers).

▷ The food cost percentage budget goal (example: 32%) was established because it brought the right quality and quantity of product needed to serve menu items according to operational standards.

▷ Payroll cost, another highly variable cost, is budgeted (see the Payroll Budget Estimate section starting on p. 154 of Chapter 8) to provide the right amount of money and labor hours to staff at levels that deliver the quality of service defined by operational standards (example: 34%).

Although payroll cost is also a **mixed controllable cost**—the *variable portion* of the cost is the number of hourly workers scheduled—according to sales forecasts, more employees are scheduled at busy times and less are scheduled at slower times. The *fixed portion* of payroll has two elements: the cost of hourly staff needed to open the business, and salaried employees—these portions of the payroll are considered fixed because they are unresponsive to sales.

It is important to know the proportion of variable and fixed costs together with the controllable costs before analyzing performance.

▶ **Mixed costs** are made up of both variable and fixed costs. For example, direct operating expenses have variable costs affected by an increase or decrease in sales, such as cleaning supplies, paper goods, uniforms, table linens, and so on, whereas the fixed costs in the direct operating expenses would be the contract service for trash removal and pest control that would not be affected by an increase or decrease in sales.

▶ Management would know the **ratio of fixed costs to variable costs** in each line item and would know if changes in a line item are attributable to a fixed portion of the cost or a variable portion. An example of a change in the fixed portion would be if there was an increase in the cost for either trash removal or pest control service.

Fixed costs have no reaction to sales increases or decreases.

▶ **Fixed costs** stay the same for a period of time. Under Occupation Costs, Rent is a fixed cost because it is a set amount each month unless it is a base amount plus a percentage of sales. Rent is payable each month regardless of the level of sales.

Reviewing Performance

LEARNING OBJECTIVE 4
Recognize favorable and unfavorable variances from forecasted amounts and budget goals.

An analysis of the Income Statement for the Period Ending: 01/31/20xx, Figure 14.1 on p. 257, is as follows:

▶ The **profit or loss line** is the last line, often referred to as the "Bottom Line"—the line that reports how well the restaurant was managed in terms of meeting the planned profit goal for the period. If the profit goal for the month of January was set at 7% and the profit line shows a 7.03% profit, then the profit goal was achieved.

		Restaurant Profit %	Restaurant Profit Goal %
Restaurant Profit before Taxes	$19,391	7.03%	7.00%

▶ The overall performance of the restaurant operation is further revealed in each component of the Income Statement beginning with **Sales**. Management prepares a sales forecast based on the sales history for the same periods (weekly, monthly, quarterly, annually) of the previous year. If the sales forecast goal for total sales for the month of January was $282,500 and the actual total sales line shows $275,849, then the total sales goal was not achieved—resulting in $6,651 less than forecasted ($282,500 − 275,849 = $6,651). Management needs to identify the reasons why the total sales were less, although the 80% food sales and 20% beverage sales ratio remained a constant. Therefore, what caused a drop in sales that did not affect the 80 and 20% ratio?

Sales			Forecasted Sales		
Food	$220,679	80.00%	Food	$226,000	80.00%
Beverage	55,170	20.00%	Beverage	56,500	20.00%
Total Sales	$275,849	100.00%	Total Forecasted Sales	$282,500	100.00%

▷ If the ratio had changed, overall profit could have been affected—beverage sales are more profitable than food sales. The **cost of goods sold** component reflects management's ability to control food cost and beverage cost in the day-to-day operation of the business. The food and beverage sales may increase or decrease, but if operating standards are maintained and strictly followed, the food cost and beverage cost percentage budgeted goals can be achieved.

▷ Although the actual sales were less than the forecasted sales, management responded in a way that kept the cost of goods sold in line with the budgeted goal of 30%—along with the budgeted goal of a 32% food cost percentage and a 22% beverage cost percentage.

Actual Cost of Goods Sold		Actual Cost %	Budget Goals %
Food Cost	$70,196	31.81%	32.00%
Beverage Cost	12,255	22.21%	22.00%
Total Cost of Goods Sold	**$82,451**	**29.89%**	**30.00%**

► The **expense detail** is also reviewed to further verify that the percentages are in line for all purchases within the food cost and beverage cost categories.

► The **controllable expenses** component is another area of the day-to-day business operation that is under the direct control of management. This particularly requires constant attention to payroll cost—and in promptly adjusting the hourly employees' work schedules in response to an increase or decrease in the level of sales.

▷ A payroll cost percentage of 33.76% is in line with a budgeted goal of 34%. The total controllable expenses percentage of 51.08% is below the budgeted 51.75%. Although the percentage amounts are favorable, the expense detail is also carefully reviewed.

Actual Controllable Expenses		Actual Expense %	Budget Goals %
Payroll Cost	$93,132	33.76%	34.00%
Direct Operating Expenses	12,715	4.61%	5.00%
Advertising & Marketing	8,280	3.00%	3.00%
Music & Entertainment	1,875	0.68%	0.50%
Utilities	13,989	5.07%	5.00%
Maintenance & Repairs	7,674	2.78%	2.75%
Administration & General	3,250	1.18%	1.50%
Total Controllable Expenses	**$140,915**	**51.08%**	**51.75%**

► The **occupation costs** component are the noncontrollable fixed costs, which remain the same—but the percentages will increase or decrease according to a decrease or increase in sales. Since there was a decrease in sales by $6,651, the percentages increased by a small amount. The actual total occupation cost percentage is 12.00%, 0.75% higher than the budgeted amount of 11.25%.

Actual Occupation Costs		Actual Cost %	Budget Goals %
Rent	$16,050	5.82%	5.25%
Property Tax	4,115	1.49%	1.45%
Other Taxes	1,769	0.64%	0.60%
Property Insurance	2,956	1.07%	1.05%
Interest Expense	2,437	0.88%	0.85%
Depreciation	5,765	2.09%	2.05%
Total Occupation Costs	**$33,092**	**12.00%**	**11.25%**

Comparing Cost Categories

▶ The **cost of goods sold** (food and beverage costs) were controlled and within an acceptable variance of being less than 00.11% of the budget goal of 30.00%.

▶ The **controllable expenses** were 00.67% under the budget amount of 51.75%.

▶ The **occupation costs** are fixed but remained within an acceptable margin of difference.

▶ The **profit goal** was achieved for the period by a + 00.03%.

	Actual %	Budget %	% Difference
Cost of Goods Sold	29.89%	30.00%	– 00.11%
Controllable Expenses	51.08%	51.75%	– 00.67%
Occupation Costs	12.00%	11.25%	+ 00.75%
Profit	7.03%	7.00%	+ 00.03%
Total	**100.00%**	**100.00%**	

LEARNING OBJECTIVE 5
Identify possible reasons for unacceptable variances.

Management must determine an acceptable percentage amount of variance from the budget goal in each component and line item of the Income Statement and expense detail:

▶ A variance can be acceptable when the difference between budget goal percentage and actual percentage is insignificant, typically less than 00.50%—and no action is required.

▶ A variance exceeding an acceptable percentage would require immediate analysis and action to identify the problem and correct it—typically more than 01.00%.

▶ A **favorable variance** is when actual sales are greater than forecasted sales, when actual expenses are less than the budget goal without compromising product quality and customer service standards, and when profit rises above the profit goal.

▶ An **unfavorable variance** is when actual sales are less than forecasted sales, when actual expenses are more than the budget goal, and when profit falls below the profit goal.

The Income Statement reflects what happened during the accounting period, and when problem areas are identified management needs to take the necessary corrective action as follows:

▶ Enforce an existing standard or standard operating procedure that may have been compromised or omitted for lack of accountability.

▶ Create a new standard or standard operating procedure that can correct a problem area.

▶ Monitor external factors that can affect the normal flow of business, such as extreme weather, increased competition from other restaurants, neighborhood or community events, sporting activities or conventions, and road construction. The impact of certain conditions can be reduced when they are anticipated.

Comparing Sales

	Actual	Forecasted	Difference
Total Sales	$275,849	$282,500	−$6,651

The sales were $6,651 less than forecasted for the month of January—an unfavorable variance attributed to several days of rain with extreme cold weather causing icy road conditions that resulted in slower than anticipated business during those days.

Complete Assignments 19, 20, and 21 on pp. 266–270.

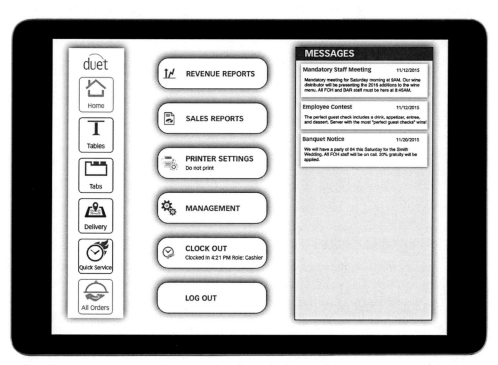

A handheld tablet/Cloud POS system that provides real-time mobile operational information, reports, and alerts—anytime, anywhere. Courtesy of Action Systems, Inc.

Cash and Card Reporting

The foodservice business is like every other business when it comes to recording sales, correctly handling cash and processing credit and debit cards, and maintaining control of the process. The function can be accomplished through a few quick and easy steps that should be performed as a simple business routine. An established procedure will also provide a comfort level of accountability for the employees handling money. Once the employees are trained to the level of management's expectations, they can perform their tasks with a certainty of correctness.

Cash and card transactions must be tightly controlled and documented through the use of appropriate control procedures. A **Cash Turn-In Report**, Figure 14.2, shows the Date: January 15, 20xx, Day: Friday, Department: Dining Room, Shift: 5:00 PM – 10:00 PM, Cashier: by name, and Manager: by name. Typically, this report is printed on the side of a cash deposit envelope. The purpose of the form is to assist the cashier in counting the amount of cash at the end of the shift. It is very similar to preparing a deposit slip for a bank deposit.

The shift begins with a Standard Opening Bank POS cash drawer that specifically identifies the Currency (Notes and Coins), Quantity and Amount of each, and Total Bank Amount: $350.00 as shown in Figure 14.2. That amount, as determined by management, is necessary to adequately service the cash change needs of customers for the shift. At the end of the shift, the cash drawer is removed from the POS terminal, taken to a secure area (manager's office), and the money is counted by both the cashier and manager. The specific Currency, Quantity, and Amounts are totaled, showing the Total Cash from the POS terminal cash drawer ($3,798.78 in the example in Figure 14.2). Less the Total Bank amount ($350.00) results in a Cash Deposit of $3,448.78, which is verified by the signature of the Manager after the cash deposit envelope is sealed. The sealed envelope may be securely placed in the business safe or placed in a locked bank-deposit bag that the manager will drop into a bank night-deposit chute.

The second part of the process is for the manager to compare the actual cash taken in by the cashier, with the POS system reporting the amount of cash that should have been taken in. The **Cash & Card Sales Report**, Figure 14.3, checks the accuracy of the cashier. The POS system software identifies Credit and Debit Card amounts processed along with Gift Card Redeemed amounts. The Report also separates Food Sales and Beverage Sales, has a combined Food & Beverage Subtotal, a Sales Tax collected amount, and Staff Tips collected amount. This analysis provides management with specific cash and card sales reporting for the shift.

Summary amounts shown on Figure 14.3 show Food & Beverage Sales ($14,585.46), Sales Tax Due to State ($1,166.84), and Tips Due to Staff ($2,215.00).

Cash Reconciliation lists the Cash End of Shift ($3,798.78), Less Cash Bank ($350.00) and Net Cash ($3,448.78), showing the actual cash taken-in. (See Figure 14.2, Cash Turn-In Report.) The Net Cash ($3,448.78) is reconciled with the POS system reporting Total Cash Collected ($3,451.23), which is the cash amount that should have been taken in. The Total Cash Collect minus the Net Cash shows $2.45 short. The Reason for the over (short): Error making change.

Cash Turn-In Report

Date: January 15, 20xx   **Department:** Dining Room   **Cashier:** Ricky (Host)
Day: Friday   **Shift:** 5:00 PM–10:00 PM   **Manager:** Mitch (Asst Mgr)

Standard Opening Bank				Ending Cash		
Currency	Quantity	Amount		Currency	Quantity	Amount
Notes				Notes		
$100	0	$0.00		$100	5	$500.00
$50	0	$0.00		$50	31	$1,550.00
$20	3	$60.00		$20	54	$1,080.00
$10	10	$100.00		$10	35	$350.00
$5	20	$100.00		$5	43	$215.00
$1	50	$50.00		$1	80	$80.00
Coins				Coins		
$0.25	80	$20.00		$0.25	49	$12.25
$0.10	100	$10.00		$0.10	58	$5.80
$0.05	120	$6.00		$0.05	94	$4.70
$0.01	400	$4.00		$0.01	103	$1.03
Total Bank		$350.00		Total Cash		$3,798.78

Total Cash	$3,798.78
Less Total Bank	($350.00)
Cash Deposit	**$3,448.78**

Signature: _____Mitch, Assistant Manager_____

Figure 14.2   Cash Turn-In Report

Cash & Card Sales Report

Date: January 15, 20xx   **Department:** Dining Room   **Cashier:** Ricky (Host)
Day: Friday   **Shift:** 5:00 PM–10:00 PM   **Manager:** Mitch (Asst Mgr)

	Food Sales	Beverage Sales	Food & Beverage Subtotal	Sales Tax at 8%	Tips
Card Sales					
Credit Cards	$7,732.18	$1,504.78	$9,236.96	$738.96	$1,390.00
Debit Cards	$1,546.33	$823.25	$2,369.58	$189.57	$375.00
Gift Cards Redeemed	$180.00	$20.00	$200.00	$16.00	$0.00
Total Cards	$9,458.51	$2,348.03	$11,806.54	$944.53	$1,765.00
Cash Sales	$2,250.68	$528.24	$2,778.92	$222.31	$450.00
TOTALS	**$11,709.19**	**$2,876.27**	**$14,585.46**	**$1,166.84**	**$2,215.00**

Summary

Food & Beverage Sales	$14,585.46
Sales Tax Due to State	$1,166.84
Tips Due to Staff	$2,215.00

Cash Reconciliation

Cash End of Shift	$3,798.78
Less Cash Bank	($350.00)
Net Cash	$3,448.78
Total Cash Collected (per POS)	$3,451.23
Total Cash Collect minus Net Cash	($2.45)

Reason for over (short): Error making change

Figure 14.3   Cash & Card Sales Report

Assignment 19

1. Calculate the missing percentages in the following Income Statement for a Casual-Dining Italian Restaurant for the one-month period ending February 28, 20xx.

Income Statement			
Period Ending: 02/28/20xx			
Sales			
Food	$237,542	_____%	Food Sales % Ratio
Beverage	61,820	_____%	Beverage Sales % Ratio
Total Sales:	**$299,362**	**100.00%**	
Cost of Goods Sold			
Food Cost	$75,167	_____%	Food Cost %
Beverage Cost	15,614	_____%	Beverage Cost %
Total Cost of Goods Sold:	**$90,781**	**_____%**	**Cost of Goods Sold %**
Gross Profit:	$208,581	_____%	Gross Profit %
Controllable Expenses			
Payroll Cost	$102,109	_____%	Payroll Cost %
Direct Operating Expenses	14,310	_____%	Direct Operating Exp.%
Advertising & Marketing	8,175	2.73%	
Music & Entertainment	1,875	0.63%	
Utilities	13,872	4.64%	
Maintenance & Repairs	7,848	2.62%	
Administration & General	3,335	1.11%	
Total Controllable Expenses:	**$151,524**	**_____%**	**Controllable Exp. %**
Income before Occupation Costs:	$57,057	_____%	Income before Occ. Cost %
Occupation Costs			
Rent	$16,050	5.36%	
Property Tax	4,115	1.37%	
Other Taxes	1,905	0.64%	
Property Insurance	2,956	0.99%	
Interest Expense	2,437	0.81%	
Depreciation	5,765	1.93%	
Total Occupation Costs:	**$33,228**	**11.10%**	
Restaurant Profit before Taxes:	**$23,829**	**_____%**	**Restaurant Profit %**

Assignment 19 (cont.)

2. Calculate the missing percentages in the following Income Statement for an Upscale Restaurant with a Cocktail Lounge for the one-month period ending March 31, 20xx.

Income Statement
Period Ending: 03/31/20xx

Sales			
Food	$735,452	_____%	Food Sales % Ratio
Beverage	137,506	_____%	Beverage Sales % Ratio
Total Sales:	**$872,958**	**100.00%**	
Cost of Goods Sold			
Food Cost	$203,115	_____%	Food Cost %
Beverage Cost	26,398	_____%	Beverage Cost %
Total Cost of Goods Sold:	**$229,513**	_____%	**Cost of Goods Sold %**
Gross Profit:	$643,445	_____%	Gross Profit %
Controllable Expenses			
Payroll Cost	$285,784	_____%	Payroll Cost %
Direct Operating Expenses	52,387	_____%	Direct Operating Exp.%
Advertising & Marketing	19,228	2.20%	
Music & Entertainment	32,950	3.77%	
Utilities	37,673	4.32%	
Maintenance & Repairs	16,826	1.93%	
Administration & General	9,849	1.13%	
Total Controllable Expenses:	**$454,697**	_____%	**Controllable Exp. %**
Income before Occupation Costs:	$188,748	_____%	Income before Occ. Cost %
Occupation Costs			
Rent	$42,150	4.83%	
Property Tax	6,212	0.71%	
Other Taxes	58,835	6.74%	
Property Insurance	9,027	1.03%	
Interest Expense	7,823	0.90%	
Depreciation	22,350	2.56%	
Total Occupation Costs:	**$146,397**	**16.77%**	
Restaurant Profit before Taxes:	**$42,351**	_____%	Restaurant Profit %

Assignment 19 (cont.)

3. Calculate the missing totals and percentages in the following Income Statement for a Mexican theme restaurant for the one-month period ending June 30, 20xx.

Income Statement
Period Ending: 06/30/20xx

Sales			
Food	$318,963	_____%	Food Sales % Ratio
Beverage	41,010	_____%	Beverage Sales % Ratio
Total Sales:	$_____	100.00%	
Cost of Goods Sold			
Food Cost	$86,971	_____%	Food Cost %
Beverage Cost	7,425	_____%	Beverage Cost %
Total Cost of Goods Sold:	$_____	_____%	**Cost of Goods Sold %**
Gross Profit:	$_____	_____%	Gross Profit %
Controllable Expenses			
Payroll Cost	$109,624	_____%	Payroll Cost %
Direct Operating Expenses	16,868	_____%	Direct Operating Exp.%
Advertising & Marketing	12,285	3.41%	
Music & Entertainment	14,500	4.03%	
Utilities	19,032	5.29%	
Maintenance & Repairs	9,794	2.72%	
Administration & General	6,360	1.77%	
Total Controllable Expenses:	$_____	_____%	**Controllable Exp. %**
Income before Occupation Costs:	$_____	_____%	Income before Occ. Cost %
Occupation Costs			
Rent	$18,950	5.26%	
Property Tax	4,715	1.31%	
Other Taxes	6,821	1.89%	
Property Insurance	4,112	1.14%	
Interest Expense	3,905	1.08%	
Depreciation	8,725	2.42%	
Total Occupation Costs:	$_____	_____%	
Restaurant Profit before Taxes:	$_____	_____%	Restaurant Profit %

Assignment 20

1. Compare the actual percentages from the Income Statement in the first problem in Assignment 19 on p. 266 to the **Budget Percentages** in the missing cost categories below and **calculate the differences.**

	Actual %	Budget %	% Difference
Cost of Goods Sold	_____ %	30.00%	_____ %
Controllable Expenses	_____ %	51.75%	_____ %
Occupation Costs	11.10%	11.25%	−00.15%
Profit	_____ %	7.00%	_____ %

2. Compare the actual percentages from the Income Statement in the second problem in Assignment 19 on p. 267 to the **Budget Percentages** in the missing cost categories below and **calculate the differences.**

	Actual %	Budget %	% Difference
Food Sales	_____ %	85.00%	_____ %
Beverage Sales	_____ %	15.00%	_____ %
Food Cost	_____ %	28.00%	_____ %
Beverage Cost	_____ %	19.00%	_____ %
Payroll Cost	_____ %	34.00%	_____ %
Direct Oper. Expenses	_____ %	6.00%	_____ %
Profit before Taxes	_____ %	5.00%	_____ %

3. Compare the actual percentages from the Income Statement in the third problem in Assignment 19 on p. 268 to the **Budget Percentages** in the missing cost categories below and **calculate the differences.**

	Actual %	Budget %	% Difference
Food Sales	_____ %	88.00%	_____ %
Beverage Sales	_____ %	12.00%	_____ %
Food Cost	_____ %	29.00%	_____ %
Beverage Cost	_____ %	18.00%	_____ %
Payroll Cost	_____ %	32.00%	_____ %
Direct Oper. Expenses	_____ %	5.00%	_____ %
Profit before Taxes	_____ %	8.00%	_____ %

Assignment 21

The actual sales for the period ending 02/28/20xx (in the first problem of Assignment 19 on p. 266) were more than the forecasted sales. **Calculate the difference.**

Comparing Sales:

	Actual	**Forecasted**	**Difference**
Total Sales	$299,362	$287,500	_____

Refer to the category differences that were calculated (in the first problem of Assignment 20 on p. 269), then write a brief analysis of how the restaurant operation performed: **actual compared to budget goal percentages.** Comment on **favorable and unfavorable variances** including the sales mix ratio variance. **The sales mix ratio budget standard is Food Sales 80% and Beverage Sales 20%.**

1. Sales Mix Ratio (as calculated on p. 266):

_____

_____

_____

_____

2. Cost of Goods Sold:

_____

_____

_____

_____

3. Controllable Expenses:

_____

_____

_____

_____

4. Occupation Costs:

_____

_____

_____

_____

5. Profit:

_____

_____

_____

_____

Summary

An Income Statement is simply subtracting expenses from income and is typically prepared for the month, quarter, and annually. The components of an Income Statement include — Sales, Cost of Goods Sold, Controllable Expenses, Occupation Costs, and Profit or Loss. It is a record of what had occurred during an accounting period.

The Expense Detail identifies costs in the major purchasing categories. Therefore, management can review and analyze the individual expenses that make up the totals for each category, such as, meat, poultry, seafood, etc. To determine the cost percentage of a particular item category is determined by dividing the total cost of that category (for example meats) by the total food sales. This would identify what percentage of the costs are attributed to (meat) purchases.

An Operating Cost is an expense incurred to generate sales, and it is controllable and variable based upon an increase or decrease in sales. Controllable Costs are within the manager's control, and are the operating costs for the day-to-day operation of the business. Standard operating procedures are in place to control each cost: food and beverage — and payroll. The prime cost categories of food, beverage, and labor are typically reported daily and weekly through a POS system software program, and when unacceptable variances occur, they can be promptly corrected.

The most important point to understand about variable costs is that even though the dollars might be changing because of sales increases or decreases, the percent-to-sales ratio must not change. Payroll is a highly variable cost, and it is also a mixed controllable cost — the variance portion of the cost is the number of hourly workers scheduled to sales forecasts (more at busy times, less at slower times). The fixed portion of the payroll has two elements: the cost of hourly staff needed to open the business, and salaried employees — those portions of the payroll are considered fixed because they are unresponsive to sales.

Occupation Costs are the noncontrollable fixed costs that remain the same, such as rent, property tax and insurance. The percentages will increase or decrease according to decrease or increase in sales. When comparing cost percentages, that is, the actual compared to budget goal percentages there will be favorable and unfavorable variances. And, when problem areas are identified, management determines the corrective action needed.

All cash and card transactions must be tightly controlled and documented through the use of appropriate control procedures. A Cash Turn-In Report assists the cashier in counting the amount of cash at the end of a shift. The second part of the process is to compare the cash taken-in by the cashier with the POS system reporting the cash amount that should have been taken-in. The Cash & Card Sales Reports reconciles the cash amounts and further details sales tax collected and staff tips.

Discussion Questions

1. Explain the purpose of an Income Statement.
2. List the five components on an Income Statement and briefly discuss each one.
3. When Sales Income is earned from two sources: Food and Beverage — the sales mix percentage of each source category is its ratio to the Total Sales. Explain how each ratio is calculated.
4. The cost of all food and beverages when added together represents a combined total that in accounting terms is called what?
5. Explain the nature of Controllable Expenses and list three examples.
6. Occupation Costs are primarily the costs associated with a building or space within a building, but how is Depreciation applied.
7. Specifically, what questions are addressed on the Income Statement when evaluating profit performance?

8. List five Expense Detail line item categories for Food Cost, and three for Beverage Cost.

9. What is the most important point to understand about variable costs?

10. Payroll cost is a mixed controllable cost — explain the difference between the variable portion and the fixed portion.

11. When comparing a budget goal to the actual performance in the Cost Categories — cost of goods sold, controllable expenses, occupation costs, and profit goal, there will be a variance in each component. Specifically, explain when a variance is favorable and when it is unfavorable.

12. The Income Statement reflects what happened during an accounting period; so, when problem areas are identified, what type of corrective action should be taken by management?

13. Describe how a Cash Turn-In Report accounts for the money taken-in at the end of a shift.

14. Discuss the function of a Cash & Card Sales Report.

Income Statements and Budgets— Cash and Card Reporting

Restaurant Reality

Financial Management Ability and Good People Skills

Fresh out of college with a business marketing degree and some retail sales experience, Ed was anxious to begin a sales career. The company that he would be working for was an innovative leader and pioneer in a product line of office machines.

The machines were popular and the first year of selling was interesting and exciting; always meeting new people. Although successful in selling the machines, his enthusiasm began to diminish. He was repeating the same sales pitch with every new account and the thrill of closing a sale with a signed contract was slowly becoming just a repetitive routine. It was clear that Ed needed to pursue something different, but that presented a difficult decision. So, he decided to further his training by applying to a well-respected business graduate school.

The year in graduate school passed quickly and he discovered a new area of interest and ability: financial analysis and management. It was a time when industries were growing and expanding, and they were aggressively looking to recruit people that could fill management positions. Among those industries was a major international airline that was expanding. That airline would be a great choice, so Ed submitted his resume and was quickly scheduled for an interview. To his surprise, the airline was only looking to hire people for management positions within their foodservice division, which included airline catering (food and beverages served on flights), and airport terminal restaurants. He had no experience in foodservice management and wondered why indeed they would want to interview him; he was about to find out.

The management philosophy of that airline was to hire people with financial management ability and proven skills in motivating people (sales skills). Their eight-week training program involved hands-on experiences, including everything from operating a dishwashing machine to helping prepare food, bussing restaurant tables and serving customers, being a cashier, working to fill requisition orders, assisting with dispensing alcohol beverages, and helping to load catering trucks prior to the food and beverages being boarded on airplanes. Quite simply, they had people working in all of those positions, but they needed management leadership that understood the requirements and needs of those positions and the people that worked them. It was an operational boot-camp that provided the foundational experience that would be essential for achieving results.

This was the something different that Ed was looking for, and it launched a rewarding and never-boring career of endless opportunities and challenges, all within the foodservice industry—including being the author of this textbook. The opportunities are more abundant than ever for people having financial management abilities and good people skills.

A Restaurant Case with Applied Exercises

A
p
p
e
n
d
i
x

The Appendix, which can be considered a capstone to the main text, is geared to a more advanced level for students who want the chance to apply what they have learned to a realistic situation. The Appendix features a restaurant case study, including a menu and menu pricing. The restaurant profiled is comprised of a casual-dining table service restaurant—Farfalle Italiane; the restaurant's full-service catering business—Upstairs Catering at Farfalle Italiane; and its "about to be opened" pizza place—Bello Pizzeria by Farfalle Italiane. Students will perform calculations, evaluations, and recommendations as would the owner of this three-tiered restaurant operation. It concludes with the opportunity to create a menu and establish an operational and marketing plan for a mobile foodservice concept.

Courtesy of NCR Corporation.

The Restaurant Profile

Farfalle Italiane—the Italian way of saying "Italian Bow Tie"—is a casual dining table service restaurant that features authentic foods from traditional recipes of southern Italy. It is open daily for lunch and dinner from 11 A.M. to 10 P.M., Friday and Saturday from 11 A.M. to 11 P.M.

Farfalle Italiane is located in an historic building within the historic business district of a mid-size city. The restaurant occupies a corner storefront with wide windows, which expose its inviting Tuscan atmosphere. Outdoor flower boxes planted with colorful asters hang below the windows. During the spring and summer months, the flowers attract colorful butterflies that fly around the asters and entertain patrons. A tall oak entrance door is located at the corner of the aged, grey-brick building. Above the door is a decorative neon sign with Farfalle Italiane in green letters centered inside an orange bow-tie. The sign, which represents the Farfalle Italiane logo, is printed on the menus and appears on the restaurant's website and in all promotional material.

The dining room comfortably seats 75 and has an overflow area—with banquet seating that can seat an additional 25 and can be reserved by groups for lunch or dinner. Large oil paintings of southern Italian landscapes accent the walls, and the lighting creates a warm and comforting glow that accentuates the room's old-world atmosphere and charm.

The menu is designed to accommodate often hurried lunch customers as well as leisurely dinner guests who prefer to order a full-course meal. The average lunch check is $23, and the average dinner check is $38; brick oven pizzas range from $19 to $24. Farfalle Italiane customers can find street parking or use a nearby public parking lot; hotels, offices and other businesses are all within a short walk. Although other restaurants are located within the historic district, Farfalle Italiane offers a distinctively different menu with exceptional customer service.

Honored restaurant guests are invited to join Farfalle Italiane's e-family. The restaurant website offers a convenient way to register a name and email address along with personal special-occasion dates, such as a birthday or wedding anniversary. The restaurant will email an e-card and gift certificate for a complimentary dessert to commemorate the occasion. A complimentary 5-inch gluten-free three-layer chocolate or white cake is provided when placing a dinner reservation for 6 or more to celebrate the occasion.

Lunch and dinner reservations, as well as pizza take-out orders, can be made through the website. The website features the complete menu with pictures of popular menu items. It further provides helpful information for travelers visiting the city and historic district via website links. Farfalle Italiane consistently earns positive customer reviews and ratings across social media.

The Menu

Appetizers—Small Plates

- *Mozzarella in Carrozza Arrabbiata* *7*

    Fresh, homemade mozzarella stuffed with prosciutto and fresh basil; breaded and pan-fried; served with a side of spicy pomodoro sauce.

- *Melanzane alla Griglia* *8*

    Baby eggplant grilled in extra virgin olive oil, served with a balsamic vinegar-honey sauce and garnished with parsley, capers, and Pecorino Romano.

- *Totanetti agli Asparagi e Menta* *6*

    Tender calamari and asparagus sautéed in extra virgin olive oil, dry white wine, cracked black pepper, and mint.

- *Bruschetta con Portobello e Manzo* *9*

    Grilled Tuscan bread topped with a pan-seared Portobello mushroom and pan-seared tenderloin tips topped with a Madeira wine and fresh thyme cream sauce.

- *Antipasti* *11*

    Mixed selection of fresh mozzarella, Roma tomatoes, black and green olives, fresh Parmigiano-Reggiano, sliced prosciutto, salami, roasted peppers, sautéed eggplant, Auricchio provolone, and grilled polenta.

- *Carpaccio di Manzo* *9*

    Paper-thin, raw beef tenderloin, arugula, and capers; finished with lemon juice, extra virgin olive oil, and shaved Parmigiano-Reggiano.

Soups

- *Pasta e Fagioli* *4.5*

    A classic, straight from the shores of Italy. Bean soup prepared from fresh chicken stock, steeped with pancetta, macaroni, garlic, and fresh herbs; served by the bowl.

- *Minestrone* *5*

    A popular Tuscan classic. A medley of vegetables, fresh chicken, prosciutto, and herbs simmered to savory perfection; served by the bowl.

Salads

- *Insalata Cesare* **6**

    Classic romaine, Parmagiano-Reggiano, fresh black pepper, croutons, and special house anchovy dressing.

- *Insalata Mista* **5.5**

    Traditional mix of radicchio, endive, frisée, romaine, red onion, and sliced Roma tomatoes; seasoned with extra virgin olive oil, aged balsamic vinegar, and garlic.

- *Portobello, Prosciutto, e Verdure* **8**

    Grilled marinated Portobello mushrooms, prosciutto, red peppers, and onions served over insalata mista; drizzled with extra virgin olive oil, crushed black pepper, and shaved Parmigiano-Reggiano.

- *Insalata Gorgonzola* **7**

    Mixed greens topped with Gorgonzola; dressed with extra virgin olive oil, aged balsamic vinegar, and sun-dried tomatoes.

Panini—Sandwiches (Lunch Only)

- *Panini al Salmone* **9**

    Salmon fillet marinated in extra virgin olive oil, white wine, garlic, and fresh thyme and grilled or broiled to order.

- *Panini Pollo Balsamico* **8**

    Grilled boneless chicken breast marinated in balsamic vinegar and extra virgin olive oil.

- *Panini Polpette* **7.5**

    Homemade meatballs, pomodoro sauce, Parmigiano-Reggiano, and fresh mozzarella.

- *Panini con Funghi Portobello alla Griglio* **7**

    Grilled Portobello mushrooms, Roma tomatoes, red onions, cucumbers, fresh mozzarella, green olives, fresh basil, extra virgin olive oil, and balsamic vinegar.

Brick Oven Pizzas—14 inch Round

- *Pizza Arrabbiata* **20**

    Pomodoro sauce made with roasted garlic, chili flakes, extra virgin olive oil, white wine, and parsley; topped with roasted peppers and onions, artichokes, eggplant, prosciutto, and Parmigiano-Reggiano.

- *Pizza al Tonno* **23**

    Pomodoro sauce, fresh grilled marinated tuna, Calamata olives, and sliced mozzarella.

- *Pizza Picante* **22**

    Picante sauce, pepperoni, sweet sausage, and mozzarella.

- *Pizza Pomodoro Caprese* **19**

    Pomodoro sauce, porcini mushrooms, vine-ripened tomatoes, and fresh mozzarella.

- *Pizza Mare e Monte* *24*

  Pomodoro sauce, grilled marinated shrimp and scallops, black Calamata olives, and fresh mozzarella slices.

- *Pizza Romaneschi.* *21*

  Sliced artichokes, prosciutto, Calamata olives, roasted eggplant, and smoked mozzarella.

Pastas

- *Farfalle Arrabbiata* *19*

  Bow tie pasta served with pomodoro sauce, fire-roasted tomatoes and peppers, Calamata olives, fresh button mushrooms, our secret blend of herbs, and grilled shrimp; topped with fresh Parmigiano-Reggiano.

- *Spaghetti Bolognese* *16*

  Spaghetti tossed with pomodoro sauce, ground veal, pancetta, mushrooms, red wine, and heavy cream.

- *Ziti al Tonno Fresco* *18*

  Fresh house-prepared ziti tossed with grilled tuna, olive oil, dry white wine, tomatoes, and Calamata olives.

- *Penne con Pollo.* *16*

  Penne pasta tossed with steamed asparagus, tender pieces of grilled chicken breast, and a fusion of chopped garlic, melted butter, and white wine.

- *Tortellini alla Nero* *15*

  Tortellini tossed with sautéed julienne red peppers, red onion, and zucchini; deglazed with white wine and finished with fire-roasted tomatoes and grilled Portobello mushrooms.

- *Risotto ai Frutti di Mare* *22*

  Arborio rice, littleneck clams, shrimp, scallops, mussels, and calamari served in a light pomodoro sauce with a fresh-herb garnish.

- *Spaghetti alla Vongole* *20*

  Al dente spaghetti topped with chopped littleneck clams sautéed in garlic, olive oil, white wine, and crushed red peppers.

- *Fettuccini Fontina* *18*

  Fettuccini generously laced with a tomato Fontina cream sauce, and topped with porcini mushrooms, sun-dried tomatoes, roasted peppers, and Parmigiano-Reggiano.

Entrées (Dinner Only)

All entrees served with your choice of any of our homemade pastas, or with one of our fresh vegetables of the day grown by our local organic farm partners.

- *Cioppino* *24*

  Classic dish with fresh calamari, lobster, shrimp, clams, sea scallops, and Gaeta olives, simmered in freshly prepared fish stock.

- *Scaloppine di Vitello*. *22*

  Tender veal scallopini, roasted red peppers, asparagus, and artichoke hearts in a lemon white wine butter sauce.

- *Salmone alla Griglia* *26*

  Norwegian salmon marinated in extra virgin olive oil, white wine, garlic, and fresh thyme, grilled or broiled to order.

- *Bistecca* *28*

  8-ounce New York sirloin steak grilled to perfection, served with aged balsamic vinegar.

- *Filetto di Maiale*. *23*

  Pork tenderloin marinated in honey, Dijon mustard, and fresh herbs, encrusted with seasoned bread crumbs; oven-roasted and served with apple brandy cream sauce.

- *Pollo con Carciofini e Limone* *22*

  Grilled chicken breast served in a lemon butter sauce, with baby artichokes, wild mushrooms, and capers.

Desserts

- *Crema Fritta con Salsa di Cioccolato* *8*

  Fried custard with chocolate sauce.

- *Tiramisu* *9*

  Mascarpone and cream cheese mix, layered between lady finger cookies soaked in dark rum; topped with slightly bitter powdered cocoa and strawberries.

- *Gelato* *8*

  Gelato prepared fresh daily, in-house.

- *Fresh Fruit of the Day* *7*

  Fresh fruit variety. Check with server for daily selection.

- *Mousse Cake* *9*

  Sumptuous three-layer cake, prepared in-house for chocolate lovers.

- *Flourless Chocolate Torte*. *8*

  Ganache topping—gluten-free.

Beverages

Espresso Drinks	4			Spirited Espresso Drinks	
Espresso	Americano	Café Amaretto	9	Bailey's Irish Cream Coffee	12
Café Latte	Macchiato	Café Bueno	11	Frangelico Coffee	11
Cappuccino	Café au Lait	Café Don Juan	10	Spanish Coffee	12

Coffee			Teas	
Coffee	regular decaffeinated	2.5	Darjeeling, Jasmine Spice, Earl Grey, Green Tea	3
French Press	(3 cup)	6	Herbal Teas: Chamomile, Mint, Lemon Ginger	3

The Restaurant Owner

Farfalle Italiane is a chef owned and managed restaurant, founded 3 years ago by Mister Dee. He began his career in the restaurant business at the age of 16, working after school as a pot and dish washer in a small neighborhood restaurant and bar. He enjoyed the fast pace and had the opportunity to work every job in that restaurant, while earning a degree in culinary and hospitality management from a well-respected college. He then worked for a growing hotel chain for almost 14 years, starting as a cook and advancing to chef, sous chef, executive chef, and food and beverage manager. Later, Mister Dee and a business partner secured a 5-year concession management contract to operate the food, beverage, and catering service at a country club. The business exceeded their expectations, and when the contract expired, Mister Dee was ready to open his own restaurant. He wanted to create a unique Italian casual-dining concept. He started by traveling to the southern region of Italy to understand the culture and cuisine. Four months later, he opened Farfalle Italiane. He refers to his employees as associates, pays above-average wages, and offers excellent benefits.

The Kitchen

The kitchen, with a conveniently located storeroom, walk-in refrigerator, and walk-in freezer, is designed to be fast and efficient. A receiving area for all food and beverage deliveries is near the back door of the kitchen where Mister Dee inspects all incoming products to verify the quantity, quality, and price.

The cooking line is set up so one or two chefs can easily prepare hot and cold foods for lunch and dinner, after completing all of the food preparation work in the morning prior to opening for lunch. The line also accommodates a third chef and a cook with work stations for sautéing and for salad and dessert preparation; reach-in refrigerators are adjacent to the cold food area. A wood-fired brick oven is located at the opposite end of the line with a work station for a cook to prepare pizzas. The dishwashing area is located toward the rear of the kitchen with glass racks and trays conveniently placed for fast pick-up and dishwashing.

The Service Bar

The dark mahogany service bar is part of the classic old Italian theme of the restaurant and is clearly visible from the dining room. It features an impressive wine rack stocked with a selection of Italian and US wines. A local craft beer and a popular premium light beer are on tap; several brands of imported bottled beers are also offered. The back bar displays the liquor call brand bottles. Spotless wine glasses are easily accessed from a rack suspended over one end of the bar. An espresso machine is located at the opposite end of the bar.

Recipe Cost Cards and Plate Cost Cards

Mister Dee and Farfalle Italiane Executive Chef Albert recently met with a food-service broker at a broadline distributor foodservice trade show. The broker encouraged them to sample a new brand of imported capers. The quality was exceptional and the cost was within their budget, so they made the decision to switch to the new brand. The capers are primarily used for the Melanzane alla Griglia recipe, but when the Recipe Cost Card for Melanzane alla Griglia was initially prepared, it reflected a lower than expected portion cost. They wanted to know what went wrong.

After examining the new 32-ounce jar of capers, it was determined that the full 32 ounces was used to calculate the per ounce portion cost [$23.50 ÷ 32 oz. = 0.734 rounded to $0.73]. Chef Albert then opened another jar of capers, drained the liquid from the jar and weighed the remaining weight, which represented the amount of product that could actually be used in the recipe: the drained weight of 22 ounces.

Complete Assignment A-1 on p. 284–285.

The Filetto di Maiale (Pork Tenderloin) is a popular dinner entrée and Executive Chef Albert consistently monitors portion cost after the pork loins are cooked. Today, Chef Dorothy has recorded the Weight after Cooking at 11.6 lb. and the Weight after Trimming at 11.1 lb.

Complete Assignment A-2 on p. 286.

Assignment A-1

Chef Albert requested you to recalculate the Recipe Cost Card and Plate Cost Card for Melanzane alla Griglia (below) as follows.

NOTE: Calculate to 3 digits past the decimal point then round to 2 digits.

Example: Honey, $14.25 ÷ 5 lb. = $2.85 lb.
$2.85 lb ÷ 16 oz. = $0.178 rounded to $0.18 per ounce.

Recipe Cost Card

Date:

Recipe Name: Melanzane alla Griglia
Yield: 8 servings (5 slices per serving)

File Code: Appetizers - 9
Spice Factor: 10%

Recipe Cost–AS: $
Portion Cost: $

RECIPE CONTENTS			PURCHASING		CONVERSION AMOUNTS			RECIPE COST
Quantity	Unit	Ingredient	Unit	Cost	Quantity	Unit	Cost	AS SERVED
3.00	lb	Eggplant, Japanese	6 lb/bag	$14.94	3.00	lb		
2.00	oz	Pecorino Romano	3 lb	$22.65	2.00	oz		
3.75	oz	Sugar, brown	25 lb/bag	$16.35	3.75	oz		
4.00	oz	Honey	5 lb	$14.25	4.00	oz		
4.00	oz	Balsamic vinegar	1 gal	$5.96	4.00	oz		
2.00	oz	Soy sauce	1 gal	$6.40	2.00	oz		
0.25	oz	Capers	32 oz*/jar	$23.50	0.25	oz		
			*22 oz drained weight					
4.00	oz	Olive Oil	SF	SF				
0.50	oz	Garlic, fresh	SF	SF				
0.50	oz	Parsley, fresh	SF	SF				

Sum of Ingredient Costs $

Sum of Ingredient Costs	x	1 + Spice Factor	=	Recipe Cost–AS
$	x	1.10	=	$

Recipe Cost–AS	÷ Number of Portions	=	Portion Cost
$	÷ 8	=	$

Calculations:

Assignment A–1, continued

Plate Cost Card

Menu Item: Melanzane alla Griglia

Yield: 1 Serving (5 slices per serving)

Food Cost Percent: 32%

Date: _____

Plate Cost: $_____

Minimum Menu Price: $_____

Recipe Portion Cost: $_____

Additional Items:

Plate Cost: $_____

Plate Cost	÷	**Food Cost Percent**	=	**Minimum Menu Price:**
$_____	÷	0.32	=	$_____

Calculations:

Assignment A-2

Chef Dorothy requested that you complete the calculations for the Cooking Loss Test that follows and deliver it to Executive Chef Albert.

Cooking Loss Test

Item: #413A, Pork Loin, Boneless

Date: _____

Prepared By: _____

COOKING PROCEDURE: Oven temperature 325°F, place on a rack fat side up, moisture added to roasting pan; approximately 1½ to 2 hours cooking time or until internal temperature reachers 145°F.

Oven Prepared Weight: **14.8 lb**

WEIGHT LOSS AFTER COOKING:

Oven Prepared Weight: 14.8 lb   **100%**
Weight after Cooking: − ____ lb
Loss after Cooking: ____ **lb**   (shrinkage)

▶ **Loss after Cooking ÷ Oven Prepared Weight = Weight Loss Percent after Cooking**
_____ lb   ÷   14.8 lb   =   _____ %

Weight Loss % after Cooking—Yield %:   (−____%)

WEIGHT LOSS AFTER TRIMMING:

Weight after Cooking: ____ lb
Weight after Trimming: − ____ lb   (Servable Weight)
Loss after Trimming: ____ **lb**

▶ **Loss after Trimming ÷ Oven Prepared Weight = Weight Loss Percent after Trimming**
_____ lb   ÷   14.8 lb   =   _____ %

Weight Loss % after Trimming—Yield %:   (−____%)

SERVABLE WEIGHT–AS (AS SERVED):

▶ **Servable Weight   ÷   Oven Prepared Weight   =   Servable Weight Percent**
_____ llb   ÷   14.8 lb   =_____ %

Servable Weight—Yield %:   ____%

PURCHASE COST:

▶ **Quantity   Unit   ×   Unit Cost   =   Purchase (Invoice) Cost**
14.8   lb   × $9.65   = $142.82

AS (AS SERVED) COST:

▶   **Purchase Cost   ÷   Servable Weight   =   Oven Prepared Cost per lb**
$142.82   ÷   ____ lb   = $ _____

AS (As Served) Cost per lb: $ _____

$$\frac{\$\ \_\_\_\_\ \text{per pound}}{16\ \text{ounces per pound}} =$$

AS Cost per oz: $ _____
(for portion costing)

Upstairs Catering

Farfalle Italiane

Mister Dee leased the 3,200-square-foot second-floor space above the restaurant six months ago so he could launch his catering business, Upstairs Catering at Farfalle Italiane. A large, open, 40 × 60-foot dining room comfortably accommodates up to 200 guests. The total square footage for banquet table seating in an open room such as this is divided by 12 to find the seating capacity that allows enough space for efficient table service and is comfortable for guests. The total square footage of the dining room is 2,400 (40 × 60 = 2,400), divided by 12 (2,400 ÷ 12 = 200), which creates seating for 200.

The remaining 20 × 40-foot space occupies the remaining 800 square feet and accommodates arriving guests, a portable bar, and an hors d'oeuvre table/dessert or special-occasion cake table. A server station is located at the far end of that area adjacent to the kitchen service elevator and is equipped with an ice maker, refrigeration unit, coffee maker and hot water urn, an espresso machine, a soft drink dispenser, and server supplies. There is also space for a portable serving-line table when used for dishing up soups and plating desserts.

To maximize the capacity of the dining room, banquet table seating (long tables lined up in a row) are used; banquet tables are 6 feet long and 30 inches wide and seat 6 (7 or 8 if chairs are added to the opposite ends of the table).

Guests arriving for catered events are easily directed to the second-floor street entrance at the side of the restaurant. Bright lights illuminate a recessed white door with frosted leaded glass and bold black letters reading "Upstairs Catering" centered within the glass just above the Farfalle Italiane green letters with orange bow-tie logo. Guests may take the elevator or may choose to walk up the classic oak staircase to the second floor.

The catering business has exceeded Mister Dee's expectations, requiring a greater emphasis on food, labor, and beverage cost control measures.

Purchasing

Farfalle Italiane is currently receiving a delivery once a week on Fridays between 8 and 9 A.M. from a broadline distributor, a once–a-week delivery on Wednesdays between 7 and 9 A.M. from a specialty Italian cheese and meat distributor, and a daily delivery between 8 and 9 A.M. from a specialty bakery distributor. The need for more products due to the increasing catering business has been adequately handled by increasing the par stock amounts for the most used products. But the storeroom and refrigeration capacity will soon be maximized, therefore requiring an additional delivery day from the broadline and specialty Italian cheese and meat distributors.

Mister Dee has discussed delivery options with the distributors. He also requested that the three distributors submit a revised price bid for the items that have been significantly increased in purchasing quantities, which should result in slightly lower purchasing costs.

- ▶ The broadline distributor proposed the following delivery schedule: Tuesdays between 10 and 11 A.M., and Fridays would remain the same between 8 and 9 A.M., with the current prices to remain in effect. The broadline distributor did not agree that the increase in purchasing quantities was enough to justify lower purchasing costs.

  - ▷ Mister Dee is pleased with a Tuesday and Friday delivery schedule from the broadline distributor, although he would prefer an earlier delivery time on Tuesdays. And he still believes that the increased purchasing quantities should receive some consideration for lower purchasing costs.

- ▶ The specialty Italian meat and cheese distributor proposed the following: If the par stock amounts could continue to increase with the Wednesday delivery day and time remaining the same, the increase in purchasing quantities for the one-day-a-week delivery could reduce the purchasing costs by 2 percent.

  - ▷ Mister Dee is pleased with a 2 percent reduction in purchasing costs from the specialty Italian meat and cheese distributor and can increase the par stock amounts for the Wednesday delivery. There would be an adequate refrigeration capacity for the increased amounts of cheeses and meats, since the broadline distributor deliveries are 2 days per week.

- ▶ The specialty bakery distributor would continue with a daily delivery between 8 and 9 A.M. and submitted a discount proposal for monthly orders that exceed designated quantity levels.

  - ▷ Mister Dee has been very pleased with the consistent quality and service from the specialty bakery distributor and is further pleased with the quantity-level discount proposal. Farfalle Italiane customers continually praise the quality of the Italian bread the distributor has been delivering from the first day of the restaurant opening.

Additional facts to consider: The restaurants within the city are serviced by three major competing broadline distributors, one specialty Italian cheese and meat distributor, and two specialty bakery distributors. A national wholesale foodservice supplier recently opened a new warehouse location within the city and has been aggressively soliciting business from independent foodservice operators. A representative from the supplier contacted Mister Dee with a price sheet showing lower purchasing costs for many of the same products he currently uses—recognizing that the wholesale foodservice supplier does not offer a delivery service.

Your Explanations . . .

How should Mister Dee respond to the fact that he will continue to have increasing quantities and will need additional help with purchasing cost control? Be specific with your written answers for the following key issues.

1. Broadline distributors:

_____

_____

_____

_____

_____

_____

_____

_____

_____

_____

2. Italian cheese and meat distributor:

_____

_____

_____

_____

_____

_____

_____

_____

_____

_____

3. Wholesale foodservice supplier:

_____

_____

_____

_____

_____

_____

_____

_____

_____

_____

_____

(continued)

4. Specialty bakery distributor:

_____

_____

_____

_____

_____

_____

_____

_____

_____

_____

_____

_____

5. Additional help with purchasing:

_____

_____

_____

_____

_____

_____

_____

_____

_____

_____

_____

_____

6. Summarize the action to be taken:

_____

_____

_____

_____

_____

_____

_____

_____

_____

_____

_____

_____

Catering Order

The Community Arts Council has reserved the third Thursday of every month for their monthly lunch meeting, beginning with the first month the catering business opened. The director for the community arts council sent an email to Mister Dee on Wednesday, October 13, 20xx, with the following order confirmation:

► Community Arts Council monthly lunch meeting for Thursday, October 14, 20xx.

► Lunch served at 12 noon followed by a meeting that will adjourn by 1:30 P.M. The menu selected from the catering lunch menu includes the following: Cup of Pasta e Fagioli with Panini Pollo Balsamico; dessert, Brownie al Cioccolato; coffee and tea.

► The confirmed number of members and guests is 42, but occasionally a few more have attended.

► The council members and guests typically arrive between 11:45 A.M. and 12 noon knowing that lunch will be served promptly at 12:00 noon.

Following dessert, coffee, and tea service, the servers are available and prepared to clear the tables, leaving pots of coffee, hot water and tea bags, sugar, sweetener, and creamers on the tables during the group's meeting time.

The Pasta e Fagioli and the Panini Pollo Balsamico are also restaurant menu items. The Brownie al Cioccolato is a catering menu item that the restaurant kitchen will specifically prepare for the event.

The serving size for the Pasta e Fagioli is a 5-ounce cup and the Panini Pollo Balsamico is served exactly the same as for the restaurant. The catering menu price for the lunch combination is $16 and the Brownie al Cioccolato is $5; Coffee and Tea are $3 each. The cost per person is $24 plus a 20% service change (gratuity) that is paid to the servers for a total cost of [$24 + $4.80] $28.80, not including sales tax.

NOTE: Catering menu prices are higher than the restaurant menu prices for the same items because it is a catered event with no additional charge for the use of the private room and for the time of the event.

| Complete Assignment A-3 on pp. 295–297. |

| Complete Assignment A-4 on pp. 298–299. |

To give you an idea of what the portion costs of coffee and tea are (this is not part of the assignment; it's for your reference): Coffee and Tea is priced at $3 per cup (unlimited refills) on the catering menu. The coffee and tea is typically estimated at 2 cups per guest, recognizing that some guests may prefer only one cup, while other guests ask for more than one refill. Also, taste preferences vary for additives, such as sugar, artificial sweetener, and cream, but are estimated as follows:

Coffee: 8 ounce cup cost		**$0.13**	**Tea:** 1 bag cost	**$0.21**
Additives:				
• Sugar packet	0.02			
• Sweetener*	0.05	0.05		0.05
• Creamer	0.05	+ 0.06		+ 0.06
		$0.24 per cup		**$0.32 per cup**

* the amount of the higher cost item is used for costing

Receiving and Issuing

Mister Dee has established tracking for Upstairs Catering with the use of Requisitions and Transfers. The catering business is treated as a separate department from the restaurant. When an event such as a wedding reception, anniversary celebration, birthday party, other special occasion or group lunch or dinner is scheduled, the tracking begins as products are delivered, requisitioned, and transferred.

Your Explanations . . .

Would Mister Dee prepare a requisition or transfer for the menu and beverage items?

Explain the procedure for tracking the Pasta e Fagioli and Panini Pollo Balsamico, restaurant menu items, and the Brownie al Cioccolato, a catering menu item prepared in-house along with the coffee and tea.

_____

_____

_____

_____

_____

_____

_____

Alcohol Beverage Service

The sales of alcohol beverages for Upstairs Catering continue to increase with the portable full-service bar used for many of the evening events. In addition to wine served with dinner, some events have a cocktail reception, prior to dinner being served. The alcohol beverage service typically includes liquor, wine, and beer and functions as an open bar paid for by the customer (host of the event), whereby the guests do not pay for the drinks. Mister Dee assists the customer in determining the brands for liquor, wine, and beer along with the quantities needed. Then Mister Dee prepares Alcohol Beverage and Supply Requisitions for the items needed to stock the portable bar.

Your Explanations . . .

Explain what happens with any remaining alcohol beverages (full and partially used bottles) along with remaining amounts of bar juices, mixers, and other bar items at the end of the catered event.

_____

_____

_____

_____

_____

_____

_____

_____

Food Cost

The Farfalle Italiane restaurant and Upstairs Catering are two separate revenue centers within the Farfalle Italiane restaurant business, each having different cost guidelines. The restaurant strives to operate within a 32% food cost percentage and the catering department within a 26% food cost percentage. Therefore, Mister Dee prepares a Food Cost Report for the restaurant and one for the catering department every Monday to assure that those food cost percentages are maintained. The period (week) ending 10/18/20xx produced the following results for Farfalle Italiane:

Farfalle Italiane Restaurant

Total Food Sales	$54,428	
Complimentary Meals	$24	(dinner for two promotional gift certificate)
Purchases	$19,025	
Transfers-In	$130	(from catering department)
Transfers-Out	$1,840	(to catering department)
Employee Meal Credit	$340	
Opening Inventory	$15,990	
Closing Inventory	$15,675	

Complete Assignment A-5 on p. 300.

The period (week) ending 10/18/20xx produced the following results for Upstairs Catering at Farfalle Italiane:

Upstairs Catering at Farfalle Italiane

Total Food Sales	$16,880	
Complimentary Meals	$72	(dinner menu item samples for catering customers)
Requisitions	$2,465	(from storeroom and restaurant kitchen)
Transfers-In	$1,840	(from restaurant kitchen)
Directs	$185	(special order birthday cake)
Transfers-Out	$130	(to restaurant kitchen)
Employee Meal Credit	$65	
Opening Inventory	$1,105	
Closing Inventory	$1,013	

Complete Assignment A-6 on p. 301.

Assignment A-3

Review the Recipe Cost Cards for the Pasta e Fagioli and Panini Pollo Balsamico and prepare a Plate Cost Card for the menu item combination, keeping in mind that a 5-ounce cup of soup is served. The food cost percentage for the catering department is 26%.

Recipe Cost Card

Date:

Recipe Name: Pasta e Fagioli	
Yield: 24 servings, 10-ounce portion	

File Code: Soup - 1	
Spice Factor: 10%	

Recipe Cost–AS: $25.33	
Portion Cost: $1.06	

RECIPE CONTENTS			PURCHASING		CONVERSION AMOUNTS			RECIPE COST
Quantity	Unit	Ingredient	Unit	Cost	Quantity	Unit	Cost	AS SERVED
1.50	gal	Chicken stock	1 gal	$8.00	1.50	gal	$8.00	$12.00
0.75	#10 can	Kidney beans, red	#10 can	$3.61	0.75	#10 can	$3.61	$2.71
0.75	lb	Onion, Spanish	50 lb/bag	$23.00	0.75	lb	$0.46	$0.35
0.75	lb	Pancetta	6 lb	$37.74	0.75	lb	$6.29	$4.72
0.75	lb	Macaroni, elbow	20 lb/case	$12.80	0.75	lb	$0.64	$0.48
2.00	oz	Butter	10 lb/case	$39.90	2.00	oz	$0.25	$0.50
0.50	lb	Parmesan	10 lb	$45.40	0.50	lb	$4.54	$2.27
4.00	oz	Olive oil	SF	SF				
0.50	oz	Thyme, fresh	SF	SF				
0.50	oz	Rosemary, fresh	SF	SF				
1.50	oz	Garlic, fresh	SF	SF				
4.00	each	Bay leaf	SF	SF				
0.25	tsp	Pepper, black	SF	SF				
0.25	tsp	Salt	SF	SF				
0.25	tsp	Pepper, red flakes	SF	SF				

Sum of Ingredient Costs	$23.03

Sum of Ingredient Costs	x	1 + Spice Factor	=	Recipe Cost–AS
$23.03	x	1.10	=	$25.33

Recipe Cost–AS	÷	Number of Portions	=	Portion Cost
$25.33	÷	24	=	$1.055 rounded to $1.06

(continued)

Assignment A-3, continued

Recipe Cost Card

Date:

Recipe Name: Panini Pollo Balsamico	**File Code:** Sandwich - 4	**Recipe Cost–AS:** $13.54
Yield: 6 sandwiches, 5-ounce chicken portion	**Spice Factor:** 10%	**Portion Cost:** $2.26

RECIPE CONTENTS			PURCHASING		CONVERSION AMOUNTS			RECIPE COST
Quantity	Unit	Ingredient	Unit	Cost	Quantity	Unit	Cost	AS SERVED
12	slices	Panini	20 slice loaf	$3.60	12	slices	$0.18	$2.16
1.87	lb	Chicken breast	B/S, 5 oz/10 lb	$48.00	1.87	lb	$4.80	$8.98
4.00	oz	Balsamic vinegar	1 gal	$5.96	4.00	oz	$0.05	$0.20
4.00	oz	Honey	5 lb	$14.25	4.00	oz	$0.18	$0.72
3.75	oz	Sugar, brown	25 lb/bag	$16.35	3.75	oz	$0.04	$0.15
2.00	oz	Soy sauce	1 gal	$6.40	2.00	oz	$0.05	$0.10
0.50	oz	Rosemary, fresh	SF	SF				
0.50	oz	Garlic, fresh	SF	SF				
0.75	oz	Sesame seeds	SF	SF				
0.30	oz	Parsley, fresh	SF	SF				

Sum of Ingredient Costs	**$12.31**

Sum of Ingredient Costs	x	1 + Spice Factor	=	Recipe Cost–AS
$12.31	x	1.10	=	$13.54

Recipe Cost–AS	÷	Number of Portions	=	Portion Cost
$13.54	÷	6	=	$2.256 rounded to $2.26

Assignment A-3, continued

Plate Cost Card

Menu Item: Pasta e Fagioli / Panini Pollo Balsamico

Yield: 1 Serving, Soup, 5 oz. / Panini, 5 oz.

Food Cost Percent: 26%

Date: _____

Plate Cost: $ _____

Minimum Menu Price: $ _____

Recipe Portion Cost: $ _____   Pasta e Fagioli

+ $ _____   Panini Pollo Balsamico

$ _____   Total Plate Cost (Both Menu Items)

Plate Cost   ÷   Food Cost Percent   =   Minimum Menu Price:

$ _____   ÷   0.26   = $ _____

NOTE: Calculate to 3 digits to the right of the decimal point then round to 2 digits.

Calculations:

Assignment A-4

Review the Recipe Cost Card for the Brownie al Cioccolato and then prepare a Plate Cost Card. The food cost percentage for the catering department is 26%.

Recipe Cost Card

Date:

| Recipe Name: Brownie al Cioccolato | File Code: Dessert - 13 | Recipe Cost–AS: $4.71 |
| Yield: 24 servings, 3" × 3¼" portion | Spice Factor: 10% | Portion Cost: $0.20 |

RECIPE CONTENTS			PURCHASING		CONVERSION AMOUNTS			RECIPE COST
Quantity	Unit	Ingredient	Unit	Cost	Quantity	Unit	Cost	AS SERVED
2.50	oz	Butter	10 lb/case	$39.90	2.50	oz	$0.25	$0.63
3.50	oz	Flour, all purpose	25 lb/bag	$11.45	3.50	oz	$0.03	$0.11
1.50	oz	Unsweetened cocoa	5 lb/bag	$14.45	1.50	oz	$0.16	$0.24
4.50	oz	Unsweetened chocolate	25 lb/bag	$52.25	4.50	oz	$0.13	$0.59
3.00	oz	Semisweet chocolate	25 lb/bag	$54.90	3.00	oz	$0.14	$0.42
6.00	oz	Chocolate chunks	25 lb/bag	$58.75	6.00	oz	$0.15	$0.90
5.00	ea	Eggs, whole	30 doz	$40.50	5.00	ea	$0.11	$0.55
10.50	oz	Sugar	25 lb/bag	$14.75	10.50	oz	$0.04	$0.42
3.00	oz	Sour cream	5 lb/tub	$11.25	3.00	oz	$0.14	$0.42
0.25	oz	Baking powder	SF	SF				
0.25	oz	Salt	SF	SF				
1.25	tsp	Vanilla extract	SF	SF				

| Sum of Ingredient Costs | $4.28 |

Sum of Ingredient Costs	x	1 + Spice Factor	=	Recipe Cost–AS
$4.28	x	1.10	=	$4.71

Recipe Cost–AS	÷	Number of Portions	=	Portion Cost
$4.71	÷	24	=	$0.196 rounded to $0.20

Assignment A-4, continued

Factoring in the additional items, prepare a Plate Cost Card.

Plate Cost Card

Menu Item: Brownie al Cioccolato

Yield: 24 servings, 3″ × 3¼″ portion

Food Cost Percent: 26%

Date: _____

Plate Cost: $_____

Minimum Menu Price: $_____

Recipe Portion Cost: $_____

Additional Items:

	Syrups:	Vanilla	$0.06
		Caramel	$0.09
		Raspberry	+ $0.09

Plate Cost: $_____

Plate Cost	÷	Food Cost Percent	=	Minimum Menu Price:
$	÷	0.26	=	$ _____

Calculations:

Assignment A-5

Mister Dee would like you to prepare the Food Cost Report for the Farfalle Italiane restaurant and compare the actual food cost percentage with his planned operating percentage.

Restaurant Food Cost Report

Period Ending: October 18, 20xx

Debits

_____

_____

_____

_____

_____

Credits

_____

_____

_____

_____

_____

Cost of Food Sold _____

_____

Total Food Sales (Sum of Customer Guest Checks) _____

_____

Food Cost Percentage _____

Calculated as follows:

Cost of Food Sold ÷ Total Food Sales = **Food Cost Percentage**

_____   _____   _____

Calculations:

Assignment A-6

Mister Dee would like you to prepare the Department Food Cost Report for Upstairs Catering at Farfalle Italiane and compare the actual food cost percentage with his planned operating percentage.

Department Food Cost Report
> Upstairs Catering <

Period Ending: October 18, 20xx

Debits

_____

_____

_____

_____

_____

Credits

_____

_____

_____

_____

_____

Cost of Food Sold _____

_____

Total Food Sales (Sum of Customer Guest Checks) _____

_____

Food Cost Percentage _____

Calculated as follows:
Cost of Food Sold ÷ Total Food Sales = **Food Cost Percentage**

_____   _____   _____

Calculations:

Assignment A-7

Payroll Budget Estimate

Mister Dee prepares a Payroll Budget Estimate every week. The software is currently installing upgrades for the next several hours and is not available, so he asked you to do the calculations for the Payroll Budget Estimate right now. Mister Dee has recorded the scheduled hours by name, position, and hourly rate for the week of October 18, 20xx. His forecasted sales for the week is $56,675.00 and his payroll cost percentage goal is 34%.

> **Complete Assignment A-7 on the following page.**

Employee scheduling and preparing a Payroll Budget Estimate that remains within an established Payroll Cost Percentage is among the first responsibilities of new managers.

Assignment A-7, continued

Payroll Budget Estimate

Name	Position	Hourly Rate	Scheduled Hours	Scheduled Overtime	Total Earned
Albert	Executive Chef	$38.00	40		$
Carl	Sous Chef	$30.00	40		
Dorothy	Chef	$24.00	40		
Herbert	Cook	$20.00	36		
Dominick	Cook-Pizza	$20.00	40		
Richard	Dishwasher	$15.00	36		
Maria	Dishwasher	$15.00	36		
Joel	Dishwasher	$15.00	24		
Antonio	Server	$15.00	28		
Helen	Server	$15.00	24		
Ralph	Server	$15.00	30		
Cathy	Server	$15.00	24		
Tina	Server	$15.00	26		
William	Server	$15.00	24		
Rosa	Server	$15.00	24		
Daniel	Servers' Assistant	$15.00	22		
Sandra	Servers' Assistant	$15.00	28		
TOTAL					$

Allowance for payroll taxes—estimate is 0.125 of total gross wages $

Allowance for health insurance, vacations, & sick days—estimate is 30% of total wages $

Allowance for employee meals—$5.00 each; hourly 66 meals $

Hourly Staff Subtotal $

Name	Position	Hourly Rate	Scheduled Hours	Scheduled Overtime	Total Earned
Mister Dee	Owner/Manager	$45.00	40		$
Annie	Assistant Manager	$35.00	40		
TOTAL					$

Allowance for payroll taxes—estimate is 0.125 of total gross wages $

Allowance for health insurance, vacations, & sick days—estimate is 30% of total wages $

Allowance for employee meals—$5.00 each; managers 10 meals $

Managers Subtotal $

Week of: October 18, 20xx	**GRAND TOTAL**	$

Forecasted sales for the week: **$56,675.00**	Payroll Cost Percentage Goal	34.00%
Estimated payroll cost percentage for hourly staff		_____%
Estimated payroll cost percentage for hourly staff & managers		_____%

The Farfalle Italiane brick oven pizzas have become such popular menu items that the restaurant could not adequately handle the increased business, especially with weekend take-out orders. So Mister Dee made the decision to open a pizza restaurant, "Bello Pizzeria by Farfalle Italiane," with seating for 28, delivery to nearby hotels and businesses, and pizza by the slice. The grand opening will be in 4 months. The location is ideal, a retail space of 750 square feet within the same building at the opposite corner from Farfalle Italiane, the restaurant. Bello Pizzeria will be operated as a separate business. Therefore, with increased kitchen space, seating, and a delivery service the pizza business will be positioned to continue to grow and expand. There are currently six different pizzas being offered on the Farfalle Italiane restaurant menu priced from $19 to $24. Mister Dee compares the menu item sales and popularity percentages every week to prepare a sales forecast and to determine food production quantities. He further reviews and analyzes the standardized HACCP Recipes, Recipe Cost Cards, and Plate Cost Cards.

Your Calculations . . .

Mister Dee has totaled the pizza sales for the week of October18, 20xx and wants you to calculate the popularity percentages. He is considering increasing the number of pizza menu items to nine for the grand opening.

Menu Item	Items Sold	Popularity Percentage
Pizza Arrabbiata	142	_____
Pizza al Tonno	63	_____
Pizza Picante	81	_____
Pizza Pomodoro Caprese	93	_____
Pizza Mare e Monte	42	_____
Pizza Romaneschi	47	_____
Total	**468**	

There has been a small increase in the price per pound for the prosciutto, and Mister Dee is concerned that the current menu selling price of $20 for the Pizza Arrabbiata may have to be increased. Therefore, he wants you to update the Recipe Cost Card for Pizza Arrabbiata and complete a Plate Cost Card and give him your recommendation for the updated minimum menu selling price for the whole pizza along with the minimum menu selling price for a slice of Pizza Arrabbiata.

Complete Assignment A-8 on pp. 308–309.

Show Mister Dee that you understand the importance of costs by quickly reviewing the Farfalle Italiane restaurant menu to identify any other menu items that describe prosciutto as an ingredient. Those menu-item Recipe Cost Cards and Plate Cost Cards would also need to be reviewed and updated, beginning with Mozzarella in Carozza Arrabbiatta.

Complete Assignment A-9 on pp. 310–312.

Bello Pizzeria will have seating for 28 comprised of 6 tables—seating for 4, and 2 two tables—seating for 2. Mister Dee has talked about tabletop tablets, but he is a bit uncertain, and has asked you to check out a few places where they are in use and let him know what you think.

Your Explanations . . .

Explain how tabletop tablets would affect the business.

_____

_____

_____

_____

_____

_____

Income Statement

Mister Dee keeps tight control over financial management and has maintained a well-respected relationship with the bank that he has been doing business with from the time he opened Farfalle Italiane. He has earned a high credit rating and is professionally knowledgeable regarding financial reporting. The Farfalle Italiane accountant prepared the current Income Statement for the period ending October 31, 20xx. Mister Dee is planning to visit with his banker next week to request an increase in the Farfalle Italiane line of credit for operating expenses. Bello Pizzeria will be opening in 4 months and Mister Dee wants to be prepared for any unexpected expenses while the new business is getting established.

Your Explanations . . .

Review the Income Statement on the facing page and comment on the following:

1. Upstairs Catering significantly contributes to increasing food and beverage sales every month. The monthly growth in sales has resulted in lower food and beverage cost percentages. Explain why this is occurring.

_____

_____

_____

_____

_____

_____

_____

_____

_____

_____

2. The payroll cost percentage has remained the same each month with only a slight variance above or below the target goal of 34%. Should Mister Dee consider options to reduce payroll cost?

_____

_____

_____

_____

_____

_____

_____

_____

_____

3. The restaurant profit of 12.49% before taxes is well above the reported restaurant industry average range of 3 to 6%. What are the contributing factors that allow Mister Dee to make this happen?

_____

_____

_____

_____

_____

_____

_____

_____

_____

Income Statement

Period Ending: 10/31/20xx

Sales		
Food	$194,570	86.00%
Beverage	31,675	14.00%
Total Sales:	**$226,245**	**100.00%**

Cost of Goods Sold		
Food Cost	$56,584	29.08%
Beverage Cost	6,296	19.88%
Total Cost of Goods Sold:	**$62,880**	**27.79%**
Gross Profit:	$163,365	72.21%

Controllable Expenses		
Payroll Cost	$76,352	33.75%
Direct Operating Expenses	8,907	3.94%
Advertising & Marketing	4,615	2.04%
Music & Entertainment	785	0.34%
Utilities	10,864	4.80%
Maintenance & Repairs	3,976	1.76%
Administration & General	1,892	0.84%
Total Controllable Expenses:	**$107,391**	**47.47%**
Income before Occupation Costs:	$55,972	24.74%

Occupation Costs		
Rent	$14,025	6.20%
Property Tax	3,118	1.38%
Other Taxes	1,236	0.55%
Property Insurance	1,997	0.88%
Interest Expense	1,652	0.73%
Depreciation	5,690	2.51%
Total Occupation Costs:	**$27,718**	**12.25%**
Restaurant Profit before Taxes:	**$28,256**	12.49%

Figure A.1   Income Statement

Assignment A-8

Complete the following Recipe Cost Card and Plate Cost Card for Pizza Arrabbiata to recommend an updated minimum menu selling price for a whole pizza, along with a minimum menu selling price for a slice.

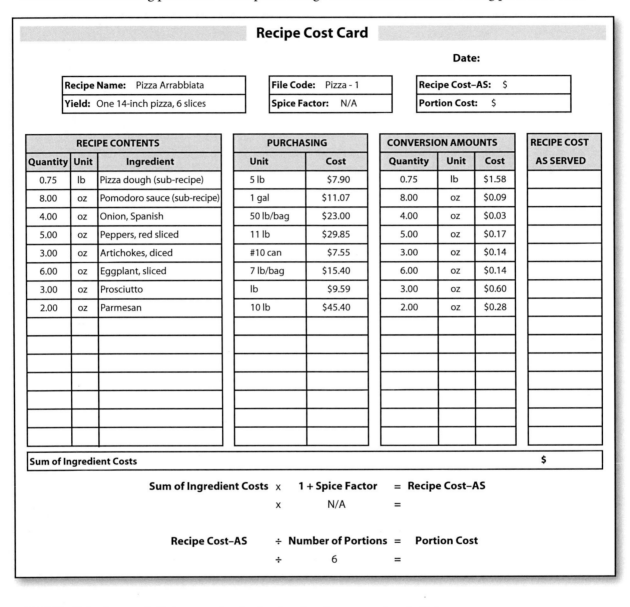

Recipe Cost Card

Date:

| Recipe Name: Pizza Arrabbiata | File Code: Pizza - 1 | Recipe Cost–AS: $ |
| Yield: One 14-inch pizza, 6 slices | Spice Factor: N/A | Portion Cost: $ |

RECIPE CONTENTS			PURCHASING		CONVERSION AMOUNTS			RECIPE COST
Quantity	Unit	Ingredient	Unit	Cost	Quantity	Unit	Cost	AS SERVED
0.75	lb	Pizza dough (sub-recipe)	5 lb	$7.90	0.75	lb	$1.58	
8.00	oz	Pomodoro sauce (sub-recipe)	1 gal	$11.07	8.00	oz	$0.09	
4.00	oz	Onion, Spanish	50 lb/bag	$23.00	4.00	oz	$0.03	
5.00	oz	Peppers, red sliced	11 lb	$29.85	5.00	oz	$0.17	
3.00	oz	Artichokes, diced	#10 can	$7.55	3.00	oz	$0.14	
6.00	oz	Eggplant, sliced	7 lb/bag	$15.40	6.00	oz	$0.14	
3.00	oz	Prosciutto	lb	$9.59	3.00	oz	$0.60	
2.00	oz	Parmesan	10 lb	$45.40	2.00	oz	$0.28	

| Sum of Ingredient Costs | $ |

Sum of Ingredient Costs x   1 + Spice Factor   = Recipe Cost–AS

x   N/A   =

Recipe Cost–AS   ÷ Number of Portions =   Portion Cost

÷   6   =

NOTE: Calculate to 3 digits past the decimal point then round to 2 digits.

| Calculations: |
| |
| |
| |
| |
| |
| |

Assignment A–8, continued

Plate Cost Card

Menu Item: Pizza Arrabbiata

Yield: One 14-inch pizza, 6 slices

Food Cost Percent: 32%

Date: _____

Plate Cost: $_____ whole pizza

Plate Cost: $_____ slice

Minimum Menu Price: $_____ whole pizza

Minimum Menu Price: $_____ slice

Recipe Portion Cost = Plate Cost:

$_____ = $_____ whole pizza

Plate Cost	**÷**	**Food Cost Percent**	**=**	**Minimum Menu Price:**	
$_____	÷	0.32	=	$_____	whole pizza
$_____	÷	0.32	=	$_____	slice

Calculations:

Recommendation:

_____

_____

_____

_____

Assignment A-9

Review and update the Recipe Cost Card and Plate Cost Card for Mozzarella in Carozza Arrabbiatta.

NOTE: Calculate to 3 digits past the decimal point then round to 2 digits.

Recipe Cost Card

Date:

Recipe Name: Mozzarella in Carrozza Arrabbiata	
Yield: 24 servings, two 1" × 4" pinwheels per serving	

File Code: Appetizers - 6
Spice Factor: 10%

Recipe Cost–AS: $
Portion Cost: $

RECIPE CONTENTS			PURCHASING		CONVERSION AMOUNTS			RECIPE COST AS SERVED
Quantity	Unit	Ingredient	Unit	Cost	Quantity	Unit	Cost	
3.00	lb	Whole milk fresh curd	5 lb/bag	$23.45	3.00	lb	$4.69	
1.00	lb	Prosciutto	lb	$9.59	1.00	lb	$9.59	
1.25	lb	Flour, all purpose	25 lb/bag	$11.45	1.25	lb	$0.46	
11.00	ea	Eggs, whole	30 doz	$40.50	11.00	ea	$0.11	
1.75	lb	Bread crumbs	25 lb/case	$18.00	1.75	lb	$0.72	
12.00	oz	Olive Oil	SF	SF				
7.50	oz	Basil, fresh	SF	SF				
0.75	oz	Salt, Kosher	SF	SF				
0.25	oz	Pepper, black	SF	SF				

Sum of Ingredient Costs	$

Sum of Ingredient Costs x   1 + Spice Factor   = Recipe Cost–AS

x   1.10   =

Recipe Cost–AS   ÷ Number of Portions =   Portion Cost

÷   24   =

Calculations:

Assignment A–9, continued

Plate Cost Card

Menu Item: Mozzarella in Carozza Arrabbiata

Yield: 1 Serving, two 1″ × 4″ pinwheels

Food Cost Percent: 32%

Date: _____

Plate Cost: $ _____

Minimum Menu Price: $ _____

Recipe Portion Cost: $ _____

Additional Items

Pomodoro sauce   +0.27

Plate Cost: $ _____

Plate Cost	÷	**Food Cost Percent**	=	**Minimum Menu Price:**
$ _____	÷	0.32	=	$ _____

Calculations:

Recommendation:

_____

_____

_____

_____

_____

_____

_____

(continued)

Assignment A-9, continued

Review the restaurant menu for Farfalle Italiane on pp. 278–281 and list the other menu items that include prosciutto as an ingredient.

_____

_____

_____

_____

_____

_____

_____

_____

_____

_____

_____

_____

Assignment A-10

Mister Dee has been following the mixed results of restaurants using customer loyalty cards and would like to know what you think about them. The questions he has been pondering are whether a customer loyalty program could be implemented for the new Bello Pizzeria; what the results might be; and what specific rewards could be offered to loyal customers.

Do some research and outline a possible loyalty program plan for Mister Dee.

_____

_____

_____

_____

_____

_____

_____

_____

_____

_____

_____

_____

_____

Mister Dee has received numerous requests to provide food and beverages for various events, ranging from the county fair to the many summer and fall festivals held at the city's waterfront park. He often responded to those requests by politely saying, "We are just not set-up for off-premise catering." After hearing him say that so many times, his wife, who is an accountant, said, "Hey, all you need is a truck or a trailer and you could take the most popular items to those events." She further added, "Let me do some research."

A month later, she had written the following informative report:

Mobile Foodservice Trucks and Trailers

The food truck and trailer segment of the quick service restaurant category is rapidly growing with upwards of 3 billion dollars in sales generated in the US annually as tracked by market research firms. This category segment of the foodservice industry offers the eating out public convenient locations with fast service. Food trucks and trailers typically operate in mid-sized to large cities and are primarily found in the following locations according to a percentage average:

- ▶ 60% – high traffic street areas and busy street corners

- ▶ 25% – fairs and festivals, holiday parades, and catered events

- ▶ 15% – construction sites and industrial work centers

A sale per customer can range from $5 to $15 dollars or more with the average revenue for a truck or trailer ranging from $200,000 to $600,000 per year, as reported by various mobile foodservice (truck and trailer) franchise organizations.

Quality Offerings, Affordable Prices

Food trucks and trailers are responding to consumer preferences for restaurant quality menu offerings and healthy food choices at affordable prices. There are food trucks and trailers selling items that include gourmet burgers and sandwiches, fresh salads and soups, fish and lobster rolls, classic bakery items and cupcakes, gelato and frozen yogurt, organic juices and smoothies, along with a variety of traditional Barbecue, Mexican, Italian, Greek, and Asian specialties.

The food items are often prepared or prepped in a commercial kitchen by chefs before being placed in the truck or trailer. Food trucks and trailers vary in size and can be efficiently designed with cooking, holding, refrigeration and freezer equipment, along with ventilation, power and gas systems, and an adequate water supply that can accommodate the menu items being offered; plus, allowing adequate space for one or more people to work. The menu items can be ready to serve, assembled from prepped items such as fresh salad and sandwich ingredients, or quickly prepared from scratch for waiting customers.

Online Ordering, Customer Data, and Social Media

Some trucks and trailers have websites or online ordering services where customers can place orders, pay in advance and quickly pick-up orders, reducing wait times and having to stand in line. The serving side of a truck or trailer may also be equipped with an adjustable awning to shield customers from uncomfortable weather conditions, and a security camera for added safety. A truck or trailer with a POS cloud-based system can track customer sales, serving times, on-board inventory levels, and relevant customer data tracking information. Successful operators maintain an established customer base and often communicate with their customers through social media, updating customers about locations, time schedules, and menu item specials, as well as being responsive to customer reviews and comments.

Although most of the food trucks and trailers are independently owned and operated, established franchising organizations provide franchisees with a brand identity that includes a standard menu, logo signage, procedures to follow for food presentation and service, worker uniforms, operations manual and training, standard recipes, ongoing development of new menu items, sales and promotional programs, purchasing discounts, and website management. The franchise organizations report that many of the franchisees are among recent college graduates, family (husband and wife teams) and retirees seeking a business adventure.

Operational Costs and Legal Requirements

The initial investment in a food truck or trailer, ranging from $50,000 to $250,000, is considerably less than that of a typical building or facility within a fixed property location. But the operating requirements, such as permits, licenses, and fees are similar. Each state, county, and city have its own laws that govern the operation of food trucks and trailers. There are regular health department and fire code inspections to ensure that safe food handling practices are being followed in a work-safe environment within the truck or trailer. Also regularly inspected is the commercial kitchen that is used to prepare or prep food items and the garage in which the food truck or trailer is kept.

A list of where food trucks and trailers can be parked, the applicable time limits, and the cost of commercial parking permits or fees is posted by each city and county under their respective parking and zoning ordinances. Food trucks and trailers are being operated during the high traffic peak selling times which is often only a few hours compared to a traditional restaurant. A truck or trailer can be restocked and moved to another high traffic location within the same day for an additional few hours, therefore avoiding the mid-morning or afternoon slow period down times.

Figure Appendix-2 is an example of a Par Requisition Form that may be used by a food truck or trailer to maintain the appropriate inventory levels in anticipation of sales. The requisition would be transmitted from the truck or trailer to the storeroom for supplies or to the commercial kitchen for prepared or prepped food items. The prepped items would receive final cooking or assembling within the truck or trailer just before being served to the customer.

Par Requisition Form

From: Truck / Trailer	**Date:** January 13, 20xx
To: Storeroom / Kitchen	**Time:** 8:00 A.M.

Product Categories	Purchasing Unit	Par Amount	On Hand	Order	Unit Cost	Extension
Horseradish Sauce	qt	2	1	1	$16.10	$16.10
BBQ Pulled Pork	lb	20	1.5	19	$4.85	$92.15
Brioche Buns	dz	6	1	5	$8.25	$41.25

Figure A.2 Par Requisition Form

The Par Requisition Form could be updated more than once per day as the truck or trailer would restock for a different location or for an additional round of business. For example, supplied for a busy lunch business and then supplied a second time for a late afternoon business, perhaps with some different food items to accommodate a dinner take-out menu. The Par Amount could also vary according to the amount of sales anticipated in any given day of the week, adjusting to certain days that may be busier.

The food cost percentages will be in direct relation to competitive market conditions and the menu items being offered. Prepackaged foods may be priced at a food cost percentage of 30 to 40 percent and foods that require chef preparation may have a food cost percentage of 25 to 35 percent. The labor cost percentages will also vary according to the level of culinary skills required to produce the food items, ranging from 25 to 30 percent. Typically, the chef prepared food items with lower food cost percentages (because of higher menu selling prices) will have higher labor cost percentages.

There are specific operating costs associated with a food truck or trailer that are very different from those of building ownership or rent. The service costs and maintenance expenses that include gas, oil, propane tanks, battery powered generators, garage ownership or rent, truck or trailer insurance, and frequent vehicle service checks. The overall profit percentage before taxes from a successfully operated food truck or trailer can exceed the average profit percentage of the typical quick service restaurant, often within the 10 to 20 percent range and far greater as reported by individual owners. Therefore, food trucks and trailers have the potential to be very profitable.

Mobile Production Delivery Trucks

Technologically equipped trucks with a kitchen that delivers freshly prepared food items are in the early stages of development and advancement, such as pizza ordering and delivery. After a customer places an order from the pizza truck's menu the technology and robotics ('bots') begin the production process. The pizza is prepared and baked during the delivery travel time to the customer. This not only shortens delivery times but provides the customer with a hot-out-of-the-oven pizza.

Mister and Misses Dee recognize that possibilities exist far beyond the county fair and festivals at the city's waterfront park. They are of the opinion that Food Trucks and Trailers represent a new growth market, much like the early 1960s with the franchised expansion of hamburger, taco, and chicken chains. Those franchise organizations created ownership opportunities for many entrepreneurial oriented people ready to invest and work in a franchised business that was rapidly responding to changing tastes and lifestyles. Consumers wanted popular food items served with consistency, uniform pricing, in convenient locations with drive-up ordering and pick-up windows.

Today, Food Trucks and Trailers just might be at the early stages of franchise growth opportunities that are responding to the current changing consumer tastes and lifestyles. Remember that Mister Dee thoroughly researched and developed his restaurant, catering, and pizza menu, which has resulted in successfully operated businesses. He believes that his brand identity, with selected menu items could possibly be developed into a franchised brand of food trucks. He is serious about taking his popular restaurant menu items on the road to customers, and the kitchen at Farfalle Italiane could initially handle an increase in production. Mister Dee would be willing to launch this new venture with a group of culinary and hospitality management program graduates, who would be interested in an entrepreneurial opportunity. If you accept the challenge, begin Assignment A – 11.

Assignment A-11

Upon successfully completing all of the chapter and appendix assignments and project exercises, you should be able to create an initial menu of popular items and then establish an operational and marketing plan. Refer to the key points that were made in the report, "Mobile Foodservice—Food Trucks and Trailers," which covers all of the essential information; then develop an outline with a checklist of questions that would need to be answered based upon the menu.

The assignment is to establish an operational and marketing plan for a Food Truck with the Farfalle Italiane brand, popular menu items (some prepared and prepped in the restaurant kitchen), and a marketing plan (who are the potential customers?).

Successful foodservice franchise organizations all began with several well-run operations that could then be duplicated.

Helpful Websites

www.nationalfoodtrucks.org

www.zume.com

Key Cost and Analysis Formulas

Determining the Portion Size When a Recipe Only Lists the Number of Servings

The following procedure determines the portion size and can be applied to any recipe to quickly find the portion size when it is not given:

Step 1— Convert the quantity for each main ingredient into ounces and then add them all up to determine Total Ounces.

Step 2— Divide the Total Ounces the recipe produces by the Number of Servings to determine the Portion Size.

$$\frac{\text{Total Number of Ounces the Recipe Produces}}{\text{Number of Servings}} = \textbf{Portion Size}$$

Recipe Conversion

When recipes have to be converted (sized) to yield a different number of servings, the following conversion procedure is used:

Step 1— Determine the multiplier:

$$\frac{\text{New Yield}}{\text{(number of servings)}} \div \frac{\text{Original Yield}}{\text{(number of servings)}} = \frac{\textbf{Conversion}}{\textbf{Multiplier}}$$

Step 2— Convert each ingredient's original recipe quantity into ounces:

$$\frac{\text{Ingredient's}}{\text{Original Measure}} \times \frac{\text{Number of Ounces}}{\text{per Unit of Measure}} = \frac{\textbf{Number of Ounces}}{\textbf{of Ingredient}}$$

Step 3— Convert ingredient quantity in ounces to sized amount:

$$\frac{\text{Ingredient Quantity}}{\text{(ounces)}} \times \frac{\text{Conversion}}{\text{Multiplier}} = \frac{\textbf{Sized Amount}}{\textbf{(in ounces)}}$$

Step 4— Convert each ingredient quantity (ounces) back to standard units of measure.

Determining the Spice Factor Percentage

$$\frac{\text{Total Cost, Spice Factor Items}}{\text{Total Cost, All Food Items}} = \textbf{Spice Factor \%}$$

Preparing a Food Cost Report

A Food Cost Report is used to accurately identify the Food Cost (Cost of Food Sold) and the Food Cost Percentage as follows:

Debits: (In-flow into an account)

Opening Inventory:	$_____	is the value of the previous Closing Inventory
Food Purchases: +	$_____	all of the food items purchased for the inventory period
Sum of Inflows:	$_____	all of the dollars spent on food for the accounting period

Credits: (Outflow from the account)

Closing Inventory:	$_____	dollar value of the inventory taken the last day of the accounting period
Employee Meal Credit:	$_____	amount charged for employee meals
Complimentary Meals:	$_____	amount of meals not charged for by the owner or manager
Sum of Outflows:	$_____	all of the outflows that did not generate sales

Sum of Inflows – Sum of Outflows = Cost of Food Sold

Cost of Food Sold	$_____
Total Food Sales:	$_____ sum of Customer Guest Checks for the accounting period

Cost of Food Sold ÷ Total Food Sales = Food Cost Percentage

Preparing a Department Food Cost Report

Debits

Opening Inventory:	$_____
Requisitions:	$_____
Directs (purchases):	$_____
Transfers-In:	$_____
Sum of Inflows:	$_____

Credits

Closing Inventory:	$_____
Employee Meal Credit:	$_____
Complimentary Meals:	$_____
Transfers-Out:	$_____
Sum of Outflows:	$_____

Sum of Inflows – Sum of Outflows = Cost of Food Sold

Cost of Food Sold	$_____
Total Food Sales:	$_____

Cost of Food Sold ÷ Total Food Sales = Food Cost Percentage

Inventory Turnover Rate

The three steps to calculating the Inventory Turnover Rate are as follows:

Step 1— Determine the Average Inventory Value

$$\text{Opening Inventory} + \text{Closing Inventory} = (\text{total}) \div 2 = \textbf{Average Inventory Value}$$

Step 2— Determine the Cost of Goods Sold

$$\text{Opening Inventory} + \text{Food Purchases} = (\text{total}) - \text{Closing Inventory} = \textbf{Cost of Goods Sold}$$

Step 3— Calculate the Inventory Turnover Rate

$$\text{Cost of Goods Sold} \div \text{Average Inventory Value} = \textbf{Inventory Turnover Rate}$$

Seat Turnover Rate

Seat Turnover represents the number of times a seat was "turned" (used by customers) during the course of a meal period and enables management to determine the average dining time during that meal period. The Seat Turnover Rate is calculated as follows:

$$\text{Customers Served in Meal Period} \div \text{Number of Seats Available} = \textbf{Seat Turnover Rate}$$

Payroll Cost Percentage

The Payroll Cost Percentage is calculated as follows:

$$\text{Payroll Cost} \div \text{Sales} = \textbf{Payroll Cost Percentage}$$

Employee Turnover Rate

The three steps to calculating the hourly Employee Turnover Rate are as follows:

Step 1— Determine the average number of hourly employees.

Number of Employees (beginning of the year)   _____

Number of Employees (end of the year)   + _____

Total: _____

Total ÷ 2 = Average Number of Employees

Step 2— Determine the number of past hourly employees.

$$\text{Number of W-2 Tax Forms} - \text{Number of Current Employees} = \textbf{Number of Past Employees}$$

Step 3— Calculate the hourly employee turnover rate.

$$\text{Number of Past Employees} \div \text{Average Number of Employees} = \textbf{Employee Turnover Rate}$$

Pour Cost (Drink Cost)

Each Alcohol Drink must have a standard portion cost, commonly referred to as the Pour Cost which is calculated as follows:

Determine the Liquor Portion Cost:

Step 1— Determine the price per ounce for each bottle:

$$\text{Purchasing Cost (bottle cost)} \div \text{Bottle Yield (number of ounces in the bottle)} = \textbf{Unit Price}$$

Step 2— Determine the liquor cost for each portion:

$$\text{Liquor Quantity Serving Size (in ounces)} \times \text{Unit Price (cost per ounce)} = \textbf{Liquor Portion Cost}$$

Alcohol Beverage Cost and Cost Percentage

The Alcohol Beverage Cost Percentage is usually separated by alcohol beverage category—liquor, wine, and beer—and is calculated as follows:

Cost of Goods Sold (Liquor) ÷ Liquor Sales = **Beverage (Liquor) Cost %**

Cost of Goods Sold (Wine) ÷ Wine Sales = **Beverage (Wine) Cost %**

Cost of Goods Sold (Beer) ÷ Beer Sales = **Beverage (Beer) Cost %**

NOTE: The Alcohol Beverage Category Sales and Cost Report would have the Cost of Goods Sold amounts for each category: liquor, wine, and beer.

Alcohol Beverage Inventory Turnover Rate

The Alcohol Beverage Inventory Turnover Rate is usually separated by alcohol beverage category—liquor, wine, and beer—and is calculated as follows:

Step 1— Determine the average inventory:

$$\text{Opening Inventory} + \text{Closing Inventory} = \text{(total)} \div 2 = \textbf{Average Inventory}$$

Step 2— Cost of Goods Sold ÷ Average Inventory = **Turnover Rate**

NOTE: The Alcohol Beverage Inventory and Sales Control Report would have the Cost of Goods Sold amounts for each category: liquor, wine, and beer.

Sales Mix Percentage

Sales revenue is often generated from two revenue centers: Food and Beverage. The Sales Mix Percentage of each source category is the ratio of each category to the Total Sales and is calculated as follows:

Food Sales ÷ Total Sales = Sales Mix %

Beverage Sales ÷ Total Sales = Sales Mix %

Website Resources

Alcohol Beverage Products

www.accardis.com	Liquor inventory control system
www.accubar.com	Alcohol beverage inventory management system
www.alcoholcontrols.com	Bottle pouring controls
www.bar-I.com	Liquor inventory system
www.barvision.com	Wireless pour spouts and inventory reports
www.berg-controls.com	Liquor dispensers and equipment
www.bjcp.org	Beer judge certification program
www.discus.org	Distilled Spirits Council of the United States
www.liquormonitor.com	Bar equipment
www.nabca.org	National Alcohol Beverage Control Association
www.partender.com	Inventory management software service
www.posi-pour.com	Bar products and pour control spouts
www.ttb.gov	Alcohol and Tobacco Tax and Trade Bureau

Coffee and Espresso

www.baristaworks.com	Coffee service supplies
www.coffeeschool.org	The American Barista & Coffee Workshops
www.coffeetalk.com	Coffee industry news and products
www.dccoffeeproducts.com	Coffee equipment/accessories
www.ico.org	International Coffee Organization
www.illyusa.com	Coffee and coffee products
www.ncausa.org	National Coffee Association USA
www.scaa.org	Specialty Coffee Association of America
www.worldbaristachampionship.com	Barista competition

Convenience Foods

www.sweetstreet.com	Sweet Street Desserts

Employee Scheduling

www.hotschedules.com	Scheduling software – labor management
www.schedulefly.com	Staff scheduling software

Food Product Information

www.ams.usda.gov	Agricultural Marketing Service USDA
www.idfa.org	International Dairy Foods Association
www.meatinstitute.org	*The Meat Buyer's Guide* from the
	American Meat Institute
www.seafoodsource.com/seafood-handbook	Seafood Handbook for all types of seafood
www.specialtyfood.com	Specialty Food Association's Fancy Food Show

Food and Wine Pairing Guide

www.foodandwinepairing.org

Foodservice Distributors / Wholesalers

www.restaurantdepot.com

www.sysco.com

www.usfoods.com

Food Trucks

www.nationalfoodtrucks.org

www.zume.com

Glassware

www.riedel.com	Wine glass guide

Kitchen Equipment

www.edlundco.com	Scales
www.hobartcorp.com	
www.rubbermaidcommercialproducts.com	
www.vollrath.com	

Market Reports

www.usfoods.com/our-services/business-trends/farmers-report

Minimum Wage Laws (Federal and State)

www.dol.gov/whd/minimumwage.htm

Nutrition

www.anfponline.org	Assoc. of Nutrition and Foodservice Professionals

POS Systems, Software, and Tablets

www.advancedhospitality.com	POS software system
www.alohancr.com	NCR/Aloha POS Systems
www.calcmenu.com	Software systems
www.caterease.com	Catering Management Software
www.elacarte.com	Presto Restaurant Tablet
www.foodsoftware.com	Restaurant software apps
www.micros.com	ORACLE/Micros
www.rmpos.com	ASI-Restaurant Manager
www.ziosk.com	ZIOSK Restaurant Tablets

Recipes

www.allrecipes.com	
www.allrecipes.com/recipes/134/drinks/coffee	
www.allrecipes.com/making-espresso.drinks/	
www.cooking.nytimes.com	
www.foodnetwork.com	
www.recipesource.com	
www.tyson.com	
www.costgenie.com	recipe and menu costing

Responsible Alcohol Server Training

www.nraef.org/ServSafeAlcohol	Manager and server training

Safe Food Handling

www.foodsafety.gov	Information and facts
www.ServSafe.com	Manager and employee food safety training

Index